FRENCH INSIL

The world-wide development of the French language in the past, present and the future

Henriette Walter

Translated by Peter Fawcett

448
.4

London and New York

First published 1994
by Routledge
11 New Fetter Lane, London EC4P 4EE

Simultaneously published in the USA and Canada
by Routledge
29 West 35th Street, New York, NY 10001

French edition, *Le français dans tous les sens*
© Éditions Robert Laffont, S.A., Paris, 1988

English edition © 1994 Routledge,
translated by Peter Fawcett

Typeset in Times by Florencetype Ltd, Kewstoke, Avon
Printed and bound in Great Britain
by T. J. Press (Padstow) Ltd, Padstow, Cornwall
Printed on acid free paper

British Library Cataloguing in Publication Data
A catalogue record for this book is available from the British
Library

Library of Congress Cataloging in Publication Data
applied for

ISBN 0-415-07669-2   ISBN 0-415-07670-6 (pbk)

CONTENTS

PREFACE

Human beings have a highly special relationship with the language they speak. They have learnt it without wanting to. It has been imposed on them by simple contact with the people around them. It coincided, for them, with their becoming conscious of the world they live in. How, in such circumstances, could they not come to identify the word with the thing? If they are afraid of the thing, then they will be afraid of the word: who has not shrunk with horror from the word *cancer*, that 'protracted disease' which usually ends in death? But on the other hand there are words which fill you with joy because they are identified with pleasure, happiness, love, or tenderness. What do the phrases 'that's a good sign' or 'that's a bad sign' mean if not that what they are describing will, at some point, become reality? Perhaps in this case, where thought is already involved, word and thing no longer coincide. But that is far from being the case in everyday life where we are confronted with concrete realities. Why should we dissociate the tree as an object from the sounds which refer to it? That would already be an act of reasoning, we would be doing 'philosophy', losing contact with reality, and common sense convinces us that a tree is a tree, just as a spade is a spade.

It is really only when we learn to read that distancing begins. Before then, a tree was only a vision of a trunk with foliage on top. Now we are given a visually perceptible equivalent in the shape of *tree*, a series of four letters that we rapidly come to perceive as a whole. It is then that, for some of us, language may take on an existence which is distinct from that of the world as we experience it. It should not, therefore, come as any surprise to learn that many people – or should I say everybody apart from a few eccentrics? – identify the French language with its written form. This language, with its spelling system which can pose so many problems for French schoolchildren, should not, of course be confused with the rough and ready writing of beginners, or even the hasty scribblings of adults. It found a respectable form only in the works of the great authors, and so represents an ideal towards which we must strive and which will, for most of us, remain unattainable.

This is where the linguists come in, the killjoys who will try to make you believe that language exists before it is written, that the language has a spoken form of which the written form was originally no more than a copy. Indeed, they go further than that. They will tell you that before we use language for thinking, we use it to try to communicate our feelings and perceptions, our needs, desires and demands to other people. But what then becomes of the ideal that we were supposed to find in the great works of literature?

There is no cause for alarm. Any language, including French, is a whole which encompasses the first babblings of the child, the lexical inventiveness of teenagers, the conversations of a housewife chatting to the milkman, the discussions of researchers and philosophers, and the year's literary prizes. All these uses, even the most humble, may well leave some trace in the development of the language. It is also everything that has gone into its making from centuries of all kinds of usage, from farm labour to literature, from camp life to diplomacy. If we want to do more than just use it, if we want to know and understand it, we have to think of it in its dynamics, both past and present, which may open a window on to its future.

Save for the sum total of works that one would have to consult to satisfy one's curiosity in the matter, there is, to date, only this book by Henriette Walter. To succeed in painting such a varied panorama, you would have had to, as she had to, conduct surveys on all kinds of French speakers, in Paris, across France, throughout the French-speaking world. You would also have had to consult the best sources, smoothly coordinate a mass of scattered data, and reproduce it simply and faithfully for the non-specialist. This book, with its wealth of informative detail, is not difficult to read, and yet anybody who has read it with the trust it deserves will have learnt what a language is *in all its aspects*; in its structure, in the way it works, in its varieties, its past and its evolution.

André Martinet

ACKNOWLEDGEMENTS

This book is the slow-growing fruit of many years of listening attentively, indiscreetly and with great delight to hundreds of people, both close friends and absolute strangers. And yet it would never have seen the light of day had it not been for Laurent Laffont, whose idea it was and who was the first to have faith in it.

In its present form it owes its originality to my two children: to my son who played a decisive part in the very conception of the work, and to my daughter who contributed constantly to its fulfilment. Each in their own way helped me to find the right language for communicating in a style more appropriate to the general public, a language that is both more pedagogical and less academic.

As for the content, every line reflects the thinking of André Martinet, in whose shadow I have had the great fortune to learn for twenty-five years, and who, in kind friendship, was good enough to read the book critically at every stage of its development.

Finally, this book, which led to many spirited family discussions, is also to a very large extent the work of my husband, who was a tireless and demanding collaborator, and who is now forever bitten by the bug of linguistics.

GRAPHIC CONVENTIONS

Following tradition, Latin words are in small capitals (e.g.: VILLA).

For the reader's convenience, a distinction is made in Latin and Old French words between *u* and *v* and *i* and *j*, but *u* and *v* were one and the same letter until the sixteenth century, as were *i* and *j*.

Words in *italics* refer to the orthographic form of a word (e.g.: *ville*).

Words between square brackets [ ] refer to phonetic notation, in other words to what is heard (e.g.:[vil]).

The meaning of words is always given between inverted commas (e.g: VILLA 'country house, farm').

The > sign indicates the result of evolution (e.g.: VILLA > *ville*).

INTRODUCTION

FRENCH AS THE LINGUISTS SEE IT

French people pass the most contradictory judgements on their language: some offer it as an example for what it was, whilst others award it a dunce's cap for what it is. They praise, correct, pity, or scold it – passionately. And they forget to look on it as a living thing. Behind these exaggerated attitudes, how can we rediscover French as it is spoken, written and loved?

If we do wish to see French for what it really is, we must examine it with a linguist's eye. Or rather, like the linguist, use our ears. Because linguists listen rather than talk. Indeed, they are frequently accused of being more interested in how people speak than in what they say. To the people they speak with, who are sometimes disturbed by this attitude, the language professionals seem much of the time to be disconcerting and even slightly unsettling characters: they do not miss a single word of what you say, they seem to know much more about your own language than you do, and yet they always seem delighted with what they hear. When you realise that their first concern is not for you to use words and grammar correctly, this somewhat amoral attitude of the mere observer can seem disconcerting.

The severity of this judgement, which is no exaggeration, will, however, not deter us from adopting the linguist's point of view in this book, the standpoint of the person who is a 'lover' of languages (in the same way that we talk about a music lover or a lover of art). Linguists are interested in all languages in all their aspects, and when they examine a particular language they are trying basically to define in what way that language is different from all other languages, how it works and how it evolves.

The aim of this book is therefore above all to show what historical, geographical and structural features characterise French. But there are so many received ideas in circulation concerning the language that we will not be able to get a clear view if we do not first deal with some of the more tenacious of them. A random list would include: 'French is Gaulish', 'French is Latin', 'dialects are a bastardised form of French', or 'the best French is spoken in Touraine'. All of these ideas are both right and wrong.

1

French is not a descendant of Gaulish

Primary schoolchildren in France are frequently told that the Gauls are their ancestors and that the Gaulish language is the ancestor of Modern French. But that is an idea that could do with closer examination.

In fact, after Gaul was conquered by the Romans, the native inhabitants adopted the language of the victors, and, apart from a few dozen words of Gaulish origin which have survived in Modern French and a certain number of place-names which can be found scattered around the country, our knowledge of Gaulish is limited and imperfect: the Druids handed down their knowledge by word of mouth and the few surviving inscriptions are short and repetitive.

It *is* a descendant of Latin, but which variety?

It is also said that *Latin* is the ancestor of French, and that can be seen quite clearly if we compare the various Romance languages, in other words the languages which perpetuate Latin: Italian, French, Spanish, etc. But we must remember that the variety of Latin which is the source of the Romance languages is not the so-called *Classical* Latin but what we call *Vulgar* Latin, the one spoken by the Romans in their daily life.[1] Among the Romance languages, French is defined as a language which derived from the Vulgar Latin imported into Gaul by the Roman conquerors.

To be more precise, we should highlight a very important event which occurred later. All the history books teach us that Julius Caesar conquered Gaul towards the middle of the first century BC, but only books about the history of language tell us that the language of the conquerors, which the Gauls learnt from their dealings with the Roman legionnaires, settlers and merchants, was subsequently influenced by the new Germanic invaders, especially the Franks.

The Franks in the region of Paris spoke Latin with a Germanic 'accent', and so modified the language and helped to shape the dialect of the Île-de-France which is the source of Modern French. But at the time it was just one dialect among so many others, different only in a small number of features from the neighbouring Romance dialects of Normandy, Picardy and Berry.

French: a dialect that made the big time

When a language divides into different varieties, it is customary to use the terms *dialects* or *patois*. Thus we speak of *Romance* dialects and patois to designate the various local or regional forms of language which all derive from the Latin of Rome. These *Romance* patois all developed from the language spoken by the *Roman* invaders. Unfortunately, the term patois has gradually become synonymous in people's minds with the all too frequently repeated idea of a rudimentary form of speech, with some people even going so far as to say that 'it isn't a language'. This is a far cry from the value-free definition given by the linguists, for whom a (Romance) patois is initially one of the forms taken by spoken Latin in a given region: *a patois is a language*.

The Latin spoken in Gaul did not culminate in a single form, but diversified over the centuries and split up into regional varieties, or *dialects*. When this diversification is such that the language spoken in one village is no longer the same as that spoken in the neighbouring village, the linguists use the more precise term *patois*. But in their eyes there is no hierarchical value to be set up between language, dialect and patois. A patois and a dialect are no less worthy of interest from the linguistic point of view, but they are normally used only in restricted circumstances and they are generally spoken only over small areas.

That is why the common idea that a patois is deformed French must be vigorously contested. In fact, French, as a particular form of Latin spoken in the Île-de-France, was itself originally a patois of Latin, and if that variety then spread to other regions and finally became the official language in the realm of France, that was only for reasons relating to institutions and the importance acquired by the capital in the political, economic and administrative spheres. The other patois simply had less luck, remaining the language of a single region or even a single village. It must, therefore, be understood that not only is a patois not deformed French, but that *French itself is only a patois that succeeded*.

In the first part of this book we shall give an overview of the history of French and show how the dialectal varieties developed over time and why nowadays they are often found to be disappearing.

The three following parts examine geographical diversity and look in some detail at the localisation of these dialectal varieties and their degree of vitality both within and outside France.

The last two parts will answer the questions: 'What is French?' and 'Where is French going?'. They will look at the structure of the language as it appears in its pronunciation, grammar and vocabulary, and will highlight the currents and trends which are affecting it.

Touraine French: foreigners just love it

Finally there is a tradition that the 'purest' French is the form spoken in Touraine. This received wisdom is all the more unexpected since all the works on the pronunciation of French have by contrast been unanimous in declaring that the model of good French is not the usage of the inhabitants of the Loire valley but that of the educated Parisian. Recent research[2] indicates that the prestige attributed to the French spoken in Touraine

3

seems to have originated in works written by foreigners, starting with the grammarian Palsgrave who produced the first French grammar book, written in English, at the beginning of the sixteenth century. But it seems mainly to have been German, Dutch and English travel guides which advised tourists to visit places like Tours, Saumur, Blois or Orléans to be sure of hearing and learning good French. To this day there are still echoes of this tradition in the region, which preserves and hands down from one generation to the next the memory of the frequent sojourns of court and king in the castles of the Loire. It has probably also been kept alive by the reputation of the writers of the Pléiade, most of whom, like Ronsard and du Bellay, came from the region.

We still need to explain the reasons which, in the sixteenth and seventeenth centuries, led foreigners to arrive at such a judgement. The linguistic situation in France at that time may offer a few clues to the mystery: at the time, each region spoke its own patois, and it was only in its written form that French was in widespread use.

When they arrived in France, foreigners, who had learnt their French from books, did not normally understand the patois spoken in the towns and villages. Touraine was an exception: near to the Île-de-France and influenced by Paris as a result of the frequent visits of the Royal Court to the region, its people probably spoke an already highly frenchified patois. Since they had no problem with the language spoken by the inhabitants of Touraine, foreigners could thus jump to the conclusion that it was the purest since it was remarkably close to the language they had learnt from their books.

Going against the grain of this tradition, which is still strong among foreigners, all studies on pronunciation which have been conducted since the beginning of the century, as well as all the research on less recent times gathered from what the grammarians have said, establish the fact that the form of French which has tended to spread for generations is the one which developed in the Parisian basin: it has given a generous welcome to elements from various sources, resulting in a constantly shifting compromise between various provincial usages and Parisian usage proper. This tendency is confirmed by studies on the ground which will be described in the last part of this book: 'Where is French going?'.

FRENCH: A MYTH AND A FEW REALITIES

Nowadays, foreigners are surprised by the attitude of the French to their own language when they tack a sentence such as: 'I don't know if that's French', or even 'I'm sorry, that's not French' onto something they have just said. French people use such phrases so often that only foreigners are surprised by them, finding it amazing, for example, that French people should ask themselves whether *taciturnité* or *cohabitateur* are really French words, since speakers of neighbouring languages make up words as they like and nobody objects as long as they make themselves understood. French people, by contrast, do not look on their language as a malleable tool to be used for expression and communication. They think of it rather as an immutable institution, constricted by its traditions and virtually untouchable. They have, in fact, been too well-trained to accept a word only if it is already in the dictionary. If it is not, they declare with the utmost conviction, but against all the evidence, since they have just used it and been understood, that the word is not French and that it simply does not exist. *Taciturnité* and *cohabitateur* are both words which conform perfectly well to the structures of French and to the traditional rules of word formation in that language. And yet the author of the first, Gabriel Garran, founder of the theatre of Aubervilliers, speaking at a colloquium in Villetaneuse on 14 May 1986, and the author of the second, the comedian Coluche, in a radio interview shortly before his death in 1986, both apologised for using them, adding that they were not French. I quote these two cases because they were heard in real-life situations, but such behaviour is absolutely normal amongst French people.

They have an equally irrational attitude with regard to pronunciation. No matter who is speaking, it is always the other person who has an 'accent', whether that accent be described as *pointu* ('northern') or 'southern', as *chtimi* ('north-eastern') or *pied noir* ('white North African'), as 'Swiss', or as 'Belgian' or 'Canadian'. And the people talking about these accents think that they themselves do not have an accent: it is always other people who are outside of the norm and who are wrong. Yet the realisation that this diversity exists, when it is only a matter of pronunciation, produces a smile rather than a rebuke.

The situation is quite different when it comes to grammar, and expressions such as 'il s'est rappelé *de* son enfance' or 'il a pallié *aux* inconvénients' are rejected at once by the purists as inadmissible. Those who notice such forms are not far from accusing those who use them of being either uneducated simpletons or responsible for harming, not to say finishing off, the French language: 'France, your language is going down the plughole!' becomes a cry of alarm and a call for help.

Those people whose mother tongue is French thus display a paradoxical combination of a keen sense of observation (since they are forever picking up on deviations from traditionally accepted forms) and a more or less conscious refusal to recognise the existence of diversity in the use of their language. Although they understand perfectly well the meaning of a given *French* expression which they think is incorrect, they have no hesitation in declaring against all logic that it *is not* French. How can we explain this irrational attitude in people who claim to be disciples of Descartes?

There seems to exist in the mind of all French speakers a duality which causes confusion. On the one hand, they have an image of this beautiful French language handed down by tradition through the works of the great writers and which takes on the aura of a myth: don't touch it, we might ruin it! And, beside this ideal, pure, perfect language, they are all vaguely aware that another French language is developing, which they all use every day with no special care or attention, a multifarious, changing language which is adapting to the modern world and to familiar situations. It is difficult to accept this second language as French, as '*the* French language' – and yet it fits perfectly into the tradition of the classical language whilst at the same time having its own dynamic: what people find shocking today will not be shocking tomorrow.

The myth is upheld perfectly in grammar books and dictionaries which teach correct usage: they are fixed points to which it is reassuring to refer when in doubt. After hearing or using a given turn of phrase or expression, the French will check to see if it is correct, but, in the heat of conversation or the haste of writing, they let themselves be carried away by the spirit of the language and they create new forms which the language permits but which usage has not yet hallowed. They express themselves more fully, but they still have a guilty conscience. And these two views of the language are so firmly planted in their minds that, when they talk about the French language, you can never tell precisely which one it is.

This duality will make its presence felt throughout this book: we shall see how the concept of a mythical French language, reputed to be beautiful, clear and perfect, could take shape and gather force whilst at the same time the French language of everyday use, with the qualities and defects of a working language, was evolving and diversifying.

1

WHERE DOES FRENCH COME FROM?

Ten landmarks in the history of French

TEN LANDMARKS

In search of origins

French has not always existed, just as France has not always had the same frontiers, but the date of birth of this offshoot of Latin remains shrouded in mystery. It was only around the ninth century, a thousand years after the conquest of Gaul in 51 BC, that the ancestors of the modern French people noticed that the Latin which they thought they were speaking had become French without their realising it.

However, it is not easy to say when that happened. What is certain is that for centuries the ancestors of the French were obliged to live with their Roman, Frankish, Burgundian, Visigoth and Norman neighbours, and they were obliged, between skirmishes, to talk to them, share their meals, and, perhaps, woo their daughters. And all of that involved communication problems, since, originally, these peoples did not speak the same language. French is to some extent a result of these encounters and contacts.

Words change pronunciation

The words used by the ancestors of the French have been handed down to modern times, but they have suffered the ravages of time and are not always easily recognised. The French word *muer* no longer bears much resemblance to the Latin word MUTARE from which it derives. But if we analyse ancient manuscripts, we can reconstitute the stages the word has gone through. In the eighth century,[3] the use of the graphic sign *dh* to represent the Latin *t* between two vowels (mutare > mu*dh*are) shows that the consonant had weakened. It was probably pronounced like the *d* of *nada* in Modern Spanish. During the centuries which followed, this consonant, which was already articulated weakly, became even more attenuated and finally disappeared completely, at the latest around the eleventh century:

7

MUTARE → *mudhare* → *mudher* → *muer*

Thus *mutare* became *muer*, but until the fourteenth century this infinitive *muer* was pronounced with the final consonant sounded, like the modern French word *fer*. This final consonant in its turn began to weaken during the fourteenth and fifteenth centuries, resulting in the modern pronunciation with no final *r* sound: *muer* in the infinitive is now pronounced like the past participle *mué*. The metamorphoses of this final consonant in the sixteenth century will be discussed later (see pp. 60–2). In this case, evolution modified the *form* of the word; in other cases, it is the *meaning* which has changed.

Words change meaning

The Romans had two words for 'head':

– a noble word, CAPUT, which evolved phonetically into the French word *chef*, first with the meaning of 'head' in Old French, and then with that of 'the person at the head of, the boss';
– a familiar word, TESTA, which originally meant 'earthen pot'.

The Romans spoke jokingly of their *testa* (their 'mug') in much the same way that modern French people say *vous vous payez ma fiole* (Courteline) or *il a pris un coup sur la cafetière*. Nowadays, the meaning of 'earthen pot' has completely disappeared from the French word *tête* (derived from TESTA). By contrast, *tête* has kept all of the meanings of the word CAPUT, both 'head' and 'the person at the head of'.

As for the word *chef*, the formal representative of the Latin CAPUT, it still retains the meaning 'head' in a few expressions such as *couvre-chef* or *opiner du chef*.

In language as in nature, nothing is ever lost completely, and the history of a language is made up of these shifts which modify sometimes the sounds, sometimes the meanings, and sometimes both the sounds and the meanings of words.

Linguists speak of *phonetic* change when it is the sounds which are altered (MUTARE becomes *muer*) and of *semantic* change in the case of *meanings* (in Latin 'earthen pot' becomes 'head'). Some of these developments will be analysed by way of example in the historical section of this book.

The history of the language

Some of these changes will be approached via the history of the peoples who spoke French, because the history of a language depends above all on the history of the people who speak or chose to speak it. Of all the facts which have marked the history of France, we shall single out only a small number of events to serve as landmarks. They will afford the opportunity to provide some information about the linguistic changes which occurred at different times and they will help to explain the origin of some of these changes. If the distance in time between these landmarks is sometimes quite considerable, that is because, when we are talking about linguistic evolution, we have usually to count in centuries, if not in millennia.

Ten landmarks

Out of the long history of the peoples who have lived and spoken on French soil, we shall select only those events which have had consequences for the language.

We shall begin with a few brief comments on the languages of various origins which were spoken in France before the Roman conquest (*Before the 'Indo-Europeans'*), and in particular on *Gaulish* (*The age of the Gauls*).

After Latin had been adopted by the inhabitants of Gaul, it was to undergo the influence of the *Germanic* languages spoken by the invaders (*The age of the 'Barbarians'*), whilst nascent *Christianity* was to become one of the best channels for spreading this common Latin language (*The age of the Christians*).

It was during the reign of Charlemagne that people suddenly realised that the language they had always spoken was no longer Latin but a different language, one which the Norman invaders would also learn to speak (*The Viking interlude*).

Throughout the entire Middle Ages, the feudal lifestyle favoured the proliferation of regional forms of language (*The age of dialects*).

In the sixteenth century, François I was to give the 'langue françoise' its letters of nobility: from that time it replaced Latin as the written language, whilst people continued to speak patois in daily life (*The triumph of French*).

But the grammarians were on the *qui vive* and, at the end of the sixteenth century, forged the rules of 'good usage', taking as their model the language spoken at the Royal Court. This was the origin of the 'classical' language (*The age of 'good usage'*).

A century went by, and it was the age of the Revolution: the Convention, enamoured of Jacobinic centralisation, was to deal the first blow to the vitality of the patois, which were deemed to be harmful to a Republic 'one and indivisible'. In the meantime, the French language had also travelled and transplanted itself overseas (Canada, the colonies). We shall come back to this in the geographical section (see *French outside France*, pp. 128–58).

Finally, in the twentieth century, compulsory state education and the First World War on the one hand (*The age of school*) and mass communication

(*The age of the media*) on the other were to play a decisive role in the shaping of Modern French.

In the following pages we shall look in greater detail at the events which we have just sketched out (see the table opposite) and see how, over the ages, the language has changed. These dips into history will be kept deliberately brief and superficial, since their sole purpose is to demonstrate the influence that events and people have had on the language. They will be an opportunity above all to present, for each of the periods under discussion, a few aspects of French in the areas of pronunciation, grammar and vocabulary.

BEFORE THE 'INDO-EUROPEANS'

The great family of the 'Indo-Europeans'

There can be no doubt that, of all the events which have had an influence on the development of the French language, chronological priority must go to the abandonment of Gaulish after the Roman conquest. But where did that Gaulish language itself come from, and what do we know about it?

Celtic peoples from the region which is modern Germany had begun to cross the Rhine from the start of the first millennium before Jesus Christ. They spoke a Celtic tongue which no longer exists today: *Gaulish*.

This language belongs to the great family of Indo-European tongues,[4] which also gave rise to French. Some six thousand years before our era, peoples who spoke so-called Indo-European languages were settled in the region of the Caucasus and the Black Sea. Some of these peoples migrated later towards India while others spread out over almost the entire area of Europe. Thus the Celts (Gauls) arrived in the region which was to become Gaul during the first millennium before Jesus Christ.

After thousands of years of evolution and entire centuries of which no written trace remains, it is difficult to draw up a real genealogical tree of these languages, but the linguists have invented a method which uses the similarities between the forms of certain words with the same meaning to produce groupings between apparently dissimilar languages, from which linguistic kinship can thus be established between them (see table 12).

As these concordances are verified by a large number of crosschecks, we can discard the hypothesis that they are no more than coincidence. In this way, it has been possible to draw up the table of Indo-European languages shown in the table on pp. 14–15.

10

TEN LANDMARKS

Guiding Concept	Era	Events
BEFORE THE 'INDO-EUROPEANS'	Before 800 BC	The inhabitants of Gaul spoke various languages before the arrival of the Gauls, who spoke an Indo-European tongue.
THE AGE OF THE GAULS	approx. 800–500 BC	After the conquest by Julius Caesar in the first century BC, Latin gradually became the language of Gaul.
THE AGE OF THE 'BARBARIANS'	2nd–6th century	The Latin spoken by the Gauls is influenced by Germanic invaders, especially the Franks.
THE AGE OF THE CHRISTIANS	2nd–9th century	The spread of Christianity and the birth of 'Old French'. Charlemagne restores the teaching of Latin.
THE VIKING INTERLUDE	9th–10th century	The arrival of the Normans has little effect on French.
THE AGE OF DIALECTS	5th–12th century	Feudal life favours dialectal fragmentation.
THE TRIUMPH OF FRENCH	12th–16th century	The spread of French. By the decree of Villers-Cotterêts, François I imposes written French, which ousts Latin.
THE AGE OF 'GOOD USAGE'	17th–18th century	The grammarians intervene to codify the language. French acquires prestige abroad.
THE AGE OF SCHOOL	19th–20th century	Abbé Grégoire reports to the Convention on the need to abolish the patois. All French people learn French at school. The Great War and the decline of the patois.
THE AGE OF THE MEDIA	20th century	The media impose uniformity.

HOW IS THE KINSHIP OF LANGUAGES ESTABLISHED?

By way of example, we shall look at the words for 'fish', 'father' and 'foot' in seven European languages:

	fish	*father*	*foot*	
Italian	PESCE	PADRE	PIEDE	
Spanish	PEZ	PADRE	PIE	initial *p*
Portuguese	PEIXE	PAI	PE	
French	POISSON	PÈRE	PIED	
English	FISH	FATHER	FOOT	
German	FISCH	VATER	FUSS	
		(*v* pronounced *f*)		initial *f*
Swedish	FISK	FADER	FOT	

We can formulate a number of hypotheses:

1. The four languages with initial *p* probably belong to one group and the three with initial *f* to another, since such coincidences cannot be the result of pure chance.
2. All the languages in the first group derive from the same mother tongue with an initial *p* for these words, and those in the second group come from another mother tongue with initial *f*.
3. By comparison with languages such as Russian, Persian, Irish, Greek, etc., linguists have managed, after long and painstaking research, to establish new groupings which have, in turn, led to the idea that all of these languages are related. In this way, they have been able to reconstruct a common ancestor for many European languages, an ancestor which they have called *Indo-European*.

THE AGE OF THE GAULS

Gaulish, a mysterious language

Whereas the stages that Latin passed through to become French can be reconstituted through the use of a large number of documents, Gaulish, in spite of Astérix, remains largely mysterious to us. We should add that little was known of the Gauls themselves before the second half of the nineteenth century.[5] Until that time, the history of France began in the fifth century AD with Clovis, king of the Franks, and not six centuries earlier with Vercingetorix, chief of the Gauls, or ten millennia before that with the inhabitants of the Lascaux caves, or with the hardy mammoth hunters who had already begun, forty thousand years earlier, to conceive of an afterlife and of whom nothing remains but their burial grounds, or even, of course, with the first traces on French soil of the hominid who was such a skilful flint cutter and who settled at Chilhac in the heart of the Massif Central almost two million years ago.[6]

But let us not linger on such a distant past. Let us rather come back to the nearest ancestors of Modern French.

Since Victor Duruy made the study of French history compulsory from primary school upwards in 1867, French school-books have devoted a chapter to what they call 'our ancestors, the Gauls', a set phrase that all French children recited without always understanding what it meant. All the school-books stress the importance of the military, political and economic conquest of Gaul by Julius Caesar in the middle of the first century BC, but they normally make no mention of another very important fact: namely, that all the inhabitants of Gaul began to learn Latin. The result is that nowadays French people speak the French language, in other words a Romance language descended from Latin, and not a Celtic language descended from Gaulish.

Before the Gauls

It must not be thought that the Celts (the Gauls) who invaded France between 700 and 500 BC had settled in an unoccupied territory. Other peoples had arrived there before them and continued to live there long after their arrival. They were the *Ligurii* in what today is called Provence, the *Iberians* on the plains of the Languedoc, and the *Aquitani* in the south-west. These peoples probably did not speak Indo-European languages. It is difficult to identify the remnants of Iberian and Ligurian because neither of these languages survived, but Basque, which is still spoken in the extreme south-west of France, perpetuates the language of the Aquitani who were settled on the land when the Celts arrived. At the time of Julius Caesar the Gauls had subjected only the borders of the Aquitanian lands: a few bridgeheads beyond the Garonne.[7]

The Gauls were not given to writing much

We know so little of Gaulish because it has left so few written remains: the Druids, who were the guardians of the religion, refused to hand down their knowledge in writing. The sixty or so inscriptions, written in the Greek or Latin alphabets, which have been discovered on the territory of ancient Gaul, are brief and give little information on the structure of the language. Amongst the longest is a calendar engraved on a bronze tablet unearthed in 1897 at Coligny (Ain).[8] Unfortunately, it contains mainly the names of people and places, and only a few words of the language, some of which are abbreviated and still pose problems of interpretation. None of which enables us really to know anything about Gaulish.

The Breton connection

Since there is no written data on this language which has disappeared, to get a more precise idea of its structure we must nowadays turn to the living language of Breton, since, as the table of Indo-European languages suggests (see pp. 14–15), Gaulish is a close relation of Breton. However,

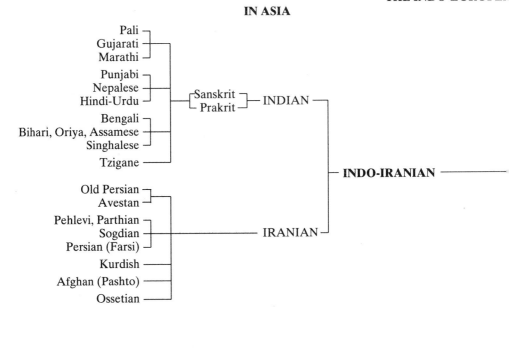

All the languages spoken in Europe are Indo-European languages with the exception of *Basque*, *Finnish*, *Hungarian*, *Turkish*, and a few languages spoken in Russia.

It should be noted:

- that *Gaulish* belongs to the *Celtic* group (Welsh, Breton, etc.);
- that *French* is classed with the languages in the *Italic* group via *Latin*;
- that the *Germanic* languages constitute another group in the Indo-European family.

† A language that has disappeared without any survivor.

IN EUROPE

CELTIC
- Celtiberian
- *Gaulish* †
- Breton
- Welsh
- Cornish †
- Irish
- Manx

ITALIC
- Venetian †, Umbrian †, Oscan †

LATIN
- Portuguese
- Spanish, Judaeo-Spanish
- Catalan
- Occitan
- French
- Italian
- Rheto-Roman (Ladin)
- Dalmatian †
- Rumanian . . .

GERMANIC

OF THE EAST
- Gothic †, Burgundian †

OF THE WEST
- German, Yiddish
- Dutch
  - Flemish
  - Dutch
  - Afrikaans
- Frisian
- English

NORDIC
- Swedish
- Danish
- Dano-Norwegian
- Norwegian
- Faroese
- Icelandic

ANCIENT GREEK — Modern Greek

ALBANIAN
- Tosk
- Gheg

BALTO-SLAVIC

BALTIC
- Old Prussian †
- Lithuanian
- Lettish

SOUTHERN SLAVIC
- Bulgarian
- Macedonian
- Serbo-Croat
- Slovenian

WESTERN SLAVIC
- Polish
- Slovak
- Czech

EASTERN SLAVIC
- Russian (Greater Russian)
- Ukranian (Lesser Russian)
- Byelorussian (White Russian)

CELTS = GAULS

The account given by Julius Caesar

In his *Commentaries on the Gallic War*, Julius Caesar bears witness to two facts which some people have refused to believe:
– that Gaulish was not the only language spoken in Gaul;
– that the terms *Gauls* and *Celts* refer to the same people.

BELLUM GALLICVM	WAR OF THE GAULS

LIBER PRIMVS

I. Gallia est omnis diuisa in partes tres, quarum unam incolunt Belgae, aliam Aquitani, tertiam qui ipsorum lingua Celtae, nostra Galli appellantur. Hi omnes lingua, institutis, legibus inter se differunt.

BOOK ONE

I. The whole of Gaul is divided into three parts: one is inhabited by the Belgae, the other by the Aquitani, and the third by those who, in their language, are called Celts, and in ours Gauls. All of these peoples differ from one another in their languages, institutions and laws.

Breton is not the direct descendant of Gaulish, for the very good reason that Brittany was repopulated in the fifth and sixth centuries AD by other Celts.

Having been forced out of Britannia, modern-day Great Britain, by Germanic invaders (the Anglo-Frisians and the Saxons),[9] these Celtic peoples subsequently settled in the north-west of Gaul in Armorica (*Are morica* must have meant '(country) near the sea' in Gaulish).

The latest research[10] suggests that when the Bretons arrived from Great Britain, the sparse populations which were then living in Armorica had not yet stopped speaking Gaulish, in spite of pressure from the Latin of Julius Caesar's Roman legions. This is the situation which the authors of *Astérix le Gaulois* were depicting when they imagined a small village of Gaulish resistance fighters.[11]

The Breton spoken today would thus be the result of the common development of insular Celtic (spoken in Great Britain) and of continental Celtic (spoken in 'little' Britain, what is now French Brittany). But it was also through contact with the Latin spoken by peoples who had become bilingual that the later development of Breton gave its appearance to the four varieties of Breton spoken in Breton-speaking Brittany today: on the one hand *Cornouaillais*, *Léonais* and *Trégorrois*, and on the other *Vannetais*, which was influenced more by the local Gaulish (see map p. 91).

Nobles and merchants first

It is almost impossible to give the precise date at which Gaulish ceased completely to be spoken in Gaul, but we know from Latin texts that the right of Gauls to become imperial magistrates encouraged the nobility from a very early date to send their children to Roman schools. Tacitus relates that in AD 21 the sons of the greatest personages in Gaul were already attending the Roman school in Autun. Together with the nobility, the merchants were certainly the first to learn Latin, which was the language of trade. It should not be thought, however, that the Gauls replaced their Celtic language by Latin overnight. Only a section of the aristocracy learnt to speak the language of Rome very rapidly, and it was only four hundred years later for example (in the fifth century AD) that, according to the poet Sidoine Apollinaire, the Gaulish nobility of the Arverne (modern-day Auvergne) finally cast off the 'rough shell of the Celtic language'.[12]

Changing one's language is like giving up a part of oneself

It always takes several generations, if not several centuries, for such an upheaval to spread to the entire population. This general principle, which may seem like a sweeping generalisation when we are talking about ancient times for which nothing can be verified, is confirmed by many cases in the history of languages.*

In Gaul, romanisation (in other words, latinisation) initially affected, for reasons of social promotion and economic interest, only the world of the nobility and the merchants, mainly in the urban centres. Gaulish must have remained the language of the home for much longer, especially among the common folk and in the country. What is more, texts of the time bear witness to the fact that, more than two hundred years after the Roman conquest, when the first Christian communities attempted to convert the Gauls to Christianity, the bishops were still obliged to preach in Celtic to the populations they were seeking to convert.[13]

* A study on the acquisition of Greek by the Turkish-speaking Muslim minority of Eastern Greece provides a contemporary example of the slow progress made by a dominant language (in this case Modern Greek) in replacing the native language of a population (in this case Turkish). In this community the more highly educated people, especially in the towns, learnt Greek very quickly. And yet two generations later the language spoken at home remains Turkish for everybody, both young and old and in both town and country, because in their eyes this language retains its symbolic value of belonging to a religion and to a culture [Hélène Sella, 'Le grec parlé par les turcophones du nord-est de la Grèce', state doctoral thesis, University René Descartes (Paris-V), Paris, 1986, unpublished].

The fact that emigrants to the United States all adopted English from the very first generation does not, contrary to appearances, invalidate this example: although they were obliged to learn English in order to find work and adapt to their adopted country, at home and in their family relations they continued to use their native tongue even after several generations.

French 'gauloiseries'

What we are almost certain of is that by the end of the sixth century, Gaulish had ceased to exist except in a few marginal cantons. However, a language does not die without leaving some vestiges of its former life, traces of which can be found in the vocabulary of the languages which succeeded it.

Some seventy Gaulish words survive in Modern French, some of which, like *bec*, *boue*, *chemin* or *mouton* are in common usage whilst others, such as *saie*, *bièvre* or *mègue* no longer have any meaning for modern French people. (See table p. 19.)

The Gaulish league: a bit like old francs

These seventy-one Gaulish words, which have survived the vicissitudes of more than two millennia to appear in Modern French, are connected mainly with the world of agriculture and reflect the kind of existence led by populations living on the products of farming, fishing and hunting. Amongst these words which tell us something about their everyday life, there is one which deserves special attention: *lieue* (the league).

If you think about it, it is quite curious that the Gauls, who had completely adopted Roman civilisation, should have managed to preserve and hand down from generation to generation over several centuries its own unit of length, the *Gaulish league* (2,222 metres), instead of the *Roman mile* (1,485 metres). Now, the Romans had positioned milestones[16] throughout the entire land along the roads they were building, and the Gallo-Romans saw them each and every day. And yet they continued to measure distances in *leagues*, refusing to use the new unit of length, the *mile*. The *league* survived for several centuries, and did not finally give way to the *kilometre* until well after the official adoption of the metric system in 1795.

The word *league* was not confined to the spoken language and continued to enjoy a brilliant literary career throughout the nineteenth century. It can be found in Stendhal, Balzac, Jules Verne and Anatole France. Even today the French speak of leagues, albeit only in a few set expressions such *les bottes de sept lieues*, *à vingt lieues à la ronde*, or *être à cent lieues de penser que* . . .

And perhaps, relatively speaking, this same kind of resistance exists in modern France, where some French people even now continue to count in old francs nearly thirty years after the official introduction of new francs.

THE HANDFUL OF WORDS OF GAULISH ORIGIN

Contrary to what one might think, French vocabulary contains very few words of Gaulish origin, and the following list is not far from being exhaustive.

Since there is dispute over the origin of some words, such as *auvent*, *chemise*, *savon*, *quatre-vingts*, *quinze-vingts*, etc., only those words whose Gaulish origin has been proven are listed here.[14] The meaning of certain words has been given only in cases of ambiguity (between brackets) or where the meaning has changed (between quotation marks).

alose (le poisson)	changer	lie
alouette	char	lieue
arpent	charpente	lotte (le poisson)
balai	charrue	marne
banne/benne	chemin	mègue 'petit-lait'
barde	chêne	mine (dans la terre)
bec	claie	mouton
bercer	cloche	orteil
bief	combe	pièce 'morceau'
bièvre 'castor'	craindre	quai
boisseau	dartre	raie 'sillon'
bonde	dru	ruche 'écorce'
bouc	druide	saie 'casaque'
boue	dune	sapin
bouge 'besace'	galet	sillon 'bande de
bouleau	glaise	terrain'
bourbier	glaner	soc
braies	gobelet	suie
bran 'excrément'	if	talus
brasser	jante	tanche (le poisson)
breuil 'champ'	jarret	tarière
briser	javelle	tonne 'outre, vase'
bruyère	lande	valet
cervoise	landier 'chenêt'	vassal

Some words in this list, such as *breuil*, *landier*, or *mègue*, may pose problems of meaning for modern French people. However, the word *breuil*, 'field, small wood', has given many place-names: *Le Breuil*, *Bruel*, etc. Much more frequent, in spite of appearances, the word *mègue* still survives to this day in the derivative *mégot*, which was formed in the nineteenth century, probably from a dialect word from Touraine, *mégauder* 'suck'.[15]

Tell me where you live and I'll tell you what sort of place it used to be

The other traces of this lost language are the place-names. The French utter them every day of the week without suspecting that they are Gaulish. There are very many place-names of Gaulish origin and they are the most living source of information on the life and language of the Gauls.

Thanks to toponymy, which is the study of place-names, we can define the four main types of town that the Gauls lived in:[17] *fortified places*, *market towns*, *holy places*, and *special situations*.

1. The fortified places: they are easily recognised by the suffixes -*dunum*, -*durum* or -*rato* 'fortress, fortified town', but only if you know that phonetic development has generally removed part of the original syllables: thus the suffixes -*dunum* are to be found in *Verdun*, -*durum* in *Nanterre* and -*rato* in *Carpentras*.[18] (See table p. 21.)

2. The market towns may be identified from their suffix -*magus* 'market': *Noyon* comes from *Noviomagus* 'new market', *Rouen* from *Rotomagus*, etc.

3. The holy places can be recognised from the form *nemeto* 'sanctuary': thus *Nanterre* comes from *Nemetodurum* 'sanctuary fortress'.

4. Special situations, identifiable from terms such as *lano* 'plain', for example in *Meulan* which comes from *Mediolanum* 'middle of the plain', or *bona* 'port' in *Lillebonne*, from *Juliobona* 'the port of Julius' (Caesar).

Tell me where you live and I'll tell you who used to live there

Although it is common knowledge that *Lutetia* was the name of a small island in the Seine around which Paris grew up, few people know that *Lutetia* was a word of pre-Celtic origin which probably meant 'marsh'. The name *Paris* comes from the name of the small Gaulish tribe known as the *Parisii* who lived on this island and in the marshlands between the forests of what is now the large modern suburb of Paris encompassing Chantilly, Fontainebleau and Compiègne.

In fact, if the names of most of the peoples who lived in Gaul have come down to modern times, it is because, from the fourth century onwards, the old town names were replaced by the names of the tribes who lived in them, probably because of the systematic destruction of the fortified towns by the barbarian invaders.

Thus, just as the *Parisii* gave their name to *Paris* (in AD 360), so the *Senones* 'the venerable' gave theirs to *Sens*, the *Pictavi* 'the cunning' to *Poitiers*, the *Bituriges* 'the kings of the world' to *Bourges*, etc.[19] (See table, p. 25 and the corresponding map p. 23.)

Some tribal names have actually given rise to different place-names according to whether they were pronounced in the Gaulish or the Latin manner. Such is the case, amongst others, of *Nîmes* and *Nemours*, which come from the same word. (See table, p. 22.)

THE GAULISH CITADELS

Here are some place-names formed with Gaulish suffixes.

-DUNUM   -DURUM   -RATO

which all mean fortress

suffix -DUNUM as in

LUGDUNUM→LYON

Autun	*fortress of Augustus*
Châteaudun	*castle fortress*
Embrun	*fortress of yews*
Issoudun	*high fortress*
Laon	
Leiden (Holland)	*fortress of Lug,*
Loudun	*god of arts and crafts*
Lyon	
Meung	*market fortress*
Nyon (Switzerland)	
Nyons	*new fortress*
Verdun	*super fortress*

Suffix -DURUM as in

NEMETODURUM→NANTERRE

Auxerre	*fortress of Autisius*
Bressuire	*fortress of Briccius*
Issoire	
Yzeure	*fortress of Iccius*
Nanterre	*sanctuary fortress*

Suffix -RATO as in

CARBANTORATO→CARPENTRAS

Tarare	*fortress of Tarus*
Tonnerre	*fortress of Turnos*
Argentré	*fortress + money*
Carpentras	*fortress + chariot*

21

NAMES OF TOWNS PRONOUNCED
IN THE GAULISH OR LATIN MANNER

According to whether the name was pronounced in the Gaulish or Latin manner, (in other words, with different syllables being stressed,) we now have two different names from the same word of origin.

GAULISH STRESS   LATIN STRESS

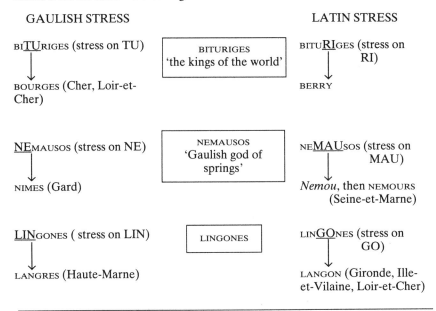

biTUriges (stress on TU) → BOURGES (Cher, Loir-et-Cher)

BITURIGES 'the kings of the world'

bituRIges (stress on RI) → BERRY

NEmausos (stress on NE) → NIMES (Gard)

NEMAUSOS 'Gaulish god of springs'

neMAUsos (stress on MAU) → *Nemou*, then NEMOURS (Seine-et-Marne)

LINgones (stress on LIN) → LANGRES (Haute-Marne)

LINGONES

linGOnes (stress on GO) → LANGON (Gironde, Ille-et-Vilaine, Loir-et-Cher)

An exception to the rule: the *Provincia*

The list on p. 24 gives the forty towns whose old name was abandoned to be replaced in the fourth century by that of the Gaulish tribe which inhabited the region.

These names have been placed on a map which, in particular, reveals a large blank in the region of the south-east, which corresponds to the ancient *Provincia Narbonensis*, which is now Provence.

The almost total absence of place-names representing the names of the Gaulish tribes in the region may be explained by the fact that they themselves had settled in the region only somewhat late and in a highly scattered way. Moreover, the *Provincia* was latinised very early on – sixty years before the rest of Gaul – and to a very considerable degree, and the Greeks had founded colonies there from the seventh century BC. The place-names in the region are therefore often of Greek (*Marseille, Nice, Antibes, Agde*) and, above all, Latin origin: *Fréjus* comes from *Forum Julii*, in memory of Julius Caesar, *Aix* from *Aquae Sextiae*,

22

TOWNS WHICH HAVE CHANGED THEIR NAMES

Lutetia: old name
PARISII: name of the Gaulish tribe
<u>Paris</u>: present name

We can see from the map that the towns which changed name to take on that of the tribes who lived there are more numerous in the north and almost non–existent in Provence.

THE CHANGING NAMES OF FRENCH TOWNS

Old name	Name of Gaulish tribe	Modern name
Samarobriva	AMBIANI	Amiens
Juliomagus	ANDECAVI	Angers
Nemetacum	ATREBATES	Arras
Igena	ABRINCATES	Avranches
Augustodurum	BAIOCASSES	Bayeux
Cossium	VASATES	Bazas (Gironde)
Cesaromagus	BELLOVACI	Beauvais
Avaricum	BITURIGES	Bourges, Berry
Divona	CADURCI	Cahors
Durotalannum	CATALAUNI	Châlons-sur-Marne
Autricum	CARNUTES	Chartres
Lugdunum	CONVENAE	(St-Bertrand-de-) Comminges
Mediolanum	EBUROVICES	Évreux
Anderitum	GABALI	Javols (Lozère)
Noviodunum	DIABLINTI	Jublains (Mayenne)
Andematunnum	LINGONES	Langres, Langon
Vindunum	CENOMANNI	Le Mans
Augustoritum	LEMOVICES	Limoges
Noviomagus	LEXOVII	Lisieux
Iatinon	MELDI	Meaux
Divodurum	MEDIOMATRICES	Metz
Condevincum	NAMNETES	Nantes
Lutetia	PARISII	Paris
Vesonna	PETROCORII	Périgueux
Limonum	PICTAVI	Poitiers
Condate	REDONES	Rennes
Durocortorum	REMI	Reims
Segodunum	RUTENI	Rodez, Rouergue
Mediolanum	SANTONES	Saintes
Noviodunum	SAGII	Sées
Augustomagus	SILVANECTES	Senlis
Agedincum	SENONES	Sens
Augusta	SUESSIONES	Soissons
Cesarodunum	TURONES	Tours
Augustobona	TRICASSES	Troyes
Noviomagus	TRICASTINI	(St-Paul-) Trois-Châteaux
Darioritum	VENETI	Vannes
Augusta	VIROMANDUI	Vermand (Aisne)
Argenue	VIDUCASSES	Vieux (Calvados)

in memory of Sextius Calvinus who conquered the *Provincia* around 120 BC.

Such then is the extent of what the Gauls, the ancestors of the French, have left of their language, and it will no doubt come as a sad surprise to many a French person to discover that, apart from a few thousand place-names, only a few dozen words of more or less common usage have survived.

THE AGE OF THE 'BARBARIANS'

From Latin to French

For over five hundred years the Roman occupation of Gaul had given the inhabitants of the country a new language as well as a different civilisation. The country had been organised, the economy had been developed, roads had been built, and everything would have been for the best in the best of all possible worlds if there had not been the great upheaval caused by the invasions. Between the fall of the Roman empire (476) and the appearance of what has been called the first 'monument' of the French language, the text of the *Strasbourg Oaths* (842), the people suffered almost four centuries of opposition to knowledge and enlightenment, which represent four centuries of darkness as far as we are concerned, because there are no documents for us to study.

And yet it was a decisive period for the history of French, because it was during this time that there developed the process of differentiation and formation of dialects which we covered rather too briefly in the preamble and to which we must now return.

In spite of the scarcity of documents relating to this period, we shall endeavour to make use of what meagre historical data we can gather together in an attempt to reconstitute the linguistic situation of the various peoples at that time and to strive to understand what could have brought about the changes which culminated in the French we find at the beginning of the ninth century.

We shall start from two historically attested facts: on the one hand, the *Germanic invasions*, and the Frankish incursions in particular, because the language of the invaders had particularly noticeable effects on what later became French; and on the other hand, as a counterpoint, *the spread of Christianity*, which had officially adopted Latin as its liturgical language in the fourth century.[20]

Provence, the first Roman province

To understand the situation as a whole, one has first of all to remember that when Julius Caesar arrived in 58 BC, the Romans had already been settled in the south of Gaul for some sixty years. Around 120 BC they had founded a province there, called *Provincia Narbonensis*, the *Narbonnaise*, which took in the regions now covered by Provence, Languedoc, Dauphiné and Savoie (apart from the high valleys). The process of romanisation had been rapid, profound and durable.[21]

This region, where the Gauls had had the least influence[22] on the Ligurian peoples who occupied it before them, was also the one that underwent the least Germanic influence. That explains to some extent why the dialects of Provence have remained very close to Latin.

The Germanic invasions

Thus, if we leave aside the area corresponding to the former *Provincia*, which seems to have resisted all later influences with particular success, the only invaders to matter for the general history of the language around the fifth century are Germanic tribes:

- the Franks;
- the Visigoths;
- the Burgundians. (See map p. 27.)

For the linguistic variety which resulted in French, it was the Franks who played the most important role, and that is understandable when you remember that they settled in Gaul for several centuries. Indeed, long before the invasions of the fifth century, the Franks were constantly to be found on Gaulish soil. They were to be found from early times in the ranks of the Roman army, in which they enrolled as mercenaries. Moreover, in the second century AD the widespread feeling of insecurity had caused the landowners to flee, leading in the third century to a virtual occupation of the entire territory of the Franks, since the Romans had given them the right to occupy the abandoned properties. By the time the Gallo-Roman nobility flooded back to the countryside at the beginning of the fourth century, these Germanic tribes had become sedentary and were farming the land.[23] The Frankish occupation was not, therefore, confined to the military, but included people who had settled permanently and who had daily contact with the Gallo-Romans.

The Frankish dominion in the north

Geographically, the Franks had moved within the space of a century from the Rhine to the Somme, and in thirty years their king, Clovis, had extended the Frankish kingdom from the Somme to the Loire. Thus, the entire northern half of modern France, with the exception of Brittany, formed the hard nucleus of the Frankish sphere of influence in the fifth century. The domination of the Franks over the rest of the territory, and in

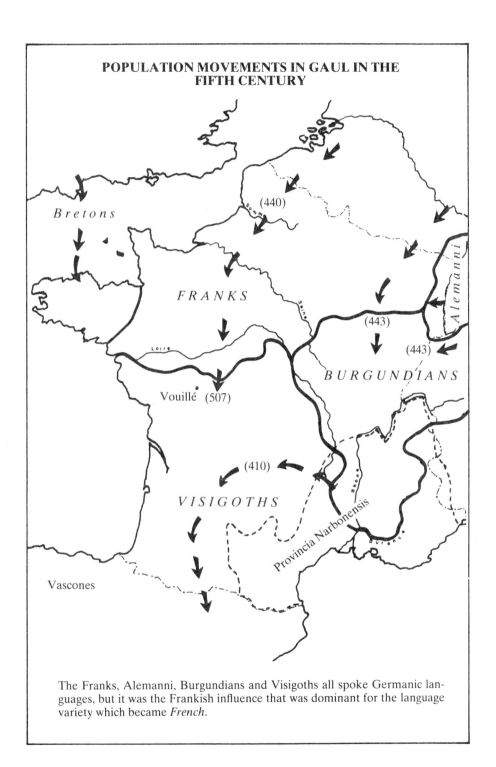

POPULATION MOVEMENTS IN GAUL IN THE FIFTH CENTURY

Bretons

FRANKS

Somme

Seine

(440)

Alemanni

(443)

(443)

BURGUNDIANS

Loire

Vouillé (507)

(410)

VISIGOTHS

Rhône

Provincia Narbonensis

Durance

Vascones

The Franks, Alemanni, Burgundians and Visigoths all spoke Germanic languages, but it was the Frankish influence that was dominant for the language variety which became *French*.

particular over that held by the Visigoths, was no more than a 'loose protectorate'.[24]

The Visigoths, who had taken Rome in AD 410, had at that time been granted the south of Gaul, from the Loire to the Durance, by the Roman emperor Honorius. One hundred years later, after the battle of Vouillé (507), Clovis, king of the Franks, extended his rule to cover their lands.

For their part, the Burgundians, who were forced to flee the region of the Rhine in 443 by the Huns, powerful barbarian hordes from Asia, were settled by Aetius, the holder in Gaul of the remnants of Roman power in the region corresponding to what is today Savoie (the name *Sapaudia* means 'fir forest'). They subsequently spread out in all directions, towards Troyes, the Loire and the Durance,[25] and settled a territory corresponding roughly to the present-day administrative regions of Bourgogne, Franche-Comté and the Rhône-Alpes.

Langue d'oïl, langue d'oc and Francoprovençal

From the linguistic point of view, this settling of the territory by peoples of various origins seems to be responsible in part for the great dialectal divisions (see map p. 29) which still split the country to this day:
- the *oïl* dialects of the north (so called because *oïl* was their word for 'yes');
- the *oc* dialects of the south (where 'yes' was *oc*)
- the *Francoprovençal* dialects in an intermediate zone, which covers the middle basin of the Rhône and scissors out from Châteldon to the south of Vichy (Allier) to take in the regions of Lyon, Geneva and Grenoble.

This differentiation into two main zones with an intermediate zone was probably completed by the end of the age of the invasions. But at that time the fragmentation into smaller dialectal varieties (Normand, Picard, Limousin, Savoyard, Provençal, Gascon, etc.) had not yet taken place.

The area where the *oïl* dialects were spoken corresponded more or less to the territory settled by the Franks, whose linguistic influence on the French language was considerable.

The southern region, which was romanised in depth at a very early age, was scarcely influenced at all linguistically by the settlement, which was in any case quite shortlived, of the Visigoths. It should be added that the *oc* region originally extended to the north of Bordeaux, taking in the Saintonge region.

The region in between, which was the Francoprovençal zone,[26] shared some features with the *oïl* and other features with the *oc* dialects.

THE MAJOR DIVISIONS OF THE ROMANCE DIALECTS

Oïl region

(oïl = yes)

Saintonge

Francoprovençal region

Oc region

(oc = yes)

Catalan

Tuscan region

It should be noted that these major dialect divisions relate only to the differentiation of Latin into Gallo-Roman dialects, and that *Catalan* is a member of the Ibero-Roman group of languages whilst the dialects of *Corsica* are related to the dialects of Italy.

Furthermore, the *oc* region originally extended to the north of Bordeaux, taking in the Saintonge region.

Everybody had something to offer

In attempting to establish the link between the Latin imported by the Romans and the Romance languages that we know today, it must by no means be imagined that the Gallo-Romans, in other words the Gauls once they had accepted Roman civilisation and the Latin language, woke up one fine day to find that they had stopped speaking Latin and were now speaking Picard, Normand, Poitevin, etc. The development of a language is an extremely slow process, and that is why it normally takes place without the language users realising what is happening, because they never actually stop understanding one another.

For the varieties that emerged from Latin in Gaul we must start from the information supplied by Julius Caesar and confirmed by Strabo[27] that the few hundred Gaulish tribes who were settled in Gaul originally did not all speak the same variety of Gaulish and that, as a result, each one was able to put a dash of its own 'accent' into the pronunciation of Latin.

Under the influence of these contacts between peoples speaking different languages, but also because of the new needs of the communities which were undergoing transformation, the Latin spoken in Gaul was modified in its turn, diversifying and giving birth to forms of language which differed more or less noticeably according to the region.

The Germanic influence on the vocabulary

The Germanic influence is to be found first of all in the vocabulary, which contains several hundred words, many of them Frankish in origin, which are indisputably Germanic. This is not surprising when you remember that the great Frankish invasion of the fifth century had been preceded by a long period of constant contact between Romans, romanised Celts and the Germanic peoples. Indeed, if we accept the idea that Gaulish had not yet completely disappeared from use during the early centuries of our era, then the three languages must have 'cohabited' in the daily exchanges between bilingual, or even trilingual, speakers, with the common language being a kind of Latin mixed with Gaulish and Germanic. Such a situation is by no means exceptional, and examples could easily be found today in several frontier regions of Europe, or even in Switzerland in the Grisons, where the people speak both Rheto-Roman and the Swiss varieties of German.

It is not easy to reconstruct the chronology of the borrowings from the Germanic, but it has been established by the latest research[28] that, of the four hundred French words listed as coming from the Germanic, at least half were introduced before the Frankish invasion in the fifth century, which means that these words were borrowed during the long period of gradual infiltration by the Franks which preceded the invasion proper.

FRENCH AND ITS ANCESTORS

To speak about the influence exerted on a given language by other languages, the linguists use the terms *substratum* and *superstratum* (*stratum* 'layer', *sub* 'below', *super* 'above').

In Gaul, Latin was subjected, amongst others, to the influence of the Gaulish *substratum* since the Gauls spoke Latin with their Gaulish 'accent'.

Subsequent contact between the inhabitants and the new invaders, whose language was neither Celtic nor Latin but Germanic, further modified the form of the Latin spoken by the Gauls.

Thus, the Latin spoken in Gaul, from which came the Gallo-Roman dialects, was subjected to the effects on the one hand of the *substrata* (languages previously spoken by the various tribes) and on the other of the Germanic *superstratum* (the language of the newcomers)

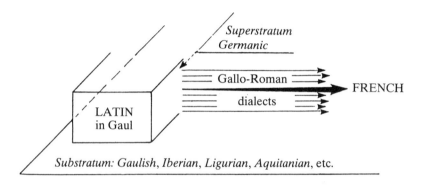

Some loan words – such as *savon* which is thought to come from Frisian – can be put down to other Germanic influences.[29] (See table p. 32.)

FRANCE: LAND OF THE FRANKS

The very word *Francia* 'France', which appears in the literature only in the third century (in Ausonius and Marcellinus Ammianus, referring solely to the region occupied by the Franks on the left bank of the River Meuse), was probably created in the second century. But it was only after the sixth century that it was used to refer to Northern Gaul.[30]

The Germanic influence on pronunciation

The Frankish influence also made itself felt in particular on the word order and the pronunciation of the language spoken in the north of Gaul. We shall take the pronunciation first, but without going into the details of the

VOCABULARY OF GERMANIC ORIGIN

The following list does not contain all[31] of the four hundred Germanic words identified in the language spoken in ancient Gaul, since many of those which appear in Old French have disappeared today and would mean nothing to modern French people (*brant* 'sword blade', *fuere* 'sheath', *rouche* 'iris', etc.).

Among those which have come down to modern times (approximately one third) are terms relating to:

war and chivalry: *bande, baron* 'brave man, husband', *bière* 'coffin', *blason, brandon, convoi, crosse, échanson, éperon, épieu, étrier, félon, fief, flèche, gain, gant, garçon* 'servant', *gars* 'soldier, valet, churl', *gonfanon* 'standard', *guerre, guet, hache, hanap, harangue, heaume, honte, lice, maréchal, marquis, orgueil, rang, sénéchal, trêve; choisir, éblouir, épargner, fournir, gagner, garder, guetter, haïr, honnir, souiller*;

life in the fields: *blé, bois, bûche, fange, fourrage, fourrure, framboise, gerbe, germe, grappe, haie, hameau, hêtre, houe, houx, jardin, marais, osier, roseau, saule, touffe, trappe, troène; caille, chouette, crapaud, frelon, hanneton, héron, laie, mésange*;

the crafts: *alène, étai, feutre, filtre, houille, maçon, tuyau; bâtir, broyer, déchirer, gratter, graver, râper*;

the life of the seafarer: *bouée, écume, falaise, flot*;

colours: *blanc, bleu, blond, brun, fauve, garance* 'scarlet', *gris, saur* 'red, brownish-yellow';

domestic life: *banc, beignet, bille, buée, crèche, cruche, écharpe, fard, fauteuil, flacon, froc, housse, lanière, louche, poche, quenotte, soupe; hanche, flanc, téton; fluet, frais, gai, laid, long; broder, danser, guérir, héberger, lécher, regarder, rôtir, téter, trépigner*.

---

phonetic developments which occurred at this time. The following are just two examples, a consonant and a vowel, which illustrate this influence.

The emergence of a new consonant; *h*

What we now call the aspirated French *h* is, in fact, neither an /h/ nor aspirated. An /h/ is, in fact, a true consonant made not by an *as*piration but by a strong *ex*piration of air, like the one we hear in the English *hair* or the German *Hund* 'dog'. In Modern French, there is simply an absence of liaison (as in *les hanches* and not *les-z-hanches*) or an absence of elision (as in *le hêtre* and not *l'hêtre*).

But have you ever wondered why there is elision in *l'homme* and obligatory liaison in *les honneurs* when there is no elision in *le hêtre* and no liaison in *les hanches*?

It is because of the Franks. The /h/ of *hêtre* or *hanche* does not now get the same treatment as the /h/ in *homme* or *honneur* because there was a time when words like *hêtre* or *hanche*, introduced into Gaul by the Germanic peoples, were pronounced with a true consonantal /h/, as in their language, whereas words'like *homme* or *honneur*, which came from Latin, were not.

To understand this apparent anomaly, you have to know that in the Latin introduced into Gaul in the first century BC[32] the written Latin consonant *h* (as in HOMO 'man', HABET 'he/she has', HONOR 'honour', etc.) was no longer pronounced by the Romans,[33] even though it was still written, and that it could not therefore be transmitted to the conquered peoples.[34]

If we draw up a list of all the words beginning with a written *h* in French, we find that nowadays elision and liaison are regularly omitted in words borrowed from the Germanic, such as *haïr, hameau, hanap, hanche, harangue, heaume, héron, hêtre, honnir, honte, houe, housse, houx, huche,* etc. Hearing them pronounced by people who had a true aspirated /h/ in their language, the Gallo-Romans borrowed them with that pronunciation.

The same phenomena are found in English, where words such as *heir, honest, honour* and *hour,* which come from Latin and were introduced by the Norman Conquest, are pronounced without an *h,* whilst *holly, holy, honey, hoof* or *horse,* of Anglo-Saxon origin, are pronounced with a true e*x*pirated consonant /h/.

Instead of this consonant /h/ Modern French now has something completely different with the totally illogical name of 'aspirate' *h,* which is utterly confusing because this so-called 'aspirate' *h* does not represent an aspiration but simply the absence of something. But since language changes are very slow and do not spread to the entire population at the same speed, if you listened carefully to what is being said around you, you would certainly be able to hear some people even today still pronouncing a true /h/ consonant in words such as *hâbleur, hachoir, haillon, haine, hâle,* etc.[35] A study carried out several years ago showed that some modern French people retain traces of this old Germanic habit.[36]

Both in the case of this pronunciation in which a proper consonant is pronounced and the case of the 'aspirate' *h* which prevents the article being elided (*la hache*) and liaison being made (*les haches* with no *s* sound before *haches*), this peculiarity of French is the result of Germanic, and in particular Frankish, influence.

Vowels disappear

Far more spectacular has been the effect of the Germanic influence on certain vowels, because these forms of pronunciation have had far more wide-reaching consequences.

We know that one characteristic of the Germanic languages is the strong stress that falls on one syllable in the word together with a weakening of neighbouring vowels. In the German word *Abend* 'evening', for example, the first vowel is heard very clearly but the second is 'swallowed', so to speak. These Germanic habits of articulation had considerable effects on all of the words in the language spoken in Gaul.

33

A single example will demonstrate the effects of this stress pattern. In Latin the word TÊLA 'cloth' was stressed on the first syllable, which had a long vowel. If we compare the Italian *tela*, the Provençal *telo*, the Francoprovençal *tala*, the Spanish *tela* and the French *toile*, we can see that only French (similar in that to all the other *oïl* languages) has today lost the final vowel (written at the end of the word but not pronounced). By contrast, Italian, Provençal and the other *oc* and Francoprovençal dialects as well as Spanish have kept the final vowel.

This way of pronouncing is still today what best distinguishes the so-called 'pointu' or northern accent without final vowels in this kind of word from the southern accent in which the so-called 'mute' *e* sounds are articulated.

Bonnet blanc or Blanc bonnet?

Finally, there is one further trace of the Frankish influence in place-names, but it is more subtle than in the names of Gaulish towns which we looked at earlier, because it is not the words themselves which have been borrowed but the way in which they are formed.

In Latin the adjective could be placed either before or after the noun, depending on whether it was being used as an epithet or an attribute. In Old French, forms like *blancs manteaux* or *rouges tabliers* were common. In Modern French it is the post-nominal position which subsequently became the norm. Now, in Germanic languages, unlike Modern French, the determiner always precedes the determined: in French it is *la langue française*, but in German *die französische Sprache* and in English *the French language*. Indeed, the authors of *Astérix chez les Bretons* fully understood just how much comic effect they could get from the front position of the adjective, which is unusual in French, in expressions such as *la gauloise cuisine*, *les romaines galères*, or *la magique potion*.

The Germanic influence can still be seen today in place-names: putting the adjective in front of the noun became the norm in regions settled by the Franks, whereas in other regions the adjective was placed after the noun. Toponyms in *-ville* (from the Latin *villa* 'farm', then 'village') are very common in the North where there is a majority of *Neuville*, *Neuvelle*, *Neuveville*, whereas in the south there are far more *Villeneuve*.

The same is true of place-names in *-court* (from the Latin *cohors* 'enclosure', 'farmyard', then 'farm' and finally 'village'), which are to be found in large numbers in the north: *Chauvoncourt* (Pas-de-Calais), *Beaudricourt* (Pas-de-Calais), *Billancourt* (Hauts-de-Seine), *Ablancourt* (Somme), *Azincourt* (Pas-de-Calais), etc., and in which the first term is usually a person's name in Germanic.[37]

The example of *Francheville* and *Villefranche*

In the *Dictionnaire des communes de France* there are twelve *Francheville* (or *Franqueville*) and twenty-one *Villefranche* (or *Villefranque*). If you placed them on a map, you would find that a large majority of the *Francheville* (nine out of twelve) are to the north of the line of maximum settlement by the Franks, whilst virtually all the *Villefranche* (nineteen out of the twenty-one) are located south of this line, albeit with one exception: the department of the Rhône contains both a *Villefranche* and a *Francheville*.

Since a large number of towns with the name *Villefranche* (and also *Villeneuve*) were created in the thirteenth century,[38] that explains why some are found in the north. But it is remarkable that up to that time, in other words several centuries after the end of the invasions, people in the north had preserved the habit of forming town names in the Germanic way.

It is significant, however, that systematic research[39] on 428 towns forming pairs of the type *Francheville–Villefranche* shows 100 per cent of formations on the Frankish model *Francheville* to the north of the oldest line of settlement of the Franks (in 440 it extended as far as the Somme), and 82 per cent to the north of the line corresponding to the advances they made up to the reign of Clovis (in 507 this line passed slightly below the Loire, as can be seen on the map p. 27).

The effects of the Germanic invasions

It is clear from all of the above that it was essentially in the region of the *oïl* languages that the Germanic, and especially the Frankish, influence left perceptible traces in the language which was to become French. But other elements were also to contribute to the formation of the language, and of these the spread of Christianity had an important role to play.

THE AGE OF THE CHRISTIANS

The spread of Christianity

While the Frankish invasion brought elements of diversification to the language spoken in Gaul, another factor, which seemed to be working in the opposite direction, towards unification, was the birth and spread of Christianity with Latin as the tool of propagation.

There is evidence of a first Christian community in Lyon at the end of the second century, but it seems to have been composed of followers of the faith who had yet to acquire a good command of Latin: their bishop Irenaeus, in a book against heresy, apologised for his unrefined Latin on

PLAYING GAMES WITH THE ROAD-MAP

You could take a road-map of France and have a bit of fun looking for symmetrical formations in which the same name is preceded or followed by the same adjective, such as *Francheville and Villefranche, Neufchâteau* and *Châteauneuf, Longchamp* and *Champlong, Bellaigue* and *Aiguebelle*, etc.

When the adjective is placed in front of the noun (e.g. *Neufchâteau*), you form the hypothesis that the formation is of the Germanic type, contrary to *Châteauneuf*, where the adjective is placed after the noun.

You could then try to verify whether the formations of the type *Francheville, Neufchâteau*, etc. are really in a majority in the north of France, where the Franks settled at a very early age, and then count the exceptions.

You must not, of course, expect to find a clear-cut and absolute opposition between the north and the south, because not all of these towns were founded at the time of the Germanic invasions.

As an example, the map opposite shows only those place-names which are first referred to in texts from before the year 1000:

10	*Neuville*	and	6	*Villeneuve*
6	*Chaumont*	and	1	*Moncaup* (formed from *Mont* and *caup* 'bald')
2	*Hautmont*	and	1	*Montaut*
1	*Hauterive*	and	1	*Ribaute* ('Rive haute')
1	*Longeville*	and	1	*Villelongue*

You must not be surprised to find *Neuville* also in the form *Nouvialle, Hautmont* also in the form *Omont*, and *Chaumont* in the form *Caumont*.

---

the grounds that his apostolic work led him to live amongst people who still spoke Gaulish.[40]

Other communities existed in the third century in Autun, Dijon, Langres and Besançon,[41] but it was in the fourth century that the new religion spread most widely. By the end of that century the majority of townspeople were converted and the evangelisation of the countryside had begun.[42] But the latter process must have been a slow one. This was the time when Saint Martin de Tours, in a fine display of efficiency, decided to christianise the popular feast days and the ancient places of pagan worship,[43] thereby bringing together under one church roof the Celtic traditions, the religious customs imported from Rome, and the new religion: in going to the same sanctuaries on the same days as before to celebrate new rites, the people remained within their normal places of residence and therefore in the same ancient administrative divisions. In particular, we know that the dioceses were created within the framework of the Roman towns.[44]

AN EXAMPLE: NEUVILLE-VILLENEUVE

Below is a map of toponyms for five pairs of towns like *Neuville* and *Villeneuve, Longeville* and *Villelongue*, etc., whose names appear in texts before the year 1000.

With the exception of one *Nouvialle* in Cantal and one *Caumont* in Aveyron, all the Germanic-type toponyms (pre-posed adjective) are indeed located in the northern half of the country, where Frankish settlement lasted longest (eighteen out of twenty), whilst all the toponyms with post-posed adjective are found in the south with the exception of a Villeneuve in Seine-et-Oise (nine out of ten).

The church was to benefit very rapidly from the support of the nobility, who respected it and frequently bequeathed their fortunes to it.[45] Becoming rich and powerful, it was able to take responsibility for running schools and ultimately universities. In this way, the Latin language, which had replaced Greek as the official language of the Christian liturgy in the West in the fourth century at the latest, must in all likelihood have begun at this time to play a unifying role among the various tribes who congregated at regular times of the year in ecclesiastical centres and the bishop's town.[46]

The spectacular conversion of Clovis

Clovis, king of the Franks, was quick to grasp the importance of this new religion, and, after his marriage to Clotilda, a Christian princess from Burgundy, he turned his conversion into an 'event': his baptism was celebrated with great pomp and circumstance by Remi, the bishop of Reims, on Christmas Day itself (probably in 496),[47] after which he became the defender of the church, which was now the only moral authority left in the land after the collapse of Rome and the fall of the Roman Empire in the West twenty years earlier in 476.

By the time of his death in 511, Clovis had founded a vast Frankish kingdom, although it did not include Brittany, Aquitaine or Provence.[48] In this kingdom, where people speaking Germanic languages rubbed shoulders with speakers of Romance languages, the church, whose language was Latin, became omnipresent: the number of monasteries increased and, with their workshops of scribes and their schools, became centres for the spread of Greco-Latin culture.

But the Latin they spoke had changed

This same church, however, was unable to prevent Latin, spoken, as we have seen, by bilinguals not to say trilinguals, from evolving and undergoing profound change. In the ninth century this spoken language had become so different from the classical Latin taught in the schools that the Council of Tours in 813 asked for the homilies to be translated into both *rustica romana lingua* and *Germanic*. It also recommended the priests to preach in these popular tongues in order to be better understood by all of the faithful.[49]

Now, not only did the faithful no longer understand Latin, but, as a result of the invasions, education had so deteriorated that even in the episcopal schools Latin was no longer taught other than for the liturgical formulae and prayers.[50] We can therefore understand why 'true' Latin was no longer understood in Gaul. But how had this happened?

Charlemagne and Latin

Outside of the constraints of school and the institutions, the spoken language had been able to develop freely. Charlemagne, a Frankish king whose language was not a Roman but a Germanic dialect, had the greatest admiration for Latin and was eager to restore it to its former glory. Faced with a form of Latin that was no longer recognisable, he attempted to redress the situation. He called upon foreign monks, mainly from Great Britain, to restore to his people a knowledge of and a taste for the Latin language that they had lost. The most famous of these monks was the scholar Alcuin, who, in the solitude of his island monastery, had been able to keep alive the knowledge of the true Latin that was his daily reading, far from the harmful changes that it had undergone on the continent in the mouths of those who spoke it every day and had been distorting it for centuries.

Installed by Charlemagne in the abbey of Saint-Martin in Tours, Alcuin[51] also had the task of giving the faithful, who no longer understood 'true' Latin, access to the text of the *Vulgate*, a Latin version of the Bible produced by Saint Jérôme four centuries earlier.

All of these efforts culminated in what has been called the *Carolingian renaissance*, especially famous for having reformed the writing of books by imposing the *Caroline minuscule*, a clearer, minuscule style of handwriting in which the words were separated and each sentence began with a capital letter. This Carolingian renaissance was also a renaissance for Latin which, through the restoration of education, had found a new lease of life and remained the only written language. In the desire to educate an illiterate population, a language confined to the written medium was reconstituted: as a result, it once again became a language restricted to the literati. In trying to educate the masses, they had recreated an élite.

They thought they were still speaking Latin, but it was already Gallo-Roman

Charlemagne's attempts resulted in the discovery of a fact which had gone unnoticed until then: that the language they were all speaking was no longer Latin as they had thought. It had imperceptibly become a different language, a Romance language and no longer a Roman one, which was to undergo even more transformations over the centuries before becoming Modern French.

Within the framework of educating the masses and in order to give them access to the *Vulgate*, written in classical school Latin, it became necessary to devise working tools which allowed the people to understand it again. The eighth and ninth centuries were the age of the *glossaries*, which are little dictionaries for going from one language to another. The most important, known as the *Reichenau Glossary*, contains over 1,300 words with the Romance translation written opposite the Latin but in Latinised form. Another document, the *Cassel Glossary*, gives the Germanic equivalents for 265 Romance words.[52]

How people spoke in the eighth and ninth centuries

When linguists declare that such and such a word had such and such a form at a given time, that it was pronounced in such and such a way or that it had such and such a meaning different from its modern meaning, they often see a gleam of amusement tinged with scepticism in the eyes of the person they are talking to. Without the help of a tape recorder, how can we claim to know the pronunciation or the nuances of meaning of ancient words? Linguists have ways of knowing, and for the Early Middle Ages they take advantage of a myriad of linguistic observations piously collected by the monks for a purpose in no way connected with keeping alive a trace of the spoken language. These glossaries then become precious mines of information.

The first dictionaries: the glossaries

The *Reichenau Glossary*[53] is therefore like a Latin-Romance dictionary giving the Romance equivalents of 1,300 Latin words. For us it provides written proof, in particular, of the existence, in eighth century spoken language, of certain words which we know today but which were unknown in classical Latin. (See table p. 41.)

These data lift a corner of the veil, but the history of words is even more difficult to reconstruct than the history of peoples, and documents such as those made by the monks of Reichenau or Cassel are only one of the elements that enable us to rediscover the various stages in language change. Many other indices must be brought together to explain, for example, why it is not the word JECUR (a Latin word taken from the Greek) which has come down to us with the meaning of 'liver', but the Romance word *ficato*, which has become the French *foie*. The word *ficato* is formed on the Latin word FICUS 'fig', and would appear to have nothing to do with the 'liver' other than that the Greeks, followed by the Romans, fattened their geese with figs to obtain particularly fleshy and tasty livers. The FICATUM JECUR or 'fig-fattened goose liver', which was very much sought after, must have become such a common expression that it was shortened to FICATUM (just as the modern French say *frites* as an abbreviation of *pommes de terre frites*). To begin with the word FICATUM probably designated only edible animal livers, with its meaning then being extended to include the human organ.[55]

DISCOVERING HOW PEOPLE SPOKE IN THE EIGHTH CENTURY

The glossaries of the monks of Reichenau and Cassel

The Reichenau Glossary takes the form of a Latin-Romance dictionary in which Romance words appear in a latinised form:

LATIN	ROMANCE	MODERN FRENCH
OVES	berbices	brebis (Old Fr. berbis)
VESPERTILIONES	calvas sorices	chauves-souris
COTURNIX	quaccola	caille
GALLIA	Francia	France
JECUR	ficato	foie

The Cassel glossary,[54] which gives the translation of a certain number of Germanic words, usefully completes the data contained in the Reichenau document.

For example, it contains a form *figido*, corresponding to the word *ficato* in the *Reichenau Glossary*, for the word 'foie'. This intermediate form gives us a better understanding of the stages in the change in pronunciation between the word *ficato*, a form very close to the Latin FICATUM, and the present form *foie*. Coming between two vowels the consonant had first weakened into a *g* and then disappeared (*ficato – figido – foie*).

The same phenomenon occurred, for example, in Gaulish place-names in *-magus*, where the *g* between two vowels has disappeared without trace in Modern French. Just as *Rotomagus* gave *Rouen*, so *figido* became *foie*, with the *g* no longer pronounced.

All the words that are glossed – in other words, translated, explained – belong to the vocabulary of daily life, which demonstrates that it was especially in this area that the Romance language had moved away from Latin. Nowadays, however, the old Latin forms are not missing from French: thus OVES 'sheep' is found in *ovin*, VESPER 'evening' in *vespéral* and *vêpres*, EQUUS 'horse' in *équestre*, etc. But it was much later, under the influence of the literati who had a good knowledge of classical Latin, that all these forms were reintroduced into French.

How a noun becomes a suffix

The *Reichenau Glossary*, which provides precious evidence for the vocabulary of Old French, also offers information on the new methods of word formation. When, for example, we see the Latin word SINGULARITER 'individually', translated into Romance by the word *solamente*, which has become *seulement* in Modern French, we are able to see that already at that time adverbs of manner were formed by means of a periphrasis with *-mente*. Now, this Latin word was originally only a noun meaning 'mind, mode of being' and was not used in classical Latin to form adverbs, which were formed with the suffix *-iter*: *suaviter* 'pleasantly', *fortiter* 'strongly, energetically'. In this respect, a story is told about Talleyrand, who knew his classical Latin well, to the effect that he tried once to seduce a young woman who seemed to have her doubts about his ageing charms, by declaring to her: '*Non fortiter in re*, Madame, *sed suaviter in modo* (literally: 'Not energetically in the act, but deliciously in the manner').

The form *solamente* in the *Reichenau Glossary* attests to the existence in the eighth century of a suffix which had become one of the most productive in the Romance languages, since it is used to form adverbs in *-ment* in French,[56] and in *-mente* in Italian, Spanish and Portuguese.

The first 'monument' of the French language

The *Strasbourg Oaths*, exchanged in 842 between two of Charlemagne's grandsons, Louis the German and Charles the Bald, to swear assistance and fidelity to one another against their brother Lothair, are generally considered to be the first 'monument' of the French language. These legal texts of just a few lines, written in the Romance and the Germanic languages, which have come down to us through a copy postdating the event by more than one hundred years, are important for the history of the language because they contain many pointers to developments of which later texts show us the end result.

Thus, for example, the copyist seems to have hesitated over t
e written form to be given to unstressed end vowels. He has transcribed them:

- by *a* in the feminine ending, as in *aiudha* 'aid' and *cadhuna* 'each',
- either by *a* or by *e* in *fradra*, *fradre* 'brother' (where classical Latin would lead us to expect an *e*),
- either by *e* or by *o* in *Karle*, *Karlo* 'Charles' (where we would expect an *o*),
- or by *o* in *nostro* 'our', *poblo* 'people'.

These hesitations in the written form might indicate that the pronunciation was uncertain, weakly articulated and not easily identifiable to the ear. This hypothesis is confirmed by later texts in which the spelling is *e* throughout. The *Strasbourg Oaths* (see table p. 43) thus gives us clues about the history of all of these unstressed vowels which, after a period of uncertainty, finally merged into the one sound *e*. The text also shows us that, in words like *chacune*, *aide*, *frère*, *Charles*, *notre* and *peuple*, the disappearance of the Latin end vowels which we see in the modern pronunciation had still not taken place at that time. Such vowels must simply have been pronounced more weakly.

THE STRASBOURG OATHS
(*Extract and Translation*)
This text of the oaths of 842 is considered to be the first written document of the French language.

Pro deo amur et pro christian poblo et nostro commun saluament d'ist di en auant, in quant Deus sauir et podir me dunat, si saluarai eo cist meon fradre Karlo, et in aiudha et in cadhuna cosa, si cum om per dreit son fradra saluar dift, in o quid il mi altresi fazet, et ab Ludher nul plaid nunquam prindrai qui meon uol cist meon fradre Karle in damno sit.

For the love of God and for the salvation of the Christian people and our common salvation, from this day in so far as God grants me knowledge and power, I shall succour this my brother Charles in aid and in all things, as one should by right succour one's brother, provided he does the same for me, and I shall never make any arrangement with Lothair, which, by my consent, may harm this my brother Charles.

Si Lodhuuigs sagrament, que son fradre Karlo iurat, conseruat, et Karlus meos sendra de suo part non lo suon tanit, si io returnar non l'int pois, ne io ne neüls cui eo returnar int pois, in nulla aiudha contra Lodhuuig non li iu er.

If Louis keeps the oath which he has sworn to his brother Charles, and if Charles, my lord, for his part does not keep his, if I can not deter him from it, neither I nor any whom I can deter from it, will give him any aid against Louis.

A new future

In spite of its brevity, this text provides us with information not only on pronunciation and vocabulary but also on certain grammatical forms.

In classical Latin the future of verbs was formed by adding to the root of the verb the endings *-bo*, *-bis*, etc. From LAVARE 'to wash' was formed LAVA-BO 'I shall wash', LAVA-BIS 'you will wash', etc. This mode of formation was abandoned in all of the Romance languages, which innovated by forming the future of their verbs from the infinitive followed by the conjugated forms of the verb *avoir*: je *laver-ai*, tu *laver-as*, etc. (See table p. 44.)

In the short text from the *Strasbourg Oaths* we can see two of these new, typically Romance future formations: *salvarai* 'je sauverai' (*salvar* 'sauver' + first person of *avoir*) and *prindrai* 'je prendrai'. This evidence allows us to establish the fact that this type of future, formed with the auxiliary verb *avoir*, already existed in the language in the second half of the ninth century. In fact, it is probably older than that, since this way of forming the future is common to the majority of Romance languages.

43

FORMATION OF A NEW FUTURE
JE LAVERAI = LAVER + AI

Because they are written as a single word, the forms of the future make us forget that they are composed of two elements: the infinitive of the verb and the present tense of the auxiliary avoir.

From the point of view of the meaning, a notion of obligation (an act that has to be done) has evolved into the notion of the future. Thus, in everyday life, people say: 'Qu'avez-vous à faire ce matin?' with the meaning of 'Que ferez-vous ce matin?'.

Infinitive	+ avoir	=	future
laver	+ *ai*	=	*laverai*
laver	+ *as*	=	*laveras*
laver	+ *a*	=	*lavera*
laver	+ *(av)ons*	=	*laverons*
laver	+ *(av)ez*	=	*laverez*
laver	+ *ont*	=	*laveront*

There is a reduction of the final form of the auxiliary in the first and second persons plural, where we do not find *laver-avons* or *laver-avez* but *laverons* and *laverez*.

Examples of linguistic change

The changes which have taken place since the first invasions and which led, more than ten centuries later, to the birth of written French are too numerous and complex for us to be able to describe them here or even list the different stages. For a more complete picture of the subject, the interested reader can consult very well-referenced and highly-detailed works of scholarship[57] as well as works written for the non-specialist and students new to the subject.[58]

You should bear in mind that for each of the periods under discussion we can give only a few illustrative examples of the history of the language, and those examples are not necessarily the most important or most significant. In many cases we take some peculiarity of Modern French, a relic of a previous state of the language, as the starting point for our discussion.

How *chevals* became *chevaux*

The formation of plurals of the type *chevaux*, for example, is very old and may have begun as early as the seventh century, but the question is much debated (was it the seventh, eighth or ninth century?). Whatever the answer, the process seems to have been completed by the middle of the twelfth century.[59]

To understand through what stages the series -als (the plural of *cheval*), in which the vowel and the two consonants *l* and *s* were sounded, can become what in Modern French is written as -aux and pronounced as *o*, you have to remember that the consonant *l* was not pronounced in Latin, and later in Old French, as it is today. You can get some idea of the old pronunciation by listening to a Portuguese pronounce the name of his or her country, Portuga*l*. After the *l* you will hear a kind of vocalic echo similar in sound to the French *ou* and to the *l* in the word *scandale* as it is pronounced by Georges Marchais, secretary of the French Communist Party (1984–5).

At the time when the French language was being formed, the articulation of the *l* in front of a vowel bore hardly any trace of this *ou* sound, whereas in front of a consonant in the same syllable it had the sound you find at the beginning of the French word *oui* (the same sound as the one at the end of the English word *cow* and the German word *Blau*). Since the plural was formed by adding an *s* (which was always sounded) to the end of the word in the singular, the pronunciation in the singular was *cheval*, *mal*, but in the plural *chevaouss*, *maouss*. This pronunciation was the norm not just before the plural *s* but also before any other consonant at the end of the syllable in a word: thus the word derived from ALBA 'aube' was pronounced *aoube*, the word derived from TALPA 'taupe' was pronounced *taoupe*, etc.

There is a similar explanation for what nowadays seem to be irregularities in the conjugation of the verb *valoir*, where the *l* had the sound *ou* before a consonant at the end of a syllable: *il vaout* (in which the final *t* was for a long time sounded), which today has become *il vaut*, whereas the *l* has remained in *va-lons*, *va-lez*, *va-loir* where it was not the final consonant of the syllable.

The reduction of the sequence *aou* to a single vowel pronounced *o* as in the Modern French *il vaut* happened much later. It seems to have become the established pronunciation in Paris in the sixteenth century.

Sans se mettre martel en tête

This same *l* suffered the same fate not only after *a* (ALBA > *aoube*), but also after other vowels. In this way, *beau* can be traced back to BELL(US) (with an intermediate form *beaou*), *marteau* to MARTELL(US) and *fou* to FOLL(IS). Given the modern pronunciation of *beau*, *marteau*, *fou* and *nouveau*, the reader may have some difficulty in accepting without discussion the idea that these words once contained an *l*, and yet consider the following: 'sans se mettre *martel* en tête, on peut *bel* et bien donner un *nouvel* élan à cette consonne *l* dans le parler d'aujourd'hui, dans un *fol* amour des formes désuètes'. In other words, *martel* survives alongside *marteau*, just as *bel*, *fol* and *nouvel* survive alongside *beau*, *fou* and *nouveau*.

45

Latin and the Carolingian renaissance

Other texts have survived from the ninth and tenth centuries in addition to the *Glossaries*. The most famous is a sequence of twenty-nine verses, the *Séquence* (or *Cantilène*) *de sainte Eulalie*, which tells of the exemplary life of a young woman martyred in the fourth century. Another text takes the form of a commentary in Romance in the middle of a sermon in Latin on Jonah, and probably represents an application of the decision of the Council of Tours which enjoined helping the faithful to better understand the liturgy. Neither the *Strasbourg Oaths*, nor the tales written in the epic style, nor the commented sermons are of any real literary interest. (See tables p. 47.) And yet what a windfall they are for the historian of language. Although they do not faithfully reflect the spoken language, these texts are still the only currently available pieces of evidence of an intermediate language state between Latin and French. Without them how could we explain the presence side by side in the first literary texts of the twelfth century of forms which seem to have evolved normally, like *frère*, and forms which seem to have undergone no change at all, like *fraternel*? For the word *frère* as it is known today has lost the *t* of the Latin FRATREM (of which we saw an intermediate form with a *d* in the *Strasbourg Oaths*: *fradre*), whereas the *t* is still present in *fraternel*. Could the rule be wrong, then, which says that a Latin *t* (or *tr*) between two vowels evolved into a *d* and then weakened and disappeared, since we find *fraternel* with a *t* in the twelfth century?

And yet there are hundreds of examples confirming this development from Latin to French:

ESPATHA > *espethe* > *épée* (the spelling *th* is found in manuscripts written in England)

VENUTA > *venude* > *venue*, as well as all the Latin past participles in *-tus*, *-ta*, *-tum* which have evolved in the same way

MATURUM > *madhur* > *meür* > *mûr*

(A)QUITANIA > *Guyenne* (pronounced *Ghienne*).

And we have already seen:

ROTAMAGUS > *Rouen*

MUTARE > *mudhare* > *mudher* > *muer*.

A nation of Latinists

So if this is a general rule, if Latin words of the type *fratrem* 'regularly' give French words of the type *frère*, what can explain words such as *fraternel* which seem to have escaped the tyranny of evolution?

The great chaos to be seen in the form of words in Modern French dates from the time of Charlemagne. The Carolingian renaissance, which sought to improve the knowledge of Latin, gradually reintroduced and controlled

THE FIRST WRITINGS IN VERY OLD FRENCH

Until the ninth century all literary works were written in *Latin*:
- in the fourth century: Ausonius (310–385), *Épîtres*;
- in the fifth century: Sidoine Apollinaire (430–486), *Lettres*;
- in the sixth century: Grégoire de Tours (538–594), *Histoire des Francs*.

We can add to these the text commenting on the *Tapisserie de Bayeux* (end of the eleventh century).

The first works written in *very old French* are rare and very short. Among them are:
- end of the ninth century: *Cantilène de sainte Eulalie* (29 verses), probably composed in the abbey of Saint-Amand near Valenciennes;
- end of the tenth century: *Vie de saint Léger* (240 verses), probably written by a Burgundian although the manuscript is attributed to a Provençal scribe;
- end of the eleventh century: *Vie de saint Alexis* (625 verses), perhaps written in Normandy.

A SAMPLE OF SOME VERY OLD FRENCH

Buona pulcella fut Eulalia,
Bel avret corps bellezour anima.

. . .

Enz enl fou la getterent, com arde tost;
Elle colpes non avret, por o no's coist.

    Eulalia was a virtuous young woman,
    She had a beautiful body and an even more beautiful soul.

    . . .

    Into the fire they threw her, so she would burn quickly;
    She had committed no sins, for that she did not burn.
           Cantilène de sainte Eulalie (verses 1–2 and 19–20)

the pronunciation of a large number of Latin words. In doing so, it repressed the pronunciation habits that had been acquired over the previous centuries and, in trying to promote Latin, had the indirect effect of influencing the vernacular. The bulk of these borrowings from the Latin were made only in the twelfth and thirteenth centuries, when the Carolingian reforms in the schools bore fruit.

But, in any event, the ninth century saw the beginning of a new attitude which has persisted to this day. Starting with Charlemagne, the history of the French language ceased to be that of an idiom which lived and changed simply according to the needs of those who spoke it: higher ecclesiastical and national authorities sought to control its destiny with the aim of improving, protecting and enriching it. Thus, Charlemagne prefigured those subsequent guardians of 'good usage' such as the French Academy, the grammarian Vaugelas, the Haut Comité de la Langue Française and the present Commissariat Général à la Langue Française.

It is because of this centuries-old habit of drawing on Latin or Greek vocabulary to renew the vocabulary of French that learned forms such as *fragile*, *hôpital* or *fraternel* occur side by side in Modern French with popular forms such as *frêle*, *hôtel* and *frère*. As a result, the French, like Molière's Monsieur Jourdain and his prose, are Latinists without knowing it, since they use 'Latin' words: *fragile* (from FRAGILIS), *hôpital* (from HOSPITALIS) and *fraternel* (from FRATERNALIS). And if educated people do not themselves always know that *fragile* is a Latinism (from the Latin word FRAGILIS) whilst *frêle* is the popular form derived from the same Latin word FRA(G)ILIS, it is because learned and popular forms have been rubbing shoulders in the language for centuries without anybody being in the slightest bit concerned about it. French speakers have, for centuries, shown no surprise that the adjective *aigu* gives the noun *acuité* (in other words that it is formed on the Latin ACUTUS and not the French *aigu*) or that the adjective for *père* is *paternel* (derived from PATER not *père*).

The rigidity of French words

Pity those who wish to learn French and who have to memorise both *entier* and *intégrité*, *vide* and *vacuité*, *proche* and *proximité*, or, even worse, *aveugle* and *cécité* (and even though *aveuglement* still exists, it no longer has the same meaning as *cécité* and so cannot be used as a synonym for it).

It is instructive to compare the rigid structures of French vocabulary with the freedom enjoyed by some of its neighbours. In English, for example, the suffix *-ness* can be used to form a whole series of nouns almost without restriction: *empty*, *emptiness*; *blind*, *blindness*, etc. In French the adjective and the corresponding noun rarely have a common root. Which explains why French has a reputation for being so difficult to learn. But there again, is that not part of its charm for some people?

THE VIKING INTERLUDE

The Vikings: Germans who came in from the cold

At the time when French was embarking on a partial re-latinisation, it was adopted by new invaders from a cold climate in place of their own language.

It was at the very beginning of the ninth century that the Vikings, those tall blond men from Scandinavia, made their first raids on the Channel coasts and pushed their attacks into the interior, sometimes as far as Paris and even Burgundy.[60] In 911, King Charles the Simple finally yielded territory to them along the Channel, land that was to become the Duchy of Normandy. As soon as these Normans ('North men') were settled on their own lands, they gave up pillaging for good and integrated with the population. Since they had come without women of their own, they married the beautiful native women, took on their customs, and finally adopted their language. Thus, their children learnt the Romance language of their mothers, to the extent that, after 940, there are no written documents to show that the Scandinavian language was still alive in the region.[61]

After three generations the integration of the Normans was complete and it was even thanks to them that French was to cross the Channel, since, when William, Duke of Normandy, conquered England in 1066 and shared the country out among his barons, French became the language of the aristocracy, the Royal Court, the law courts and the Church. One can, in fact, easily spot the French origin of a whole series of terms introduced into the vocabulary of English at that time: in politics (*crown, council, count, court, duke, justice, obedience*, etc.), in religion (*abbot, cardinal, charity, grace, mercy, pilgrim, sacrament*, etc.), or everyday life (*catch, county, pay, peace, poor, poverty, rich, treasure, wait*, etc.).[62]

French was the language spoken by Richard the Lionheart, who was king of England at the end of the twelfth century and on whose side fought his legendary contemporary Robin Hood. It is true that Richard was the son of Eleanor of Aquitaine, who had become Queen of England after her divorce from Louis VII, King of France. It was not until the beginning of the fifteenth century that a king of England, Henry IV of Lancaster, had English as his mother tongue.[63] Even today the coat of arms of the British monarchy bears the words 'Dieu et mon droit', while the highest rank of knighthood in the land, the Order of the Garter, respectfully preserves as its motto King Edward III's exclamation as he retied the garter of his mistress at a ball: 'Honni soit qui mal y pense'. That was in 1347, right in the middle of the fourteenth century, and the king of England, like the rest of his court, spoke French no less than did his cousin King Philip VI of France, whom he had just defeated at the battle of Crécy.

Moreover, it was in England in 1530 that Palsgrave produced the first French grammar, albeit written in English since it was intended for the English, and England continued to use French in its law courts until the middle of the eighteenth century (1731).[64]

One wonders what might have happened to the linguistic situation in France and England if Joan of Arc had not managed to 'boot the English out of France', and if the English had finally triumphed. In that case, the king of England would have become the legal king of France and French might well have become the official language of both kingdoms. But one can also imagine that there might have been a protracted battle between the two languages which could have led to the present situation.

English enriched by French (or *franglais* in reverse)

In any event, the Normans left a strong French imprint on the English language, whose vocabulary even today shows signs of their passing.

Generally speaking, the words of French (Norman) origin are found in more sophisticated, often more specialised, usages, whereas the words of Anglo-Saxon origin relate to more familiar usages, are more adapted to practical realities. You only have to compare, for example:

to combat and to fight	to finish and to end
to conceal and to hide	to gain and to win
cordial and hearty	to mount and to go up
economy and thrift	to perish and to die
egotism and selfishness	to retard and to keep back
to expectorate and to spit	to tolerate and to put up with

Similarly, a cultivated flower is designated by the word *flower*, from the French *fleur*, whereas *bloom* and *blossom*, of Germanic origin, designate the flowers on trees. For elaborate culinary dishes we find *veal, mutton* and *beef* (from the French *veau, mouton* and *bœuf*), as opposed to the traditional Germanic forms *calf, sheep* and *ox*, which designate the animals themselves.

Borrowing has continued to this day. It occurred on a large scale in the thirteenth and fourteenth centuries, when the upper classes were effectively bilingual. We can quote, among many others:

- *bachelor* (Old French *bachelier* 'aspirant chevalier', then 'célibataire');
- *bargain* (Old French *bargaignier* 'commercer, hésiter' > *barguigner*);
- *constable* (Old French *cunestable* > *connétable*);
- *foreign* (Old French *forain*);
- *purchase* (Old French *pourchacier* 'tenter d'obtenir');
- *squire* (Old French *esquier* > *écuyer*), etc.

The following, in their English spelling, are just a few of the thousands of other words which found their way from French into English:

in the sixteenth century – *promenade, colonel, portmanteau, moustache, scene, vogue*, etc.
in the seventeenth century – *dishabille, liaison, repartee, burlesque, bureau, brunette, cabaret, concierge, fiacre, double entendre, nom-de-plume, faux pas*, etc.

REVERSE 'FRANGLAIS'

It was after the Norman Conquest (1066) in particular that hundreds of French words were introduced into English. French was the language of the ruling classes in England for several centuries, and it could still be said in 1298 that 'unless you knew French, you were a person of no consequence' in England.

Some borrowings from Old French are unrecognisable nowadays:

caterpillar from the Old French *chatepelose* 'hairy cat'
duty from *dueté*, an old derivative of *devoir*
parson from *personne* (person of high rank)
match from the Old French *meiche* 'wick'
mushroom from *mousseron*
plenty from the Old French *a plente* 'in abundance'
toast from the Old French *toster* 'to roast'
fuel from the Old French *fouaille* 'what feeds the hearth'.

The borrowing from French in the following words is easier to recognise. They normally form doublets with words of Anglo-Saxon origin.

French origin	Anglo-Saxon origin
meagre	lean
to demand	to ask for
to abandon	to give up
to labour	to work

in the eighteenth century – *bouquet, boulevard, connoisseur, liqueur, envelope, nuance, souvenir, carte blanche, fauteuil, brochure, picnic*, etc.
in the nineteenth century – *format, cliché, chef, menu, restaurant, gourmet, secretaire, entente, parvenu, blasé, bête noire*, etc.
in the twentieth century – *garage, crêpe, dressage, existentialism*, etc.[65]

Even now there are daily manifestations in English of the effects of the French language transported to England by the Normans more than 900 years ago. (See table above and also p. 132.)

Signs of the Norman invasion

So these Norman pillagers-turned-gentlemen very quickly abandoned their own Scandinavian language, a Germanic cousin of English and German. It was not learnt by the children, who were brought up by their French mothers. And yet this Scandinavian language did not disappear without leaving a few traces, small but still there, in Modern French (see table p. 52): a few dozen names of people and places, as well as a small number of lexical items, mainly to do with the sea.

51

SOME PLACE-NAMES OF SCANDINAVIAN ORIGIN

Place-names as French-sounding as *Honfleur*, *Harfleur* or *Barfleur* have nothing to do with flowers, because their final syllable comes from a Scandinavian word meaning 'bay, creek'.

In the place name *Le Houlme*, we find the same suffix *-holm* 'shore, island' as in Stockholm, and in *Le Torp Mesnil*, *torp* means 'village'.

Another word, *toft*, meaning 'farm' and then 'village', was used to form a large number of Norman place-names:

Esquetot (Eure) 'ash-tree farm' (compare *Esque* and *ash*).

Appetot (Eure) 'apple-tree farm' (compare *appe* and *apple*).

(The same place-name is also found in Denmark, in fact, in the form *Æbeltoft* 'apple-tree farm', in Jutland.)

Lintot (Seine-Maritime) 'lime-tree farm' (compare with German *Linden* 'lime tree').

Robertot (Seine-Maritime) 'Robert's farm', as well as *Yvetot* etc.[66]

Balbec, or the imaginary geography of Marcel Proust

The word meaning 'stream' appears in the form *-bec* (compare with the German *Bach* 'stream') in many Norman place-names: *Caudebec* (Eure), *Annebec* (Calvados), *Bolbec* (Seine-Maritime), *Houlbec* (Seine-Maritime), *Beaubec* (Seine-Maritime), etc. But we should resist the temptation to add to this list of place-names the most famous of them all, *Balbec*, which occupies such an important place in *A la recherche du temps perdu*. You won't find it on any map, because it doesn't exist.

Perhaps only Proust experts know that *Balbec* is the author's creation, a town in which he impressionistically merges and blends the landscapes and monuments of *Trouville*, *Cabourg*, *Dives*, and maybe other places too.[67]

The handful of French words of Scandinavian origin

Through contact with the Vikings, the language of the sea was enriched by a series of words which nowadays are used mainly by sailing enthusiasts: *cingler* 'to set sail', *hauban* 'ropes supporting the mast', *hune* 'platform resting on a mast', (prendre un) *ris* '(to reduce) the surface of the sails'. In more common use are words such as *turbot* (the fish) and especially *vague* 'wave'. Such are the small posthumous presents bequeathed to the French heritage by the people who came originally to steal and plunder.

THE AGE OF DIALECTS

The linguistic diversification of the Middle Ages

The influence of the Germanic invaders can, as we have seen, explain some of the regional differences that existed in the languages spoken in the Middle Ages. (See *Langue d'oïl, langue d'oc* and *Francoprovençal*, p. 28–9.) It cannot, however, explain all of them. In fact, how is it possible that the Latin imported from Rome could have led several centuries later to a linguistic diversification such that every region had its own dialect, since it is the case that, in the Middle Ages, an inhabitant of Limousin would have understood very little of the language spoken by a Burgundian, and neither would have understood a Parisian. They each spoke just the language of their own region and only the scholars knew Latin, which was the sole written language.

To understand how this diversification into different dialects could have happened one has to remember how people lived under feudalism. Based on the relationship of vassal to suzerain (feudal overlord), life was organised around the lord's land and castle. As a result, the lord entertained a variety of relationships with the peasants, by whom he had to make himself understood, but he encountered his peers only on rare occasions. It was thus within the boundaries of the fiefdom that linguistic differences arose and developed. These differences were initially minimal but grew larger when geographical conditions increased the isolation of two adjoining domains. Conversely, when two neighbouring communities were able to establish and develop contact, each one adapted its language to that of the other, so ensuring that any differences did not widen. Market towns (with their fairs which periodically attracted people from different domains) also favoured uniformity.

There were thus more or less accidental differences between the neighbouring dialectal regions that we are able to reconstruct in the Middle Ages. But we cannot be sure of their precise boundaries, which depended not only on natural geographical conditions and paths of communication but also on ecclesiastical frontiers and political relationships between lords.

Paris begins to stir

The survival of these various dialects in modern France, especially in the countryside, gives only a very rough idea of what the country was like in the Middle Ages. Nowadays French is spoken everywhere, whereas at that time it was just one dialect among others.

The common language might not now have been French were it not for an event which occurred at the end of the tenth century which was to be of the utmost importance in the history of the dialect: in 987 Hugh Capet was *elected* king by the grandees of the realm with the support of the Church. Hugh Capet was the Duke of France (that is to say in other words of what is now called the Île-de-France), and his duchy, which was to become the royal domain, was very small. You can see from the map (p. 55) that it was restricted to Paris and its immediate vicinity, a part of the Orléanais and the Vermandois, the region of Attigny on the Aisne and a small window on the Channel near Montreuil (Pas-de-Calais).

Some two hundred years later, on the accession of Philippe Auguste in 1180, the royal domain had expanded considerably around Paris, especially towards the south and the east.

If you look at a road-map of France, you can easily find around Paris a whole series of places, such as *Baillet-en-France*, *Belloy-en-France*, *Bonneuil-en-France*, *Châtenay-en-France*, *Puiseux-en-France* and, of course, *Roissy-en-France*, which bear witness to the location of the ancient duchy and which are a reminder of the oldest Frankish settlement in the country. (See enlarged section on p. 55.)

Why Paris?

It still remains to be explained why the dialect of Paris should have become the dominant one. The development must have have been the result of a set of circumstances.

Paris was very favourably situated from the geographical point of view. Located near the confluence of three major waterways, the Seine, the Oise and the Marne – hence the name 'Île' de France – the Parisian region seems very quickly to have become the natural centre of a linguistic area which, at the end of the Middle Ages, extended as far as the Loire. Blois and Tours to the west, Troyes and Rheims to the east had dialects not very different from those spoken in Paris.[68]

To this exceptional geographical situation must be added economic and cultural reasons: the immediate proximity of a highly fertile region, the bread basket of Beauce and Brie, and, a little later, the literary movement supported by the court which contributed to raising the prestige of the language of the Île-de-France. The literature born in this region at the end of the eleventh century initially included, above all, the *chanson de geste*, a kind of long epic poem sung by minstrels at fairs and popular gatherings. It was a literature which extolled the deeds of exceptional men and was written in a language that was not too sophisticated because it had to be understood by the common people.

In the twelfth century a new genre was born, the 'courtly' novel, which, under the influence of the literature of the *oc*-speaking countries, gave expression to delicate sentiments, with linguistic refinements of a kind not seen in the *chanson de geste*. In these novels, the poet – called a *troubadour* in the south, a *trouvère* in the north – tirelessly paid court to the lady of his

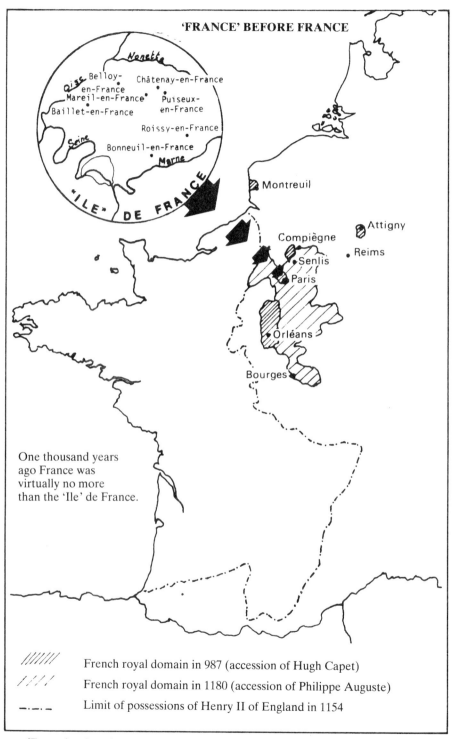

'FRANCE' BEFORE FRANCE

Nonette

Oise

Belloy-en-France
Châtenay-en-France
Mareil-en-France
Puiseux-en-France
Baillet-en-France
Roissy-en-France
Bonneuil-en-France
Seine
Marne

"ILE" DE FRANCE

Montreuil

Attigny

Compiègne
Reims
Senlis
Paris

Orléans

Bourges

One thousand years
ago France was
virtually no more
than the 'Ile' de France.

/////// French royal domain in 987 (accession of Hugh Capet)

/ / / / French royal domain in 1180 (accession of Philippe Auguste)

—·—·— Limit of possessions of Henry II of England in 1154

(From the *Grand atlas de l'histoire mondiale*, Paris, Albin Michel, 1979, p. 125) dreams in a language full of subtleties which delighted the nobility in their castles. It was the age of the crusades, the lords were far away and their wives, left alone in their domains, had more appreciation for love stories than tales of war. Introduced to the king's court by Marie de Champagne, the daughter of Eleanor of Aquitaine, this new literary genre came into its own with poets such as Chrétien de Troyes (c.1135–c.1183), who was himself the protégé of Marie de Champagne. (See table p. 57.)

Loan words from the *langue d'oc*

This delicate, refined literature, which drew its inspiration from the literature of the south of France, also made many borrowings from the *oc* language. They were mainly lexical, like: *aubade*, *ballade*, *bastide*, *cabane*, *ciboule*, *escargot*, *estrade*, *salade*, etc.[69] (See table p. 116.)

It is probably also because of the influence of southern pronunciation that the French now say *amour* (from the Latin AMOR) and not *ameur*, whereas they say *chaleur* (from CALOR) and *douleur* (from DOLOR).

They all wanted to sound like Parisians

The new prestige attached to the language of the court, which had become more refined, strengthened the already favourable situation which the dialect of the Ile-de-France owed to its geographical situation at the heart of a vast network of communications. Subjected to the continual migrations of the populations, this language had also acquired a reputation for being a 'happy medium' which people of quality were beginning to see as a kind of ideal to strive for.

Towards the second half of the twelfth century, it seemed preferable to avoid anything that was specific to a small region, and the common base seemed well and truly to be identified with the French of Paris.[70] It was at this time, in 1180, that Conon de Béthune complained of being ridiculed at court because he had used words from his native Artois. The poet Guernes de Pont-Sainte-Maxence, for his part, however, reassured his readers by writing:

'Mis langages est buens, car en France sui nez.'
[My language is correct, for I was born in (Île-de-)France.][71]

Thus began the slow movement which, by pushing all the other dialects into the background, was gradually to make French, the dialect of the Parisian region, into the common language of the whole country.

SOME WORKS WRITTEN IN OLD FRENCH
(twelfth and thirteenth centuries)

The literature of this period is characterised by two great trends: on the one hand the great epic tales in which the knights confronted one another in the clash of arms, and the long novels of chivalry which celebrated courtly love; and on the other hand the popular, so-called bourgeois literature, represented by the *Roman de Renart* and, slightly later, by the *fabliaux*, short poems which were invariably satirical and occasionally bawdy.

The *Chansons de geste*
Eighty *chansons de geste* have survived, falling into three groups:
La Geste de Charlemagne, which includes, among others:
La Chanson de Roland (eleventh–twelfth centuries), by an unknown author, although it mentions a certain Turoldus: was he the author, a *trouvère*, or a scribe?
La Geste de Guillaume d'Orange, of which the best known episode, used by Victor Hugo in *La Légende des siècles*, *Aimeri de Narbonne* (thirteenth century), is attributed to Bertrand, of Bar-sur-Aube.
La Geste de Doon de Mayence, of which the main *chanson de geste* is *Renaud de Montauban* (thirteenth century), which later became the novel *Quatre Fils Aymon*.

Courtly literature
It was influenced by the literature of the south of France and was characterised above all by the depiction of *courtly love*.
Tristan (twelfth century), a long poem by two Anglo-Norman authors, Beroul (*c*.1150) and Thomas (*c*.1170), of which only fragments are preserved (3,000 verses). The legend of *Tristan* was taken up again in the form of a novel at the beginning of the thirteenth century.
Lancelot and *Perceval* (twelfth century), two works by Chrétien de Troyes.
Aucassin et Nicolette (thirteenth century).
The *Roman de la Rose* (thirteenth century), an allegorical poem of 22,000 verses, begun *c*.1236 by Guillaume de Lorris and finished forty years later by Jean de Meung.

Bourgois literature
The *Roman de Renart* (twelfth–thirteenth centuries), a collection of fifty seven poems in which animals take the stage.
The *fabliaux* (thirteenth–fourteenth centuries), short poems (300–400 verses) of a satirical nature. There are over 150 of them.

* * *

Chrétien de Troyes (*c*.1135–*c*.1183), a poet from the Champagne region.
Geoffroy de Villehardouin (1165–1213), a chronicler from the Champagne region, *La Conquête de Constantinople*.
Jean, sire de Joinville (1224–1317), a chronicler from the Champagne region, *Vie de Saint Louis*.
Adam de La Halle (1230–1287), *trouvère* and playwright from Picardy, *Le Jeu d'Adam*.
Rutebeuf (thirteenth century), Parisian *trouvère*, poet and playwright, *Le Miracle de Théophile*.

SOME WORKS WRITTEN IN MIDDLE FRENCH
(fourteenth and fifteenth centuries)

The linguistic system which gave birth to Modern French was actually put in place between 1350 and 1610. This form of the language is usually called *Middle French* (Pierre Guiraud, *Le Moyen français*, Paris, PUF, Que sais-je?, no. 1086).

In the fourteenth and fifteenth centuries, the main genres used by writers were poems, chronicles and comic or religious plays.

Jean Froissart (1317–1410), *Chroniques* (Flanders)
Christine de Pisan (1363–1431), *Œuvres poétiques* (Paris, born in Venice)
Charles d'Orléans (1394–1465), *Œuvres poétiques*, (Blois)
François Villon (1430–1463), *Le Grand Testament* (Paris)
Philippe de Commynes (1445–1511), *Mémoires* (Flanders)

Religious theatre

From the fourteenth century we have some fifty plays on religious subjects, almost all on the theme of the *Miracle of Our Lady*.

In the fifteenth century the *Mysteries* flourished, of which some sixty have been rediscovered, including the *Mystère de la Passion* by Arnoul Gréban, which, in spite of its 35,574 verses, is still sometimes performed today.

Comic theatre

In the fifteenth century the *Farces*: *Farce du cuvier*, *Farce de Maître Pathelin*, etc.

A sample of middle French

La pluye nous a buez et lavez
Et le soleil dessechez et noircis;
Pies, corbeaulx nous ont les yeux cavez
Et arraché la barbe et les sourcilz;
Jamais, nul temps, nous ne sommes rassis;
Puis ça, puis la, comme le vent varie,
A son plaisir sans cesser nous charie,
Plus becquetez d'oiseaulx que dez à coudre
Ne soiez donc de nostre confrarie
Mais priez Dieu que tous nous vueille absouldre.

Villon, *La Ballade des pendus*

THE TRIUMPH OF FRENCH

Latin climbs down from its pedestal

We shall skip the next three or four centuries, during which time everyone spoke their own dialect, whilst those who could write wrote in Latin. In school, children learnt Latin. At the Sorbonne, the guardian of the

58

tradition since its foundation in 1227 by Robert de Sorbon, not only were all subjects taught in Latin, but the students also had to write and be vivaed on a thesis in Latin. This habit was to last until the end of the nineteenth century.

In the face of a Sorbonne populated by traditionalist ecclesiastics fiercely attached to Latin, François I was to create a stir when, in 1530, he founded a competing institution, the Collège des Trois Langues (Hebrew, Greek and Latin), which was later to become the Collège Royal and is now called the Collège de France. For the first time, a small number of lecturers were innovative in giving a high-level education in French.[72]

This first blow against Latin's monopoly within education was also the official recognition of French as the instrument of knowledge, and above all it was the first time that the world of scholars distanced itself from the Church.

French becomes the language of writing

In everything to do with practical life, French was to replace Latin in all administrative documents from 1539 onwards, when François I passed the famous decree of Villers-Cotterêts. So that there should be no more uncertainty or ambiguity in administrative texts, official documents, decrees and laws, they all had to be written in the 'langage maternel françois' and no other language.

In fact, the decree of Villers-Cotterêts simply made obligatory a practice that already existed for notarial deeds in most of the country, since people had already begun in the thirteenth century to write such deeds in the vulgar tongue, in other words in Occitan in the south, in Picard in the Beauvaisis, and in French in Paris,[73] etc. From this time onwards, Latin was excluded, but so also were the dialects.

In this great movement of the Renaissance, other areas opened up to French: geography with Jacques Cartier, whose *Bref recit de la nauigation faicte es isles de Canada* dates from 1545; medicine, when Ambroise Paré, the founder of modern surgery, scandalised his colleagues by publishing all of his scientific works in French; astrology, with the *Prophéties* of Nostradamus, which was printed in 1555.[74]

Finally, the *Défense et illustration de la langue française*, published by du Bellay in 1549, was an enthusiastic manifesto of the young writers and grammarians of the period, supporting the use of French as the national literary language. Du Bellay may be thought of as the initiator of this literary protest movement, of what today would be called 'le droit à la francité', alongside the other poets of the Pléiade: Ronsard, Baïf and Belleau, to whom should be added the grammarians Pontus de Tyard and Peletier du Mans.

Thus promoted to the rank of a language worthy of study, the French language acquired its first grammar book in 1530, although written in English by Palsgrave. Jacques Dubois, known as Sylvius, also wrote a grammar of French in 1531, but it was in Latin. Finally, around 1550, the Lyonnais Meigret[75] published a French grammar written, this time, in French: in it, he distinguished between good and bad usage and proposed a writing system that was close to the pronunciation of his contemporaries.

Natural and guided evolution

After the sixteenth century it is hard to discover the natural tendencies of the language from its manifestations, because the grammarians were constantly intervening to unify and fix it.

From the seventeenth century onwards, then, allowances have to be made for the interventions 'from on high' which halt, channel or go against the linguistic changes arising out of new communicative needs.

The following pages describe the tendencies which manifested themselves in the course of the sixteenth century in pronunciation, grammar and vocabulary just before the lovers of 'good usage' confused things by working against those tendencies.

The hesitation waltz of final consonants

The French now easily and unconsciously pronounce the final *r* in *mer* or *enfer* but not in *aimer* or *chauffer*, which are pronounced like *aimé* or *chauffé*. But why is that?

Could it be a special rule for infinitives? No, since the final *r is* pronounced in *mourir* and *pouvoir*. On the other hand, in the words *cahier*, *fusil*, *tabac* and *bonnet* the final consonant is not sounded, but in *hier*, *péril*, *sac*, and *net* it is. In all these cases, oral usage is now perfectly fixed and takes no account of the spelling, which in all cases includes a final consonant.

For other words the usage is not so well-established, and the final consonant is pronounced by some people but not by others:

almanach	*chenil*	*nombril*
ananas	*circonspect*	*persil*
août	*exact*	*sourcil*
but	*fait (un)*	*suspect . . .*
cerf	*gril*	

How can we know which is the correct usage? A recent survey[76] on the pronunciation of a group of highly educated people of all ages living in Paris shows that, for all these words, usage varies considerably: it is the less frequent words (such as *chenil* or *cerf*) which are pronounced for the most part with the final consonant sounded, whereas, for the more frequent words (such as *persil* or *sourcil*), it is the pronunciation without a final consonant which is most widespread.

This is a reflection of the reality today, showing that on this score usage is not completely established.

The chaos of liaisons

To understand the present anarchic situation, you have to go back to the end of the twelfth century, a time from which every consonant at the end of a word was:
- pronounced only when the following word began with a vowel;
- was not pronounced when the following word began with a consonant.
  Example: *petit-t-enfant* but *peti garçon*.

We can see there the beginnings of what is called *liaison*, which knew no exception for many centuries. Such was the rule in the sixteenth century: no final consonant was pronounced unless it was followed by a vowel. (See table on p. 62.)

Should the final consonant be pronounced or not?

Nowadays, only the final consonants of certain words are governed by the rule of liaison, since words such as *bac*, *péril*, *bonheur* or *nef* are never subjected to the phenomena of liaison given that their final consonant is always pronounced. But words such as *trop*, *heureux*, *tout*, *petit* (and many others), which also end in a written consonant, are pronounced as in the old tongue, in other words with no final consonant except in liaison, when the following word begins with a vowel: *j'en ai tro*, *tro grand* but *tro-p-étroit*; *père heureu*, *heureu père* but *heureu-z-événement*, etc. Moreover, there is not always liaison in front of a vowel.

How was it possible to go from the regularity described by the grammarians of the sixteenth century, when all words received the same treatment, to the arbitrariness of modern pronunciation, which defies spelling and confuses foreigners trying to learn French?

The breaking point comes towards the middle of the sixteenth century: we note that at that time final consonants are gradually reintroduced into pronunciation, partly under the influence of the grammarians. However, they were not all of the same opinion, and ultimately each word has its own history. We know, for example, that the purists of the seventeenth century recommended saying *mouchoi* for *mouchoir*, and that Vaugelas recommended saying *couri* and not *courir*. Similarly, *i faut* was at that time considered to be the correct pronunciation, while *il faut* was thought to be pedantic and provincial.[78] Conversely, in the eighteenth century, some grammarians branded the pronunciation *tiroi* (for *tiroir*) vulgar.[79]

Closer to our own times we know that, until the middle of the nineteenth

LIAISONS IN THE SIXTEENTH CENTURY

Grammarians of the sixteenth century gave very precise rules for the use of liaisons.

Sylvius (Jacques Dubois) wrote in 1531: 'At the end of words, we write but do not pronounce the *s* or other consonants, except when they are followed by a vowel or come at the end of a sentence, thus we write *les femmes sont bonnes* but we pronounce *les* with a sound elided, *femmes* without *s*, *son* without *t*, *bones*.' (*sic*).

In 1582, another grammarian, Henri Estienne, gave an almost phonetic transcription of liaison:

. . . *que nou ne vivon depui troi mois en cete ville.*

Note that in this sentence only the word *mois* is written with the final consonant *s*, which is pronounced, since this word comes before a word beginning with a vowel, which is not the case for *nou*, *vivon*, *depui* and *troi*.[77]

---

century *péril* was pronounced *péri* and that in the middle of the twentieth century there was hesitation between *bari* and *baril*.[80] In 1987, the form *bari* (without the *l*) had still not entirely disappeared from usage, since it was used by the journalist Jean Amadou during a television programme.

Each word has its own history

When you look at the language today, you can see that the grammarians' attempts to reintroduce these final consonants into the pronunciation were not successful in every case: all the verbs in *-er*, which are the most numerous, have in fact kept the pronunciation without the final *r*, whereas those in *-ir* and *-oir*, after being pronounced without the final *r*, then followed the rules of spelling, which is why the French now always pronounce the *r* in *finir* and *pouvoir* but not in *aimer* or *chanter*.

Some of these restorations of the final consonant took effect immediately, whilst others, like the suffix *-eur*, did not happen until the eighteenth century. The modern language still bears traces of the old pronunciation without *r*, firstly in *monsieur* but also in *piqueur*, which is still pronounced *piqueu* by hunting enthusiasts but *piqueur* by those who know nothing about the traditions of the sport. The form *boueux* for *éboueur* is less well accepted and seems to be on the way out.

e becomes mute

It is difficult to impose by arbitrary decision pronunciations which go against the natural tendencies of language users, and if the grammarians' interventions were successful in part, it must be because they were assisted by favourable circumstances: liaisons must have played a part in the restoration of final consonants because they constantly reminded the language users of the existence of these latent consonants. One must probably

62

add to this the written form, which is the guardian of formal identity. But there was more to it than that.

The sixteenth century also saw the spread of another tendency, which had begun in the previous century, of not pronouncing a final *e*, that most frequent vowel in the language. In *mère*, *faire* or *dire*, words that had until then been pronounced as two syllables, the final vowel became mute in spite of the grammarians' continued recommendation that it be sounded, even if only weakly. At the end of the seventeenth and in the eighteenth century, the disappearance of this vowel was so widespread in the usages that were taken as reference points that the grammarians were finally unanimous in accepting reality.[81]

The most immediate consequence of the fall of this final vowel (the 'mute' *e*) was that the preceding consonant became, in its turn, the final consonant: *dire* is pronounced *dir* with no final *e*.

The existence of verbs like *dire* or *faire*, where the *r* had become final in pronunciation, favoured the return of the pronounced *r* in infinitives ending in *-ir* and *-oir* (*finir*, *pouvoir*, etc.). The fact that this did not happen for infinitives in *-er* (*aimer*, *chanter*, etc.) was because their great frequency in the language meant that they offered unsurmountable resistance to the purists' prescriptions.[82]

An aborted phonetic change

Another tendency that was repressed with much greater severity was the trend at this time towards pronouncing a single *r* between two vowels as a *z*. If Erasmus is to be believed, the 'petites dames' of those days said *mazi* for *mari*, and *Pazi* for *Paris*.[83]

There are those who believe that this was no more than a passing fad started by high-society ladies in Paris, but the pronunciation has also been observed in the dialects of the south and of the north-east of Paris. It must have been fairly rapidly rejected, since, by the beginning of the seventeenth century, only two words remained in which *r* was pronounced as *z*, words which have survived in that pronunciation today: *chaise* from its doublet *chaire* (both derived from the Latin CATHEDRA), and *bésicles*, formed from *béryl* (German Brille 'glasses') and with an end component influenced by that of *escarboucle* and *binocle*.

Pas, point, mie, goutte . . .

It was at roughly the same time that the use of the double negative *ne* . . . *pas* became firmly established in French, which is an innovation compared with the other Romance languages. The French say *je **ne** vois **pas***, whereas they say simply ***non** vedo* in Italian, ***no** veo* in Spanish and ***não** vejo* in Portuguese.

In Old French the simple negation sufficed. It existed first in its full form *non*, which is found in the *Strasbourg Oaths* (*si io returnar non l'int pois* 'if I cannot dissuade him from it' – see table p. 43), and then in the twelfth century in its weakened form *ne*. The old texts already give evidence of cases in which the negative particle *ne* was strengthened by a term designating an object of little or no value, such as *pas*, *point*, *mie*, *goutte*, or even *ail*, *clou*, *miette* and *grain*.[84] Originally, *pas* kept its first meaning in *il ne marche pas* 'he does not walk a step'. But people probably preferred to say *il ne mange mie* (or *miette*) 'he does not eat a crumb', *il ne boit goutte* 'he does not drink a drop', *il ne coud point* 'he does not sew a stitch, *il ne moud grain* 'he does not grind a grain', etc.

From the fifteenth century onwards, *pas* and *point* began to eclipse the various other forms. The great authors of the sixteenth and seventeenth centuries continued to use the forms *mie*, *goutte* and *grain*, but the etymological meaning was usually absent: 'Ces messieurs de l'Académie ne me le pardonneraient mie' (Scarron); 'Pour moi *je ne vois* goutte en ce raisonnement' (Corneille, *Nicomède*, III, 4); 'Le cierge ne savait grain de la philosophie' (La Fontaine, *Fables*, IX, 12); and 'Je n'entends goutte à l'être simple' (Voltaire).

Nowadays, in spite of a few surviving traces of these old forms in set expressions such as *on n'y voit goutte*, *pas* has replaced all the others. Strangely enough, *point* is found both in mannered language ('Va, je ne te hais point') and in the country vernaculars of some regions such as Beauce and Romance Brittany and in some dialects spoken in the west of the country ('Y fait point chaud').

The negative form *pas* even seems now to have ousted its former partner *ne* since, in the spoken language, it now bears the whole weight of the negative on its own: *je sais pas*, *je vois pas* are much more frequent in speech than *je ne sais pas* or *je ne vois pas*, both among the best educated – although they deny it – and among those with very little education.

In this respect, linguists like to recount the following anecdote, which is passed on by word of mouth (I got it from André Martinet who was told it by another linguist). The great phonetician Paul Passy, who founded the International Phonetics Association at the end of the nineteenth century, was a witness to the following scene between his own father, Frédéric Passy, an important politician and the first winner of the Nobel peace prize in 1901, and Otto Jespersen, the great Danish linguist. Rather mischievously, the latter wanted to have it confirmed to him that the French do not pronounce the *l* of *il* in front of a verb beginning with a consonant (*y vient*, *y dit*). Frédéric Passy fell unwittingly into the trap:

'Mon cher ami, ceux qui vous ont dit ça, *y savent pas c'qu'y disent*.'

This answer is interesting in more ways than one: it shows that the absence of the -*l* (*y savent*, *y disent*) was natural even in the language of an educated man from the very best society. It also confirms that forms which are still considered to be loose today were already frequent in educated circles almost a century ago.

You could try Jespersen's experiment (I have often done it myself) on people who are convinced that they speak refined French: they will be surprised (to say the least) when they realise what their true pronunciation is like.

The language acquires new riches

The gradual introduction of French into the sciences and literature in the sixteenth century created a new interest in the language as such: people theorised about it, devised the first grammars, tried to simplify and fix the spelling, and did not hesitate to enrich the language with new words. Ronsard declared: 'The more words we have in our language, the more perfect it will be.' Rabelais, for his part, borrowed unashamedly not only from Hebrew, Greek and Latin, but also from foreign languages, slang and the dialects. Du Bellay encouraged the poets to bold innovation. (See table p. 67.) As a result, in spite of the opposition of a large number of men and women of letters and people at the court, who remained faithful to the traditional language, the sixteenth century was a time when the French vocabulary was increased by several hundred words. This happened by resuscitating some which had fallen into disuse, by drawing largely on the scholarly Greek and Latin stock, but also by borrowing from foreign languages, from Spanish, Dutch, German, and above all, Italian. Most borrowings from Arabic were made before the fifteenth century (see table p. 66) and many of them came via Italian or Spanish.[85]

The memory of the Medicis

Italian was drawn on for loan words most eagerly, since it was in fashion, especially at the court. When Catherine de Medici became regent in 1560, its influence had already been felt for over thirty years. Although there was some resistance, the list of words borrowed from Italian during the sixteenth century was a long one, between 250 and 300 words according to the lists drawn up by Ferdinand Brunot. (See table p. 68.)

Doublets which don't double up

The most unexpected result of this renewal of the vocabulary was the creation of a large number of *doublets*: these are two words which are derived from the same source word, one of which has followed the normal phonetic evolution whilst the other has been borrowed directly from the Greek or Latin word. We have already seen the case in the twelfth century of *frêle* which evolved normally from the Latin word FRAGILEM, whilst

65

SOME LOAN WORDS FROM ARABIC

French borrowed words very early from Arabic (*amiral* can already be found in the *Chanson de Roland*), but very few of the hundreds of French loan words from Arabic were imported directly. For the most part they came via the Low Latin of the Middle Ages used by the scholars, or via Italian, Provençal, Portuguese, and above all Spanish. What is more, some of these words had themselves been borrowed by Arabic from other languages such as Turkish, Persian and Greek.

alambic (Gk.)	gilet (Sp.)	orange (Prov.)
algarade (Sp.)	harem	sucre (Ital.)
carafe (Ital./Sp.)	masser (*v.*) (Turk.)	zénith
coton (Lat./Ital.)	nénuphar (Lat.)	alcôve (Sp.)
gazelle	sirop (Lat.)	azur (Pers./Lat.)
guitare (Sp.)	tasse	chiffre
laquais (Sp.)	alchimie (Gk.)	estragon (Gk./Lat.)
nacre (Ital.)	azimut	goudron
romaine (Prov.)	chamarrer (Sp.)	jupe
talisman (Gk.)	épinard (Sp.)	momie
alcool (Lat.)	girafe (Ital.)	récif (Sp.)
amiral	hasard	talc
carat (Lat.)	matraque	zéro (Ital.)
élixir (Gk.)		

A bit of etymology:
amiral in Arabic means 'the emir [of the sea]';
chiffre and *zéro* come from the same Arabic word which originally meant 'void';
harem means 'that which is forbidden';
hasard means a 'dice';
momie originally meant 'bitumen' (used to coat corpses);
romaine has nothing to do with Rome but comes from an Arabic word for 'weighing machine' (the French *balance romaine*);
zénith derives from a misreading of the Arabic word *samt* 'path' which was read as *senit*. The same word preceded by the article (*as-samt*) gave the astronomical term *azimut*.

fragile was borrowed unmodified from Latin at a later date.

There are hundreds of doublets: some of them are quite transparent, like *camp* and *champ* from the Latin CAMPUS, and others more unexpected, like *aigre* and *âcre* from the Latin ACER.

With only a few exceptions, like MONASTERIUM, which gave *moutier* and *monastère*, one of the interesting peculiarities of these doublets is that both terms never have the same meaning even though they have the same origin. The most recent term is usually a calque on the Greek or Latin root, whereas the older word has not only undergone a *phonetic* change involving the loss of a few syllables, but has also undergone a *semantic* change, in other words a change of meaning: a *clavicule* is not the same as a *cheville*, a *potion* is only occasionally a *poison*, and a *friction* does not necessarily give you a *frisson*. (See table p. 69.)

66

THE REAL BEGINNINGS OF CLASSICAL FRENCH
(Sixteenth century)

In the sixteenth century, French really asserted itself over Latin, whilst at the same time drawing on it for some of the elements which have survived in the language today. The features of this new form of the language can be seen clearly in:

Marguerite de Navarre	1492–1549	*Heptaméron*
François Rabelais	1495–1553	*Pantagruel, Gargantua*
Clément Marot	1496–1544	*Epîtres, Epigrammes*
Blaise de Montluc	1502–1572	*Commentaires*
Jean Calvin	1509–1564	*Institution chrétienne*
Joachim du Bellay	1522–1560	*Défense et illustration de la langue française, Regrets*
Pierre de Ronsard	1524–1585	*Odes, Amours de Marie, Amours d'Hélène*
Louise Labbé	1526–1566	*Elégies, Sonnets*
Rémy Belleau	1528–1577	*Les Bergeries*
Michel de Montaigne	1533–1592	*Essais*
Jean-Antoine du Baïf	1532–1589	*Amours de Méline*
Robert Garnier	1534–1590	*Antigone, Bradamante, Les Juives*
Abbé de Brantôme	1540–1614	*Vie des dames illustres*
Guillaume du Bartas	1544–1590	*La Création du monde*
Pierre de l'Estoile	1546–1611	*Journal*

THE AGE OF 'GOOD USAGE'

French in a straitjacket

After a century of expansion in which the French language welcomed with open arms everything that could enrich it, the seventeenth century saw an attempt to stem this tide of innovation by formulating rules, fixing the spelling, and attempting to standardise pronunciation. The language as an instrument of centralisation became a matter for the state: in 1635 Richelieu founded the Académie Française, the first 'scholarly society' to be directly regulated by the state. The mission of its forty hand-picked members was to observe the language, supervise it, channel its development and contain its excesses, with the production of a grammar and especially a dictionary as part of its programme.

Bel usage and *bon usage*

Work began on the *Dictionnaire de l'Académie* in 1639. Once Chapelain's project had been accepted, responsibility for it was handed to Vaugelas. But he died before he could complete his labours. Work on the dictionary then began to drag, and it was not until fifty-five years later that the first edition finally appeared in 1694.

THE ENRICHING OF FRENCH VOCABULARY IN THE SIXTEENTH CENTURY

The French language was enriched in the sixteenth century by hundreds of new words borrowed from ancient and foreign languages, especially Italian. The following are a few examples. Some of them may be older than the sixteenth century but were not attested until then.

GREEK	GERMAN	ITALIAN	caresse	Military terms
académie	halte	altesse	carnaval	cartouche
enthousiasme	hère	arcade	carrosse	casemate
épithète	matois	artisan	charlatan	embuscade
hygiène	DUTCH	bagatelle	concert	escadron
larynx	cauchemar	balcon	courtisan	escalade
orgie	chaloupe	banque	disgrâce	escorte
sympathie	colin	banqueroute	douche	fantassin
LATIN	espiègle	batifoler	escapade	forçat
agriculteur	SCANDINAVIAN	bosquet	façade	frégate
captif	étrave	bouffon	faïence	poltron
colombe	homard	bourrasque	festin	risque
docile	SPANISH	bulletin	gazette	soldat
fidèle	anchois	burlesque	gondole	
funèbre	bandoulière	cabinet	passager	
gratuit	bizarre	caleçon	salsifis	
pudique	camarade	calepin	sonnet	
torréfié	nègre	caprice		

In theory it was neither an encyclopaedic nor an etymological dictionary. Its aim was to be a dictionary of usage. But there should be no mistake about what the aim really was: the usage it described was not that of the greatest number but what was called the *bel usage*,[86] meaning that of the court and of people of quality, who mainly frequented the Parisian *salons*, in particular those of the Hôtel de Rambouillet. A large part of the vocabulary (several hundred words) was omitted from the dictionary on the grounds that it was vulgar or old-fashioned: words like *angoisse* and *immense* which were deemed to be 'old', and *poitrine* and *épingle* which were thought to be too 'popular'.[87]

Judgments were just as peremptory outside the Academy: Ménage decided in 1650 that the word *urbanité* which Guez de Balzac had just invented was indeed a French word but not an everyday one, and should therefore be used no more than two or three times a month (*sic*).[88]

In its first edition (1694), the *Dictionnaire de l'Académie* contained 24,000 words classified by their 'roots', but the second edition (1718) adopted alphabetical order. As for technical words, they were to be avoided both in court and the salons, but a list of 15,000 of them was drawn up and published separately in 1694 by Thomas Corneille.[89]

DOUBLETS ARE NOT CLONES

Forms like *fragile* and *frêle* are called doublets because they derive from the same Latin word. One of the forms results from the phonetic evolution of the original word (FRAGILEM > *frêle*), whilst the other is a direct borrowing from Latin in a later time (FRAGILIS > *fragile*). But doublets are not clones, in other words not copies of one another. They usually have different meanings.

Doublets formed in the 16th century

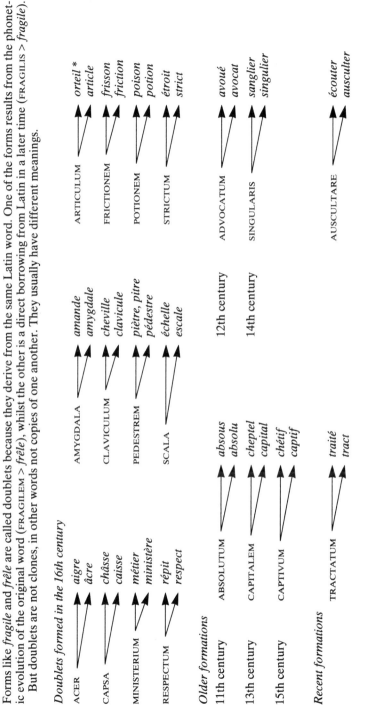

ACER	aigre / âcre	AMYGDALA	amande / amygdale	ARTICULUM	orteil * / article
CAPSA	châsse / caisse	CLAVICULUM	cheville / clavicule	FRICTIONEM	frisson / friction
MINISTERIUM	métier / ministère	PEDESTREM	piètre, pitre / pédestre	POTIONEM	poison / potion
RESPECTUM	répit / respect	SCALA	échelle / escale	STRICTUM	étroit / strict

Older formations

11th century	ABSOLUTUM	absous / absolu	12th century	ADVOCATUM	avoué / avocat
13th century	CAPITALEM	cheptel / capital	14th century	SINGULARIS	sanglier / singulier
15th century	CAPTIVUM	chétif / captif			

Recent formations

	TRACTATUM	traité / tract		AUSCULTARE	écouter / ausculter

* *Orteil* probably under the influence of Gaulish. (See table p. 19.)

The period also saw the publication of *l'Essai d'un dictionnaire universel, contenant généralement tous les mots français, tant vieux que modernes, et les termes de toutes les Sciences et Arts*, in which Furetière showed himself opposed to the purism of the Academy, of which he had been a member and from which he was now expelled for disloyal competition, so to speak. This example clearly demonstrates the difference between other dictionaries and the one produced by the Academy: the former accepted all words, whilst the latter strove to set a standard based on a particular usage.

Martyrs to spelling

All those children who today struggle to learn the spelling of French can curse Monday 8 May 1673, that dreaded day on which the members of the Academy decided to adopt a single, standardised spelling for themselves and which they then tried to force on the public.[90] This spelling, which was both abhorred and venerated, continues even today to have its martyrs, living in dread of a zero for dictation, and its admirers. (See *The written word*, p. 180.)

The academicians of the seventeenth century had another problem to solve: certainly they wished to impose an official orthography, but they first had to work it out, because different forms of spelling had been sprouting chaotically for several centuries. There had already been attempts at simplification in the sixteenth century, but the printers had always managed to scupper them.[91]

The spelling of each word was discussed at the Academy's meetings, but all the proposals for simplification were fiercely resisted because 'généralement parlant, la Compagnie prefere (*sic*) l'ancienne Orthographe, qui distingue les gens de Lettres d'avec les ignorans' (*sic*).[92] That is why archaic forms were reintroduced with superfluous consonants, as in *corps, temps, teste, ptisane, poulmon*, etc. Occasionally, however, a few rare concessions were made to usage: *devoir* and *fevrier* (*sic*) were adopted in place of *debvoir* and *febvrier*.[93] But the decisions usually went in favour of the unsimplified spellings.

Fixing the pronunciation

Just as they tried to devise a single spelling for each word, so the academicians sought also to fix on a uniform and regular pronunciation. Entire sessions were devoted to the problem of whether forms in *e* or forms in *a* should be accepted in words where usage hesitated between the two. It was finally decided to keep *asperge* rather than *asparge* and *guérir* rather than *guarir*, but *hargneux* was retained instead of *hergneux* and *marquer* instead of *merquer*. The reasons Vaugelas gave for these choices are disarming: '*e* is softer than *a*, but it should not be used too frequently'.[94] The academicians also pronounced on the choice between *formage* and *fromage*, *matelas* and *materas*, *venin* and *velin*. They also decided to take part in the quarrel of the 'ou-ists' and the 'non-ou-ists': should one say *corbeau* or *courbeau*, *forbu* or *fourbu*, *reposer* or *repouser*, *arroser* or *arrouser*, *coleuvre* or *couleuvre*, *cossin* or *coussin*?[95] We know what the result of the quarrel was: there was no general solution to the problem, and each word was resolved individually. The 'ou-ists' had their way with *fourbu*, *couleuvre* and *coussin* while the 'non-ou-ists' carried the day with *corbeau*, *reposer* and *arroser*.

Working on the meaning of words

Perhaps the most important contribution, or at least the least disputable, of the seventeenth century was the search for precision in the meaning of words, the setting up of nuances, such as the ones which allowed a distinction to be made between *souillé* and *taché*, *sommeiller* and *dormir*, etc. If the century left little space for individual inspiration, it did at least strive to turn the French language into an instrument which allowed subtleties of thought to be expressed adequately with the right words. 'Of all the different expressions which may render a single one of our thoughts', said La Bruyère, 'there is only one which is the right one'.[96]

'Usage' unthroned by 'universal reason'

In the second half of the century, the attitude of the grammarians changed. The *Grammaire de Port-Royal*, which appeared in 1660, had the great ambition of rediscovering universal reason behind the forms of the language. Whereas, at the beginning of the century, the grammarians had willingly bowed to usage ('good usage', of course), after 1660 they dared to declare themselves against it. They became the supreme authority whose judgements were accepted even by the greatest writers. Witness this message from Racine to Father Bouhours, to whom he sent the first acts of one of his tragedies: 'I beg you, Reverend Father, to take the trouble to read them, and to mark the mistakes I may have made against the language of which you are one of the most excellent masters.'[97]

Respect for good writers and politeness formulae

It is this unconditional respect for the grammatical authorities that the French have inherited from the seventeenth century, a century which they have been taught for generations to look upon as the one in which the French language reached its most complete degree of perfection, the language of the great classical authors which the schools have set up as models to be imitated. (See table p. 72.)

CLASSICAL FRENCH
(SEVENTEENTH CENTURY)

Since, from the seventeenth century onwards, references to 'good usage' always mean references to 'good writers', the following are some of those authors who gave lustre to the century which is always quoted as an example.

François Malherbe	1550–1630	*Odes, Stances à du Périer*
Honoré d'Urfé	1555–1628	*L'Astrée*
Mathurin Régnier	1573–1653	*Satires*
Claude Favre de Vaugelas	1585–1653	*Remarques sur la langue française*
René Descartes	1596–1650	*Discours de la méthode*
Vincent Voiture	1598–1648	*Lettres*
Pierre de Corneille	1606–1684	*Le Cid, Horace, Cinna* etc.
Scarron	1610–1660	*Le Roman comique*
François de La Rochefoucauld	1613–1680	*Maximes*
Gilles Ménage	1613–1692	*Observations sur la langue française*
Cyrano de Bergerac	1620–1655	*Histoire comique*
Jean de La Fontaine	1621–1695	*Fables, Contes*
Molière	1622–1673	*L'Avare, Tartuffe, Le Misanthrope*, etc.
Blaise Pascal	1623–1662	*Pensées, Les Provinciales*
Mme de Sévigné	1626–1696	*Lettres*
Bossuet	1637–1704	*Sermons, Oraisons funèbres*
Charles Perrault	1628–1703	*Les Contes de ma mère l'Oye*
Bourdaloue	1632–1704	*Sermons*
Mme de La Fayette	1634–1693	*La Princesse de Clèves*
Nicolas Boileau	1636–1711	*Epîtres, Art poétique*
Jean Racine	1639–1699	*Andromaque, Britannicus, Phèdre*, etc.
Jean de La Bruyère	1645–1696	*Les Caractères*
François Fénelon	1651–1715	*L'Education des filles*
Louis de Saint-Simon	1675–1755	*Mémoires*

If this century was the one in which the sounds and meanings of words were regulated, it was also the one which had strict rules of etiquette and which fixed the forms of politeness that the French still continue to observe. In particular, it was in this century that the forms of greeting were defined for beginning and ending letters, forms from which the French dare not depart even to this day.

Meanwhile, the patois . . .

We have just devoted quite a number of pages to the language of the people in high society, the one which took shape in Paris, torn between the fashions of the court and the injunctions of the grammarians and modelling itself on the great writers of the age. But who in the rest of the country knew how to speak French?

The different patois derived from Latin, which had gone from strength to strength in the feudal period, continued for a long time afterwards to be

72

the only languages spoken by the populace. The edict of Villers-Cotterêts issued by François I in 1539 had simply replaced one written language, Latin, by another, French. Notaries, for example, had simply adopted the habit of drawing up in French the wills of people who continued to speak the patois, as we can see from the writings of seventeenth-century authors.

Racine didn't understand a word south of Lyon

In a letter written in 1661 to his friend La Fontaine, Racine describes a journey he made to Uzès in the following terms:

> Already in Lyon I had begun scarcely to comprehend the local language and could hardly make myself understood. This misfortune increased in Valence, and as God would have it, when I asked the serving girl for a chamber pot, she put a stove under my bed. You can imagine the consequences of this accursed adventure, and what may happen to a man half-asleep who relieves himself on a stove in the middle of the night.[98]

He continued his journey and by the time he reached Uzès he could at first understand nothing of what was being said around him. After some time, he recognised in what he was hearing something that resembled a mixture of Italian and Spanish, and was then able to establish communication.[99]

At the same time, La Fontaine got somewhat lost in the region of Bellac during a journey to Limousin:

> As Bellac is distant from Limoges by no more than a short day's travel, we had all the time in the world to get lost, in which we acquitted ourselves most well and in the manner of people who knew neither the language nor the region.[100]

Death to the patois!

This same situation persisted throughout the eighteenth century: while French gradually took hold in the towns, the patois continued to be used by most of the rural population. This became abundantly clear during the Revolution.

Concerned to consolidate the Republic 'One and Indivisible', the members of the Convention attempted to do away with these local languages, which were too reminiscent of the Ancien Régime and represented an obstacle to revolutionary propaganda. After doing away with the provinces, measures had to be taken to do away with the patois named after them.

Before proposing this to the Convention, Abbé Grégoire[101], Bishop of Blois, decided in 1790 to do a detailed survey to find the number and extent

of these patois in the country. The 'circular' which he sent 'to the consti-
tuted authorities, to popular associations and to all the communes of the
Republic' contained forty-three questions, of which the following are a
sample:

'Does everybody in your region speak French?'
'Do they speak one or more patois?'
'Does this patois vary much from village to village?'
'Is it spoken in the towns?'
'What would be the religious and political importance of completely des-
troying this patois?'

Other questions bear more precisely on the linguistic forms themselves,
which allows us to see Abbé Grégoire's survey as the first real linguistic
survey on a large scale that we know of.

The answers he received in 1790 and 1791 led him to conclude that at
least six million French people, especially in the rural areas, did not know
the national language, that another six million were not capable of holding
a sustained conversation in the language, and that 'the number of those
who speak it correctly is no higher than three million'.

But Grégoire gives no details on the way in which he calculated these
results: did he or did he not include women, and did he exclude children?
If, in 1790, France had a population of some twenty-five million,[102] we
could conclude that only twelve out of a hundred French people spoke
French properly and that less than one in four could understand it.

Nowadays, when so many people believe that the search for their own
identity involves a return to the dialects, some of the answers to Grégoire's
questionnaire are not without surprise, since they contain letters witnessing
to a real desire on the part of people in the regions to be 'delivered' from
their patois. Several letters ask expressly and emphatically for central
government to organise serious teaching of the national language in the
regions as quickly as possible.[103]

The answers to his circular also enabled Grégoire to count thirty different dialects in France, which caused him to exclaim: 'We have no more
provinces and we still have thirty patois which remind us of their names
and which make thirty peoples instead of one.'

Elected constitutional bishop by his diocese of Blois, it was in 1794 that
Abbé Grégoire submitted to the Convention his 'Rapport sur la nécessité et
les moyens d'anéantir les patois et d'universaliser l'usage de la langue
française'. In this report he effectively recommended the 'sole and in-
variable use of the language of liberty in a Republic one and indivisible'.
To achieve this, he suggested producing short works, songs and newspapers in French which would be sent into all the communes. He proposed
that only the national language be permitted in all the municipalities, and
he even went so far as to ask – with the utmost seriousness – that future

PRIMARY SCHOOL VERSUS THE DIALECTS

'The primary schools will finally put an end to this bizarre inequality: they will teach the language of the Constitution and the laws to all, and that horde of corrupt dialects, the last remnant of feudalism, will be forced to disappear: the force of things demands it.'

Report by Talleyrand-Périgord, former Bishop of Autun, to the Constituent Assembly, 10 September 1791. (Quoted by Charles Bruneau, *Histoire de la langue française*, volume 9, book 1, ch. 2, pp. 13–14.)

spouses 'should be subjected to the obligation to prove that they can read, write and speak the national language' before they got married.[104]

A primary school teacher in every village: the impossible dream

Having learnt from Grégoire's survey, the revolutionaries wished, after Talleyrand had presented the report to the Convention (see table above, to take measures to spread *primary* (the word dates from 1791) education by setting up in each commune a school where the teaching would be done in French. Unfortunately, it was not possible at the time to find enough people who knew French, let alone be able to teach it.

It was therefore decided to set up *Écoles normales* (always this idea of a 'norm') to train teachers for primary school teaching, but attempts to do this did not lead to immediate results. It was only in 1794 that the *École normale supérieure* was founded in the rue d'Ulm to train teachers for secondary education. As for the *École normale supérieure* for girls, that was not to open until 1881, almost a century later.

During this time, the universities remained faithful to Latin, since the Faculties of Letters at the time still required all students to write a thesis in Latin as well as one in French. This requirement was not lifted until 1905.

Between 1789 and 1815, there was a considerable increase in the number of people in the population who could speak French, whilst the patois began to lose ground.

What eighteenth-century French was like

When French people are confronted with a text from the eighteenth century, they have no feelings of strangeness and they even have the impression that the language is scarcely different from Modern French. Nonetheless, two centuries of evolution have produced perceptible changes. If the French do not see these changes at once, it is more than anything because they are seeing it in the written form, as fixed by the

NOTHING IS EVER LOST IN A LANGUAGE

We can express in these somewhat simplistic terms one of the great contributions of functional and structural linguistics to the understanding of the phenomena of phonetic change.

In *Économie des changements phonétiques*,[105] André Martinet put forward the principles of a theory which allows us to grasp the complex conditioning of phonetic changes. One of them relates to the maintaining of sound differences which are useful for distinguishing words from one another: *blanc* and *blond* are distinguished from one another by the same lip movements as *brin* is from *brun*. But there are large numbers of word pairs of the type *blanc–blond, il fend–il fond, il range–il ronge, les bancs–les bonds* whereas the words which appear in the rare pairs of the type *brin–brun, empreinte–emprunte* cannot occur in the same contexts. As a result, the difference between *an* (*en*) and *on* is well maintained, whereas in Paris *un* sounds exactly the same as *in*.

It may happen that over the centuries a highly useful distinction tends to weaken and disappear under the influence of certain changes in the rhythm of speech. In French, for example, there was a time when the consonant following the vowel in a syllable tended to weaken. But when this consonant was useful for distinguishing words from one another, it did not purely and simply disappear: *pâte* used to be pronounced and written as *paste* (English has retained this form in the word borrowed from the French), just as *bête* was pronounced *beste* (English *beast*), *hâte* was pronounced *haste* (English *haste*). In all these words the *-s-* tended to disappear. But its disappearance pure and simple would lead to conflicts. The length of articulation of the *-s-* was transferred to the preceding vowel, so permitting a distinction between *pâte* and *patte*, *bête* and *bette*. This is what the circumflex accent in the spelling shows.

The same tendency to reduce the consonants at the end of the syllable is found for the *n* and *m* in words like *chante* or *lampe*, which Parisians used to pronounce as they are still pronounced today in the south, *chan'te, lam'pe*, with the *n* and *m* sounded. The need to distinguish *chan'ce* from *chasse*, *ren'te* from *rate*, etc. led to the lowering of the soft palate characteristic of *n* and *m* being maintained. But this lowering was anticipated and was produced at the same time as the articulation of the preceding vowel, hence what is called the nasal vowel, written as *an* (*en*) or *am*, in these words.

---

grammarians with an orthography close to that of the modern language.

What impression would they have if they could hear the same text being spoken by somebody living at the time of the Revolution? Amongst other characteristics, they would probably have a sense of heaviness. But why?

Drawn-out vowels

Without doubt because of the frequency of long vowels. Unlike the contemporary Parisian pronunciation, the language spoken two centuries ago had a large number of long vowels. Alongside the short vowels in words like *vit, bout, la*, there were long vowels in *vie, boue, las*. Some of these long vowels were already to be found in the language in the twelfth

TOPAZE'S 'MOUTONSS'

Topaze (*dictating as he walks around the classroom*)

'Des moutons . . . Des moutons . . . étaient en sûreté . . . dans un parc . . . dans un parc. (*He looks over the shoulder of one of the children and starts again.*) Des moutons . . . moutonss . . . (*The child stares vacantly at him.*) Come along, boy, make an effort. I said *moutonsse*. Étaient (*he begins again with delicacy*) *étai-eannt*. In other words there wasn't just one *moutonne*. There were several *moutonnse*.'

Marcel Pagnol, *Topaze*,
Act I, Scene i.

century, since the fall of the *s* in words like *beste* and *teste*, which became *bête* and *tête*, pronounced with long vowels. (See table p. 76.)

Between the fourteenth and the sixteenth centuries, the natural tendency of the language had been to eliminate all final consonants, at the same time as another change was taking place: the disappearance of the most frequent vowel, the *e*. That is why since then the term 'mute *e*' has been applied to a vowel which was pronounced in all positions in the Middle Ages. To get some idea of what the older pronunciation was like, you simply have to think of the contemporary pronunciation of words like *porte* or *mère* in the south of France, where they are pronounced as two syllables.

The fall of this vowel in the unstressed position had begun in the fourteenth century within words, leading to a lengthening of the preceding vowel. A word like *prierai*, formerly pronounced *pri-e-rai*, became *pri-rai* with a long *i*.

In the sixteenth and seventeenth centuries, the vowel began to fall at the end of words as well, at first after a vowel (*fée, amie*), and then also after a consonant, as in *tête* and *perte*, which were now pronounced with a final consonant as they still are today. A century later we find that the vowel is long in *las, mots, je peux* and *maître*, as well as in *armée* or *amie*, but remains short in *là, mot, peu* and *mètre*, as well as in *armé* or *ami*. Thus we can see that length replaced the fallen consonant or vowel.

At this stage in the development, the vowel length becomes *pertinent* since it allows *las* (with long *a*) to be distinguished from *là* (with a short *a*), *mots* (long in the plural) from *mot* (short in the singular), *armée* (long in the feminine) from *armé* (short in the masculine), etc.

At a time when the singular and the plural of nouns, or the masculine and the feminine of adjectives, were pronounced differently, the attempts made by the primary school teacher Topaze to teach the plural of *mouton* would have been unnecessary. (See table above)

77

Giles Vaudelin, a precursor

Evidence for the existence of these long vowels is found in the writings of all the grammarians of the eighteenth century, and in particular in the very precise description given by a Father of the Reformed Augustinians who attempted to 'immortalise the true pronunciation' in two works[106] intended to preserve the correct reading of religious books. Using twenty-nine signs inspired by the letters of the Latin alphabet and four accents, Giles Vaudelin tried to give everybody, including the less well educated, a writing system to make French easier to read.

In Vaudelin's texts, the vowels are marked with a given accent depending on whether they are long or short: the final vowels of *oublient*, *désolée*, *prononçaient*, *je trouvais*, *mots*, and *tous* (*les beaux-arts*) are marked long, while those in *ici*, *pensé*, *prononçait*, *aurait* and *mot* are marked short.

Vaudelin adds that this way of writing 'immortalises' the true pronunciation of the words of his time 'because it will never be possible with this spelling to read them and pronounce them differently'.[107] And indeed, thanks to him we can have an exact idea of the pronunciation in use in the eighteenth century.

Nowadays, we hear fewer and fewer long vowels in the most common of contemporary usages. However, if you go to Franche-Comté, Bourgogne, Champagne, Belgium or Switzerland, you will have occasion to hear drawn-out vowels. What may now seem like a regional peculiarity was once the pronunciation of the majority of the non-southern population around the year 1700.

Thus there are important differences of pronunciation between eighteenth-century and twentieth-century French. There are also differences in the way sentences were constructed.

The 'simple' past: too complicated for the French

Nowadays, forms like vous *aimâtes*, nous *cousîmes* or vous *résolûtes* have become curiosities which are only ever seen in the written language, where they are usually intended to be playful or ridiculous. Some forms of the past historic (*passé simple* in French) are still to be found in literary language, but only in narrative and usually only in the third person: we find *il vécut*, *ils vécurent* but rarely *nous vécûmes*, *vous vécûtes*.

As far as the spoken language is concerned, we do not know exactly when the forms of the past historic began to disappear from use. At the beginning of the seventeenth century, Vaugelas[108] hesitated between the forms *vescut* and *vesquit*, but he noted that the past historic was already avoided at that time and that the perfect, the compound past, was preferred instead. Furthermore, although Mme de Sévigné still made frequent use of the forms of the past historic, they were not used with the value of a past historic but rather as an equivalent of the perfect tense.[109] It is in any case quite clear that by the end of the eighteenth century, in Paris at least, the past historic was no longer used in the spoken language.

It was probably because of the complexity of its forms that the past historic finally disappeared completely from the spoken language. People took to the habit of preferring the perfect tense, out of fear of making a mistake or of not having on the tip of the tongue the correct forms of commonly used verbs such as *retenir, s'enfuir, bouillir, résoudre, distraire* or *promouvoir*. The danger was a very real one. Amongst many others, barbarisms such as *ils s'enfuyèrent* or *il dissolva* have been noted in written and published texts, and *ils conquérirent* has been heard on the radio.[110]

And those with a nostalgic love of these perilous past historics which remind them of the great classical authors ('Vous mourûtes aux bords où vous fûtes laissée') will probably find it the height of irony that this so-called *simple* past was doomed to die because it was too complicated.

But even more than the past historic, the imperfect subjunctive was very quickly to become a rarity in conversation.

'J'eusse été fâché que vous m'imputassiez cette connerie!'

The imperfect subjunctives in the title of this section clash somewhat with the noun at the end of it: according to Jean Duché,[111] the sentence was uttered by a mischievous academician, Jacques de Lacretelle, who used the refined and outmoded verbal forms to make the indecency, or, as we would say nowadays, the colloquialism, of the last word more palatable.

The disappearance of the imperfect subjunctive, which began at the beginning of the seventeenth century, seems to have reached Paris by the end of the eighteenth.[112] In Modern French it is avoided for reasons of euphony and is replaced by the present subjunctive, disregarding the sequence of tenses: instead of *je voulais que nous nous comprissions et que vous m'aimassiez*, a French person would usually prefer to say *je voulais que nous nous comprenions et que vous m'aimiez*.

There are, however, certain well-read people of refined taste who insist on using it but who would perhaps do better not to, because they get it wrong half of the time. In the twentieth century, the subjunctive has thus become a superfluous ornament which is intended to indicate refinement and cultivation but in fact only too often indicates an imperfect knowledge of the norm.

The spirit of the *Encyclopédistes*

Unlike the seventeenth century, when a desire to purify the language led to the suppression of any hint of invention, the eighteenth century seems to have been a time when the vocabulary increased with most freedom. The rise of new technology, the proliferation of philosophical ideas and the transformation of social structures gave rise to a pressing need to name the new objects and concepts.

This need was satisfied with the publication of the *Encyclopédie* in 1751. Inspired by Bayle's *Dictionnaire historique et critique* (1697) and under the editorship of Diderot and d'Alembert, it brought together articles by all the great writers and thinkers of the century: Rousseau, Voltaire, Condillac, Marmontel, Turgot, Helvétius, etc.

The *Encyclopédie* is the clearest reflection of a new state of mind, eager to know about everything that concerned human activity. 'Bel usage' and 'bon usage' were no longer on the agenda. The *Encyclopédie* welcomed without restriction professional, scientific and technical terms, and, in response to the new thirst for knowledge, provided not only the meanings of the words but also a precise description of the objects.

The proliferation of new words in the eighteenth century

The sheer number of lexical innovations in the eighteenth century is such that it is not possible to draw up even an approximate list of them. They are found in every sphere:

- politics: *exécutif, plébiscite, député, bureaucratie*, etc.
- finance: *bourse, cote, agio, transfert*, etc.
- agriculture: *agronomie, excédent, primeur*, etc.

   Towards the end of the century the word *pomme de terre* made its appearance, replacing its rivals *patate, cartoufle, troufle, trouffe* and even *topinambour* and *truffe*. The new name for the tuber, which seems to be a calque on the Dutch *aardappel* 'potato', spread largely thanks to the efforts of Parmentier, who introduced the court and Parisians of quality to the incomparable qualities of the vegetable.
- commerce: among other innovations, a distinction was made at that time between *commerce* 'the sale of what one produces oneself' and *trafic* or *négoce* 'the sale of what others produce'.
- industry, the sciences, the arts, etc.[113]

THE AGE OF SCHOOL

People learn to speak French, but they don't forget the patois

In nineteenth-century France, the French language gained ground but 80 per cent of people still spoke the patois in most of the situations of daily life. We have an idea of what patois were spoken at the time, thanks to a survey conducted in 1807 by Coquebert de Montbret, who was the

Director of Statistics at the Ministry of the Interior. He asked each locality to provide him with a sample of its dialect by listing the names of numbers and giving a patois version of the 'parable of the prodigal son'. The results were published twenty-four years later by his son.[114] Although no real use can be made of them because the phonetic notation is inadequate, these texts still constitute the most precise evidence of the vitality of the patois during that period.

At the same time, the French language was making progress. In Provence, for example, in the period before the Revolution, French became the language of the aristocrats, the bourgeoisie and all those who wanted to 'rise' in society, while Provençal remained in common use in daily life. Many people were thus becoming bilinguals.[115]

This bilingualism persisted throughout the nineteenth century in most regions, although the use of the patois gradually became restricted to certain situations, losing ground to the invasion of French.[116]

In 1832, Guizot founded the primary schools.[117] Fifty years later (1880–6), Jules Ferry created the system of non-religious, free and compulsory state education where the teaching was naturally done in French and where the study of French had a privileged position.

. . . and all French children had to be taught how to write

This is the title of a book[118] in which André Chervel reviews the history of French grammar. Anybody who wants to write French must know how to spell it, and the school grammar books were written essentially for the purpose of teaching that treacherous orthography.

The sixth edition of the *Dictionnaire de l'Académie* appeared in 1835 and became the spelling bible for the 36,000 words it contained. Whilst rejecting words such as *abat* or *embêter*,[119] the academicians restored a number of consonants in the orthography, such as the *t* at the end of the word *enfant*, which at the time was written without a *t* in the plural *enfans*,[120] and they accepted the spelling proposed by Voltaire for words previously spelt with *-ois* (the endings of the imperfect tense, words such as *français*, etc.), which now had to be spelt with *-ais*[121] in conformity with Parisian pronunciation.

To be sure that everybody would conform to the new orthography, the government decreed in 1832 that it was to be compulsory in all examinations, in all official documents and to gain access to all state employment.

French people in all walks of life have had this system of spelling so impressed upon them for four hundred years that, as Chervel says, they have come to identify French orthography with the French language itself. (See *The written word*, p. 180.)

Mutual incomprehension in the ranks

The nineteenth century saw French increase in importance because, as a result of compulsory schooling, it found its way into every household. But the patois were not dead. The revolutionaries had loudly proclaimed the need to abolish them, but plans to do so had proven impossible to implement and the most spontaneous forms of communication were still made in the local dialect.

French was spoken at school, but in the playground the patois was used between friends. Even when the patois of the nearby village was slightly different, all it took was a little bit of adapting to establish mutual comprehension.

This situation persisted until the First World War. The conscripts, who were enrolled in the regional regiments of their respective provinces, were still able to speak the patois to one another at the beginning of the war. But the terrible losses suffered during the first battles led to the formation of new units consisting of soldiers from every part of France. It consequently became easier to speak the common language that everybody had learnt at school, in other words French, rather than trying to make oneself understood in one's native dialect. It was these regroupings ordered by the General Staff which were to deal a fatal blow to the patois which the Revolution had been unable to do away with.

After four years of this regime, the habit had taken root, and when they returned home, the men continued to speak French in the house. As a result, their children had less and less occasion to hear and speak the patois.

Abandoning the patois

It was then that the real decline of the patois began, a process encouraged by the orders given by schoolteachers, who, since the start of the century, had been punishing any child who spoke the dialect in the classroom.

In the course of a linguistic survey[122] which I carried out several years ago in various French-speaking regions, more than a few of the older participants recalled the somewhat sadistic custom of handing an object, which varied according to the region, to the first child who used a patois word in class. The guilty pupil would then pass the object to the next child who used the patois, and so on until the end of the lesson, when punishment would befall the last unfortunate who had not been able to get rid of the object before the bell sounded for break.

This left the bilingual child with mixed feelings of shame and attachment towards the patois. In *Les tilleuls de Lautenbach*,[123] the author Jean Egen recounts that as a child he spoke Alsacien only at home.

When I was playing outside with little Gaulard or little Parrot, if I saw

82

my mother coming, before she could even open her mouth I would begin speaking to her in French because I was afraid that she would speak to me in dialect.

He also said of his mother: 'To her husband and children she spoke only the dialect. To God she spoke German, and a little French to please Dad.'

In the chapter on geography we shall see the place that the regional languages still occupy today in a country where French has taken first place throughout. (See the map, p. 84.)

THE AGE OF THE MEDIA

In the twentieth century, it is French, that is to say the common language, that has benefited from the new broadcasting technologies: nowadays we naturally think of television, but before that there was the radio, or rather the wireless.

When the wireless became the radio

The wireless (in French TSF, an acronym that young French people have never even heard of) evokes memories of that heroic age of 'steam broadcasting' which transformed the lives of those who are now old enough to be grandparents.

Radio receivers were exhibited for the first time in France at the Paris Fair in 1921. Sales to private individuals must have increased very rapidly because the first advertisement was broadcast on French radio in 1929. The fact that the operation was considered to be profitable at that time means that there must already have been a sizeable listening audience. French radio never looked back after that, and by 1939 there were no less than five million radio sets in a population of forty-one million.

It was probably at about that time that the word *radio* superseded the acronym TSF,[124] which has now completely disappeared from ordinary usage. But for a long time after the war, authors like Jean-Paul Sartre evoking their childhood memories still used the term as a matter of course to describe the apparatus.

To begin with, they were enormous boxes for producing speech and music, more like items of furniture which, from the 1930s onwards, began to introduce the life of the great wide world into French homes, until, in the decades that followed, they became no more than background noise to most of our activities.

In this way, from the beginning of the 1930s, people who had only ever heard French spoken with the 'accent' of their native region found themselves exposed every day to hearing new ways of talking from elsewhere

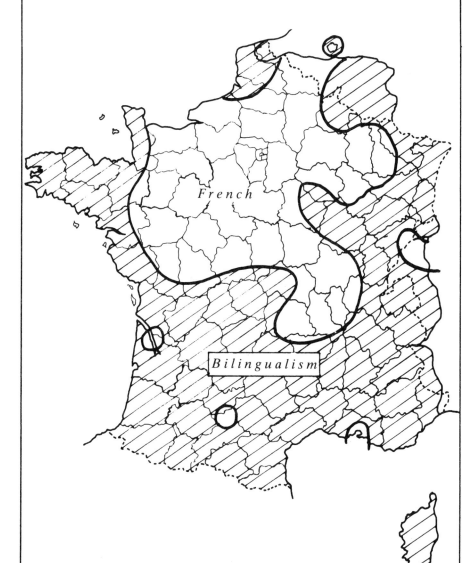

WHERE THE PATOIS ARE SPOKEN

French

Bilingualism

There are no general surveys which allow us to locate with precision the people who still speak the regional languages.

The above map, based on a survey of the regional varieties of French conducted between 1974 and 1978, is purely indicative and relates to people who are sedentary and of a fairly high average age.

(See Henriette Walter, *Enquête phonologique et variétés régionales du français*, Paris, PUF, 1982.)

and in another 'accent'. The French heard on the radio was now to influence the language of everybody.

Twenty years on: pictures with sound

Television merely followed, slowly at first, the movement already begun by the radio. Regular television broadcasts were transmitted from the Eiffel Tower in 1935, but fifteen years later there were still very few viewers. The first televised news bulletin presented by Pierre Sabbagh in 1949 marked an important date in the history of French television, but by 1950 there were still only a few hundred TV sets in France. Ten years on and the triumph was complete: in 1960 there were one and a half million, in 1970 ten million and in 1985 more than twenty-three million.[125]

It was from the 1960s onwards, therefore, that television began gradually to play a central part in the lives of all French people. It has thus become, alongside radio, one of the prime motors of change in the language, demoting the cinema, which started to make talkies in 1927, to second place.

The French of the media

By 1985, 93 per cent of homes were equipped with at least one television set, and the French spent, on average, two hours and forty five minutes a day in front of the small screen.[126]

Thus, the words spoken by a small group of people are listened to every day by millions of others who, as a result, become accustomed to hearing them and subsequently use them themselves. Television and radio presenters thus bear a great responsibility, and are forgiven no departure from the norm, whether great or small.

A 1986 book, *Le français télé . . . visé*,[127] which notes the mistakes made by presenters, actors and politicians against the French of the Academy, reveals a set of tendencies which are already fairly widespread in modern French usage and which, being aired daily on the television channels and the radio waves, will spread even further. In denouncing mistakes picked up on the airwaves, the author of the book wants to sound a warning note so that steps may be taken to remedy the situation. But the history of languages has frequently shown that a form denounced as a mistake in one period often appears in the next generation as a form to be imitated.

Pronunciation and the media

With the same keen observation but in a completely different spirit, the linguist Anne Lefebvre has studied a sample of twelve hours of recorded speech from various types of broadcast (news, games, adverts) with the voices of 111 different people.[128]

Without wishing to make value judgements, she attempted to observe the pronunciation of words which reach us daily over the airwaves and which influence us in spite of ourselves. The results of this study show how the various 'accents' are fading and slowly converging on a more neutral pronunciation, such as the one which is developing in and around Paris but which is not the same as the Paris 'accent'.

The situation today

At the end of this twentieth century, the spread of mass communication, by increasing contact between different linguistic usages, is indisputably becoming a channel for unifying these usages. We could even go so far as to ask to what extent the features which characterise each of these usages have not already begun to blur, and sometimes even to disappear completely.

But let us not be too hasty. We do not have to conduct even more surveys to realise that beside these 'media' pressures which cause different usages to converge, there are others acting in the opposite direction. In particular, we should not forget the attachment individuals feel, consciously or unconsciously, to the way people speak in their native region and which makes them resist the levelling process taking shape around them. If we analyse the situation in the French language community, we can see that a single version of French identical for everybody is still a long way off.

But what remains of the dialectal diversity of the Middle Ages in today's world? What new varieties of French have come into the world in more recent times? The next chapter will examine one of the most striking aspects of this diversity, one which is defined most clearly by geographical criteria.

2

DIALECTS AND PATOIS
The regional languages

THE NON-ROMANCE LANGUAGES

Who speaks what?

As we have just seen, the linguistic usage of the Île-de-France has for centuries imposed its domination on the other regional languages. However, fortified by well-established traditions, these latter languages have been able to some extent to withstand the uniforming effects of school and, more recently, the media. Happily, we can still find today people who speak these regional languages, which have become favourite objects of study for the language specialists. These experts are losing no time in seeking out the last speakers of these languages threatened with extinction in order to collect the linguistic riches they have preserved right up to the end of the twentieth century, so giving the lie to the dialectologists Gilliéron and Rousselot, who were already proclaiming, nearly one hundred years ago, 'the imminent destruction of the patois'.[129]

We must begin by giving a separate place to the non-Romance languages: *Basque*, *Breton*, *Flamand*, *Alsacien* and the Germanic dialect of *Lorrain*. (See map p. 88.)

Basque – surviving the Indo-European invasion

Of all the languages of France, the *Basque* language is the most ancient, since it was spoken before the arrival of the Gauls, in other words before the arrival of the Indo-Europeans. Its ancestor was the language of the Aquitani who seem to have yielded to the Gauls when the Romans arrived. *Basque* is still spoken today in part of the Pyrénées-Atlantiques and above all in Spain. In 1972 the total number of Bascophones was estimated to be half a million,[130] of which some 80,000 were in France.[131]

NON–ROMANCE LANGUAGES SPOKEN IN FRANCE

Flamand

Germanic Lorrain

Alsacien

Breton

Basque

The non-Romance languages spoken in France seem to have taken refuge on the edges of the country: *Flamand* in the north, and *Lorrain* and *Alsacien* in the east are Germanic languages, while *Breton* in the west is a Celtic language.

Basque in the extreme south-west is the only non-Indo-European language still spoken in France.

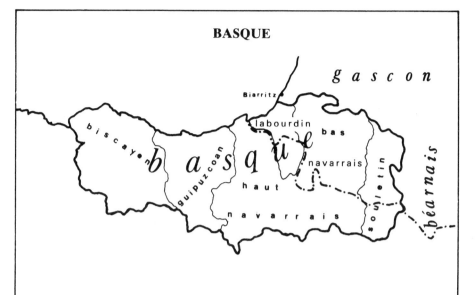

BASQUE

Basque is the only non-Indo-European language still spoken in France. On French territory it is subdivided into three dialects: *Souletin, Bas-Navarrais* and *Labourdin*. These dialects extend into Spain through Haut-Navarrais, Guipuzcoan and Biscayen.

The other non-Romance languages

Among the Indo-European languages – but not including the Romance languages, which will be discussed below – we find:

– in the extreme west, *Breton*, which we have already looked at and which belongs to the Celtic family;
– in the extreme north, *Flamand*, which belongs to the Germanic family and is a variety of Dutch;
– in the east, *Alsacien* and *Lorrain*, which also belong to the Germanic family but which are closer to German.

These languages have lived alongside French for varying lengths of time and have managed to varying degrees to withstand being dominated by it.

Who speaks Breton today?

Breton is spoken in the furthermost part of Brittany, which is also called Lower Brittany, Celtic Brittany or Breton-speaking Brittany, in the departments of North and South Finistère as well as in the western part of Côtes-d'Armor and Morbihan.

There are some one and a half million people living in this region but there is no census to tell us how many are true Breton speakers. Estimates made in 1950 were in the region of 700,000,[132] but it is unlikely that there are more than half that number nowadays. And even then a distinction must be made between those who speak it naturally in their everyday communications and those who have learnt it later in life almost as a foreign language.

For Breton, which was once the language of peasants and craftsmen, has for several years been the object of increased interest on the part of intellectuals and young people in search of their cultural identity. Students can now learn Breton to degree level and obtain a CAPES in the subject (Certificat d'aptitude pédagogique à l'enseignement secondaire).[133] In addition, almost a century after the creation in 1876 of the first Head of Studies in Celtic at the École Pratique des Hautes Études,[134] research centres were set up in Rennes and Brest. However, in spite of the vitality and competence of these centres, there is a real problem for the survival of the language since there is a perceptible gap between the Breton taught in the universities and the language of Breton speakers by birth.[135]

Flemish

Flemish is still spoken in a small enclave in the extreme north of the Nord department, but at the beginning of the thirteenth century it covered a good part of the Artois and extended to beyond Boulogne. More than fifty place-names ending in -ghem, -ghen (or -hem, -hen), meaning 'house, village' in Flemish and corresponding to heim in German, confirm this (see map p. 93).

In the fourteenth century, the area in which Flemish languages were spoken was already not as geographically extensive and did not go beyond Calais. France annexed Flanders in 1678 and six years later a royal edict made the use of French compulsory in the law courts. Flemish has constantly lost ground to French since then, but the infiltration was a slow process, since French at that time was used only in cultivated circles.

During the eighteenth century, French became the language of education and in the nineteenth century even the peasants were beginning to understand and speak it.[136] During this time the geographical extension of Flemish was further reduced and went no further than Gravelines.

Nowadays, we can still find people who speak Flemish in the Dunkerque district, but not in the towns or along the coast. Anyway it is difficult to hazard even an approximate figure, since no survey allows us to establish one. One of the habits most frequently noted in bilingual French–Flemish speakers is the fact that in conversation or in the same sentence they pass

BRETON

Breton is still spoken in so-called Celtic or Breton-speaking Brittany to the west of a line which now extends roughly from Paimpol to Vannes but which was much further east in the ninth century (from around Dol-de-Bretagne to Pornic). We can see that Rennes was not a part of the Breton-speaking area even in the ninth century. It should also be noted that the decline in Breton since 1886 is no longer the result of geographical shrinkage but rather of a gradual slow reduction in the number of Breton speakers within the one area.

Breton is subdivided into four main dialects: Cornouaillais, Léonais and Trégorrois on the one hand, and Vannetais on the other. The badge that you can sometimes see on the back of cars registered in Brittany bears the name of the province Breizh which is a combination of the word Breiz from the first three of these dialects and the word Breih from the fourth.

from one language to the other without realising it.[137] However, that is not something specific to the region or to the language.

The vitality of Alsacien and Lorrain

It is perhaps in Alsace and German Lorraine that the traditional language of the region, the *vernacular* language to use the scholarly term, has retained most of its vitality.

The Germanic Alsacien dialect is still in daily use throughout Alsace. You can often hear people in Strasbourg speaking Alsacien, to which the people in the region, even in the large towns, still feel strongly attached. Several years ago, less than twenty kilometres from Strasbourg, when we stopped to ask a peasant the way in French we had some difficulty in making ourselves understood.

This situation is understandable when you remember that after the annexation of Alsace-Lorraine by Germany, French was no longer taught for almost fifty years, from 1870 to 1918, and again for the five years from 1940 to 1945. Since then, French has made progress, but Alsacien has yielded only slowly, with most Alsaciens becoming bilingual.

The same situation is to be found in Germanic-speaking Lorraine (in the north and east of the department of Moselle), where a survey carried out in 1968[138] showed not only widespread bilingualism but also, outside the younger generations, a frequently superficial knowledge of French. Generally speaking, although French was making advances, the dialect was standing up well and was only clearly in decline in the towns. The survey also showed that there were a small number of monolinguals who could speak only the dialect. The author of the survey highlighted the curious behaviour of a woman farmer who spoke good French:[139] in switching from French to the Germanic Lorrain dialect, her voice changed tone and became deeper.[140] In making this unconscious change of pitch, this inhabitant of the Moselle was probably expressing her feeling of belonging to two different linguistic worlds.

THE ROMANCE DIALECTS

Listening out for differences in the Romance zone

The great dialectal divisions which cut the country into the *oïl*, *oc*, and *Francoprovençal* zones have already been discussed (see pp. 28–9), but with no mention of the criteria which allow the dialectologists to establish these divisions.

The various situations are, in fact, so complicated and interconnected that the dialectologists themselves are still debating certain groupings, and it would thus be presumptuous for me to take sides. None the less, it would

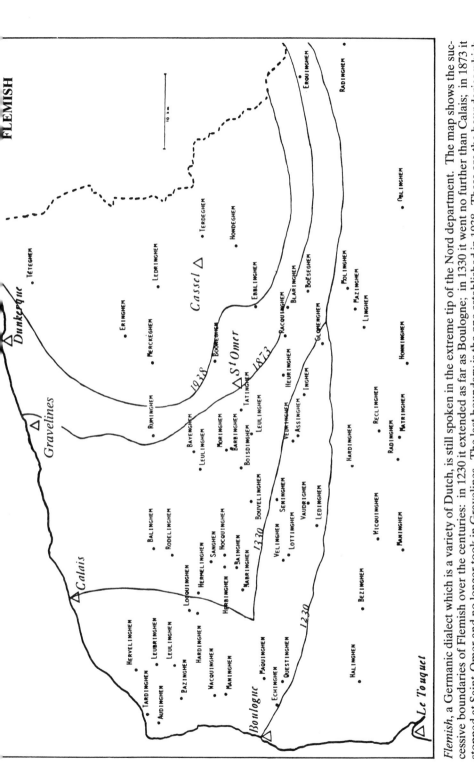

FLEMISH

Flemish, a Germanic dialect which is a variety of Dutch, is still spoken in the extreme tip of the Nord department. The map shows the successive boundaries of Flemish over the centuries: in 1230 it extended as far as Boulogne; in 1330 it went no further than Calais; in 1873 it stopped at Saint-Omer and no longer took in Gravelines. The last boundary is the one established in 1938. These are the boundaries which are given in *Le Guide de Flandre et Artois mystérieux* (Paris, Tchou, 1966, p. 29).

Place-names ending in -*ghem* (and -*ghen*), in which the suffix means 'village' (German *Heim*), attest to the earlier existence of Flemish, not only in Flanders but also in Artois and Picardy.

The research for these placenames of Flemish origin was conducted by Gérard Walter using a Michelin map with a scale of 1:200,000.

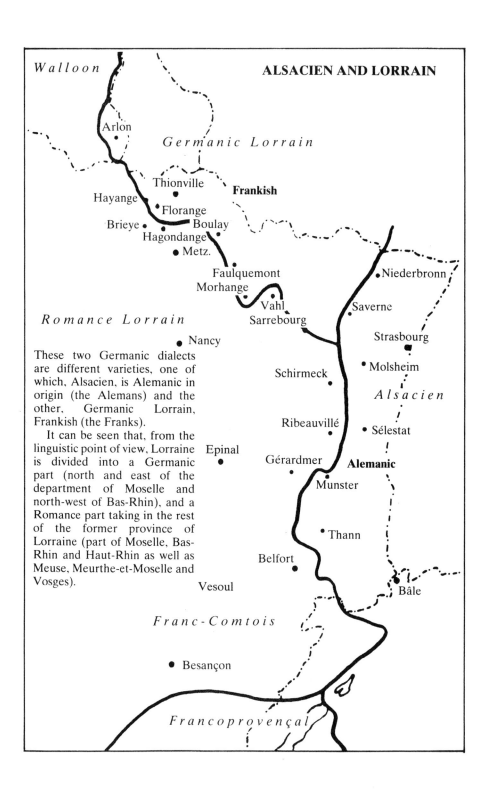

ALSACIEN AND LORRAIN

Walloon

Germanic Lorrain

Arlon

Thionville

Frankish

Hayange

Florange

Brieye · · Boulay

Hagondange

· Metz.

Faulquemont

Morhange

Vahl

Sarrebourg

· Niederbronn

Saverne

Romance Lorrain

· Nancy

Strasbourg

· Molsheim

Schirmeck

Alsacien

Ribeauvillé

· Sélestat

Epinal

Gérardmer

Alemanic

Munster

· Thann

Belfort

Vesoul

Bâle

Franc-Comtois

· Besançon

Francoprovençal

These two Germanic dialects are different varieties, one of which, Alsacien, is Alemanic in origin (the Alemans) and the other, Germanic Lorrain, Frankish (the Franks).

It can be seen that, from the linguistic point of view, Lorraine is divided into a Germanic part (north and east of the department of Moselle and north-west of Bas-Rhin), and a Romance part taking in the rest of the former province of Lorraine (part of Moselle, Bas-Rhin and Haut-Rhin as well as Meuse, Meurthe-et-Moselle and Vosges).

FRANCE ON A BIKE OR THE BIRTH OF LINGUISTIC GEOGRAPHY

At the end of the nineteenth century, the dialectologist Jules Gilliéron, a geologist by training, asked Edmond Edmont, a pharmacist whose hearing was highly sensitive, to ride around France on a bicycle collecting the different forms of a list of 1,400 words in 639 villages. Of course, Edmont did not have a tape recorder. He immediately wrote down in phonetic script the pronunciations he heard, and, in order to avoid the temptation of correcting his first impression, sent the information he had harvested to Gilliéron each evening.

The results of this 'survey on a bike', which took four years to complete, were published by Gilliéron between 1902 and 1910 as the *Atlas linguistique de la France*. The atlas contains a separate map for each of the words studied with the form of the word in phonetic notation at the place where it was heard.

This first cartographic collection of the dialects of France was followed by a series of smaller-scale atlases, the twenty-five *Atlas linguistiques par région*, produced by teams from the CNRS and currently nearing completion (*sic*).

---

be a pity not to present some of the data highlighted by linguistic geography, a discipline which relates linguistic phenomena to the places where they are found. (See table above.)

There are linguistic atlases of France which show on a map of the country the linguistic forms for one concept, which have been gathered locally by the researcher and written on the map in phonetic notation at the places covered by the survey. Thus you have all the words used to designate, for example, 'cat', 'cockerel' or 'to rain' on one map, and so on. Using data like this, it is possible to map out dialectal areas in which the same words or the same pronunciation is used.

Let's speak a little patois

The following pages give information which will be inadequate for anybody looking for a real initiation into dialectology but which may be able to arouse the curiosity of those readers who have so far been indifferent to regional languages simply because they knew absolutely nothing about them. And then, when they are travelling in France or watching French television and they hear somebody say words like *canchon*, *cabro* or the surname *Martí*, perhaps they will remember that *canchon* is 'chanson' in Picard, *cabro* is 'chèvre' in Provençal, and *Martí* is Catalan for *Martin*.

THE OC *DIALECTS*

In order to describe how these dialects differ from the other Romance languages, dialectologists make use of some twenty criteria,[141] which combine in different ways in different areas, thus giving rise to internal subdivisions. (See map p. 101.)

CATEAU = CHÂTEAU = CASTEL

Linguistic geography allows us to represent on the ground the diversity of the dialects that evolved from Latin. Thus, all Latin words in CA- (like CAPRA 'chèvre') have kept the initial Latin consonant both in the far north (*kèvre* in Picard) and in the far south (*cabro* in Provençal). But in a vast area in between, highly modified initial consonants are found: *chèvre* in French, *chieuve* in Gallo, *tchabra* in Haut-Limousin, *tsabra* in Bas-Limousin, *sièbre* in the Forez, and even *thevra* in Savoyard.

Confirmation of these evolutionary phenomena is found in toponymy, except for the fact that throughout the central area the initial consonant has converged on the French form *Ch-*. Thus, we have:

– in the north, *Le Cateau* (formerly *Cateau-Cambrésis*), *Catillon*, *Le Catelet*, etc.

– in the south, *Castelnaudary, Castillon, Castelet*, etc.

– and in between, *Châteauroux, Châtillon, Châtelet*, etc.

You can see that the line which divides the central region (*Cha-*) from the southern region (*Ca-*) does not coincide with the frontier (dotted line) of the *oïl* and *oc* regions. It therefore allows us to set up a subdivision of the *oc* dialects (see p. 101).

Who speaks Occitan nowadays?

The generic term *langue d'oc* or *Occitan* is used to designate the dialects spoken in the south of France over a vast area, which goes from the department of Gironde in the west to the department of Hautes-Alpes in the east. They are still spoken, in competition with French, by numbers of people which vary according to place, but it is well nigh impossible to calculate the number of people who can speak or simply understand an Occitan dialect, and the figures vary with the chosen criterion. In 1963, it was estimated that twelve million people could at least understand the dialect.[142] A more recent estimate revolves around eight million, of which two million claim to be 'full-time' users.[143]

No systematic census has been undertaken, but there have been a number of limited surveys which allow us to see the vitality of the regional languages,[144] which are more widely used in Roussillon than in Gascony, usually better preserved in rural circles than in the large towns and especially among the elderly. Gilliéron's surveys of the whole of France at the end of the nineteenth century still included a large number of people under forty, whereas the latest surveys conducted by the CNRS teams tended to collect evidence from people whose average age was over seventy.[145]

The memory of Mistral

The dialects of southern France make most people think immediately of the Provence and Mistral, a reaction which quite wrongly ignores the other *oc* dialects.

The language of the southern troubadours, whose literary prestige goes back to the Middle Ages, enjoyed some degree of unity to begin with, but *langue d'oc* nowadays is not synonymous with *Provençal*, since differences began to emerge as early as the thirteenth century, culminating in the subdivisions which exist today: Provençal, Languedocien, Auvergnat, Limousin, Gascon, and so on.

This fragmentation had taken place a long time ago when, in the middle of the nineteenth century, seven young Provençal poets, including Frédéric Mistral, gathered in a castle belonging to one of them to create the *Félibrige*. The aim of this Provençal 'Pléiade' was essentially to bring back to life a common language with the first objective of creating a unified orthography to represent the pronunciation of the language as faithfully as possible.

Spelling problems

You must remember that at the time there was not just *one oc* language, as there had been in the Middle Ages, but several dialectal varieties. So for each word to have its own *unique* spelling, one dialect had to be chosen as a point of reference. Since all the early *félibres* came from the same region between Arles and Avignon, they quite naturally took as their model the dialect of Mistral's birthplace, Maillane.

Any subsequent success Félibrige may have enjoyed outside Provence stemmed mainly from Mistral's reputation. In 1904 he was awarded the Nobel prize for literature, and in October 1913 President Raymond Poincaré had the presidential train stopped near Maillane where he invited the writer to join him in his carriage for dinner.

However, the truth had to be faced. In spite of the honours bestowed on its most famous representative, Félibrige did not bring about the hoped-for dialectal unity: on the one hand the chosen form of spelling was too close to the dialect of Maillane and could not be adapted easily to the other Occitanian dialects; on the other hand the movement did not enjoy the support of a political force powerful enough to impose the dialect of Maillane as a common basis for all of Occitan. After the failure of Félibrige, other spelling systems were proposed, since the need for a written language remained the major concern of all those who spoke one or other of the dialectal varieties of the *langue d'oc*.

The Institute for Occitanian Studies

Towards the end of the nineteenth century, another spelling system, which was as close as possible to the ancient orthography of the troubadours, in other words of the period before dialectal fragmentation, was created outside Provence. In 1935, Louis Alibert published an enormous 500-page grammar of Occitan based not on Provençal but Languedocien. Benefiting from Mistral's unfortunate experience, Alibert took as his point of departure not the dialect of a given village, but the traditional spellings that went back to the troubadours, before differentiation had taken place, and which allowed for various readings adapted to the variations of each of the dialects.

These same principles were adopted and improved upon in 1945 by the Institut d'Études Occitanes (IEO), which has its headquarters in Toulouse but also has numerous regional centres. In 1951 the Occitan specialist Robert Lafont published a work which applied this Occitanian spelling to the dialects of Provence, thus competing with Mistral's spelling system on his own ground. Attempts were also made in the 1970s to devise a kind of standard language, based on Languedocien, which is closest to the classical language, to act as a common Occitan.

SOME PROVENÇAL

Lou Mas di Falabrego	*The House of Micocoules*
Cante uno chato de Prouvènço	I sing of a girl of Provence
Dins lis amour de sa jouvènço	In the loves of her youth
A travès de la Crau, vers la mar, dins li blad.	Across Crau, towards the sea, in the corn;
Umble escoulan dou grand Oumèro	Humble pupil of great Homer
Iéu la vole segui. Coume èro	I want to follow her. As she was
Rèn qu'uno chato de la terro	Only a daughter of the soil
En foro de la Crau se n'es gaire parla.	Outside Crau there was little talk of her.

(Frédéric Mistral, *Mireio*, first song, Paris, Fasquelle, 1968, pp. 2–3)

Although the spelling system produced by the IEO, one feature of which is its independence from French spelling, seems to be favoured by most contemporary young southern writers, there are still some unreconstructed Mistralians in Provence who remain faithful to the spelling of Félibrige.

But spelling is only one aspect of the phenomenon. These 'Mistralians' are also fiercely opposed to the very word *Occitan*, which, through its generalising nature, would have the effect, if adopted, of shifting the centre of gravity of Occitanism from Provence to Languedoc.[146]

THE LANGUAGE OF MISTRAL

'Why is Mistral not Virgil? Because he did not write in French.'
(André Suares, Letter to an unknown person)

*

'A great epic poet is born . . . a poet who has taken a vulgar patois and made it into a classical language, with image and harmony, delighting the imagination and the ear.'
(Alphonse de Lamartine, *Cours familier de littérature*, 1859)

Divisions within Occitan

Writers in the nineteenth and twentieth centuries felt the need to unify the system of spelling, because Occitan does not exist as a common language. In fact, the Occitan area includes several different varieties (see map p. 101):

– *North Occitan*, which comprises *Limousin*, *Auvergnat* and *Provençal Alpin*;

- *South Occitan* (called 'middle Occitan') which includes *Languedocien* and *Provençal (Maritime)*, to which can be added *Niçart*;
- *Gascon* and *Béarnais* in the west.

A few of Ariadne's threads

To penetrate the maze of Occitan dialectology without losing your way in the tangle of diverse forms to be found there and to get as quickly as possible to the essentials, you have to remember that Occitan generally stayed closer to Latin, whereas French frequently contains greatly modified forms. The following is an easy example to remember: the stressed Latin vowel A in words like SALE(M) remained *a* in the south but took on a different timbre in the *oïl* zone. Thus you find: *sau* (pronounced *saou*) in Gascon, Limousin and Provençal, *sal* in Languedocien, but *sel* in French.

And, provided you don't make mistakes with the original Latin word – the A of SALE(M) did not develop like the A of CASTELLU(M) or LUNA because it was not in the same position in the word – you can amuse yourself finding the Occitan equivalents of words like *père*, *mère*, *tel*, *chèvre*, *mer*, *chef*, *nef*, *clé*, *pré*, and all the infinitives in *-er*. The vowel, as you will have guessed, remained *a* as in Latin.

Not only are Latin vowels better preserved in the Occitan area, but a large number of Latin consonants which are mute in Modern French are still to be heard in Occitan, albeit in a slightly modified form. Thus, the Latin intervocalic T (for example in VITELLUM) has completely disappeared in *veau* but survives as a *d* in Languedocien (*vedèl*) and Provençal (*vedèu*). In the French words *salade* and *daurade*, pronounced with a final consonant *d*, we can recognise borrowings from Occitan, since the French forms derived normally from Latin are *salée* and *dorée* with no consonant.

We should also remember (see table p. 96) another feature which enables us to distinguish North Occitan (Limousin, Auvergnat, Provençal Alpin) from Middle Occitan (Languedocien, Provençal): the *c* which derives from the CA combination in Latin (CANTARE 'to sing') remained *c* in Languedocien and Provençal (*cantar*) but developed into *tch*, *ts*, etc. in North Occitan (*tchantar*, *tsantar*). Note that these forms are intermediate between the Latin CA and the French *cha-*.

Gascon, for its part, is characterised by a totally specific trait: it is the only dialect, together with Béarnais, to have an *h* (a true pronounced consonant). It should be pointed out, however, that this does not mean that it has retained the Latin *h*, which, as we have already seen, did not even reach Gaul since it was already no longer pronounced by the time of Julius Caesar's conquest. (See *The emergence of a new consonant*, pp. 32–3.) This Gascon *h* corresponds to the Latin F: FILIU(M), FARINA have given *hiu*, *harìa* in Gascon. The last of these two words shows another typical feature of Gascon, which, like Portuguese, lost the Latin N between

100

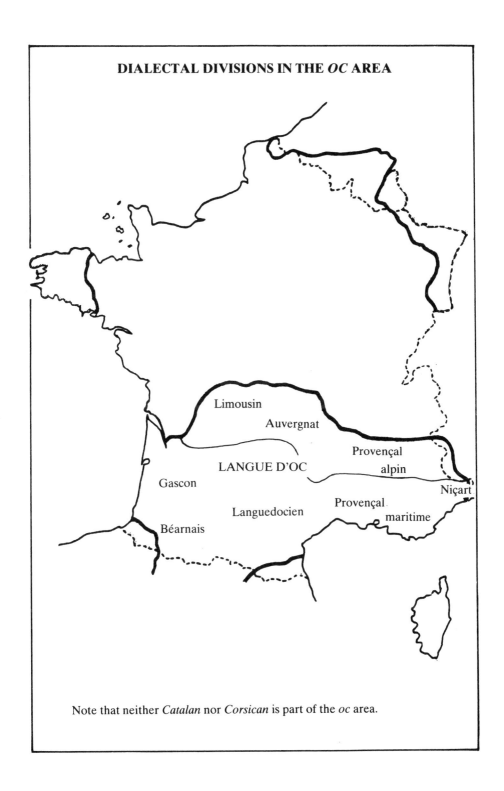

DIALECTAL DIVISIONS IN THE *OC* AREA

Limousin

Auvergnat

Provençal
alpin

LANGUE D'OC

Gascon

Niçart

Provençal
maritime

Languedocien

Béarnais

Note that neither *Catalan* nor *Corsican* is part of the *oc* area.

two vowels: LUNA gave *lua* 'moon', GALLINA gave *garía* 'hen', etc.

We can also point to the presence in Gascon of a *b* corresponding to the French *v* (as in Spanish and Catalan today), a characteristic which is also found in Languedocien and which reminds us of the remark made by Scaliger, a Renaissance humanist, who said: 'Oh happy people, for whom *vivere est bibere.*'

Catalan, which is spoken in Roussillon in France, along the entire Mediterranean coast as far as Valencia in Spain, and in the Balearic Islands, is not one of the *oc* languages. It is distinguished from neighbouring languages in particular:

– by the maintenance of the Latin U (pronounced like the French *ou* sound): DURU(M) gave *dur* (pronounced *dour*), MATURU(M) gave *madur* (pronounced *madour*),
– and by the fall of the Latin N when it evolved into final position, in words like MANU(M) which became *má* 'hand' and *bé* 'well'. You can now see why the surname *Martin* is *Martí* in Catalan (which itself, as you will already have guessed, is pronounced *catalá* in Catalan).

Corsican dialects – the Italian connection

Corsica fell under French rule in 1769, in the very year when its most famous child, Napoleone Buonaparte, was born. For the preceding five centuries, from the end of the eleventh to the end of the thirteenth century, it had been dominated first by Pisa and then by Genoa. It was this Pisan occupation that left the most durable imprint on the island. Although it was highly Tuscanised, especially in the north-east, by numerous contacts with Pisan settlers, the Corsican language is not the same as Tuscan, which has become today's Italian.

The various Corsican dialects are very close to Tuscan in the north of the island, but in the south they have a great deal in common with Sardinian. Like Sardinian, Corsican has preserved certain Latin forms which have disappeared elsewhere.[147]

It has maintained distinctions which are not found in Italian, such as, for example, the final *-u* from the Latin U which became *-o* in Italian: 'mur' is *muru* in Corsican but *muro* in Italian, 'livre' is *libru* in Corsican and *libro* in Italian, while 'année' is *annu* and *anno* respectively, etc.

Whereas, when he arrived in Marseille at the age of nine, Napoleone did not understand a word of French – which he always spoke with an 'accent', in fact – nowadays all Corsicans understand and speak it perfectly. But, contrary to what has happened elsewhere, with the exception of Alsace and Lorraine, the universal use of French has not caused any noticeable decline in the local dialect, and the fidelity of Corsicans to their language remains exemplary.

102

FRANCOPROVENÇAL

Francoprovençal extends over three European countries:

- *in France*, in the Lyonnais, Savoie, the north of Dauphiné and part of Forez and Franche-Comté;
- *in French-speaking Switzerland*, in other words in the cantons of Neuchâtel, Vaud, Genève , Fribourg and Valais;
- *in Italy*, in the Val d'Aoste.

Although we can justify making a division between a northern section (Fribourg, Neuchâtel, Valais, Vaud) and a southern section (Lyonnais, Dauphiné, Savoie, Genève, Val d'Aoste),[148] the dialectal fragmentation is such that we have thought it preferable to give only geographical markings on the map.

The specificity of this area was recognised only a century ago, and the spelling *Francoprovençal* in a single word with no hyphen, is a means for the specialists to show the unity of an area which is not a mixture of French and Provençal and which, according to André Martinet, it would be more apt to call *Rhodanian*.

Who speaks Francoprovençal?

The number of people who speak patois is diminishing by the day, but the patois are not dead, as recent surveys have shown. In 1975, for example, in Saint-Thurin, a small parish in the department of Loire, 96 per cent of the three hundred inhabitants still understood Francoprovençal and 73 per cent spoke it.[149] However, whereas the language was still spoken by most farmers (93 per cent), only 45 percent of workers could still speak it. Other surveys in the Francoprovençal-speaking region[150] demonstrate how the dialect is gradually being abandoned by the population.

How to recognise Francoprovençal

It is not easy to define Francoprovençal as a whole because it has fragmented into many different varieties. We can say that in many ways it has evolved in the same direction as the oïl dialects but with quite different results. In Savoie, for example, for the Latin combination CA- we find neither the *ca-* of Provençal nor the *cha-* of French but a consonant *th-* (as in the English word *thin*). Thus, CARBONE(M) developed into *tharbon* and CANTARE into *thantò* 'to sing'.

In relation to the other Gallo-Roman dialects we can give a rough definition of Francoprovençal by saying that it is an *oc* language that was influenced at an early stage by the Northern dialects: *oc* 'yes' became *wa* in Francoprovençal,[151] just as *foc* 'fire' became *fwa*. In an open syllable, in

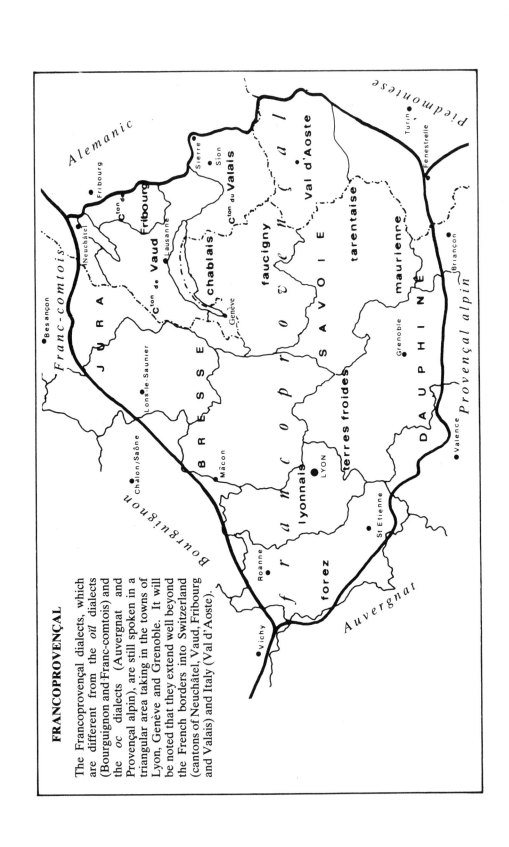

FRANCOPROVENÇAL

The Francoprovençal dialects, which are different from the *oïl* dialects (Bourguignon and Franc-comtois) and the *oc* dialects (Auvergnat and Provençal alpin), are still spoken in a triangular area taking in the towns of Lyon, Genève and Grenoble. It will be noted that they extend well beyond the French borders into Switzerland (cantons of Neuchâtel, Vaud, Fribourg and Valais) and Italy (Val d'Aoste).

Alemanic

Piedmontese

Franc-comtois

Turin

Fenestrelle

Fribourg

C.ton d.

Sierre

Sion

Neuchâtel

C.ton de Fribourg

Val d'Aoste

Lausanne

C.ton du Valais

Vaud

chablais

faucigny

tarentaise

maurienne

Besançon

J U R A

Genève

Briançon

C.ton de Vaud

SAVOIE

Provençal alpin

Lons-le-Saunier

Grenoble

B R E S S E

terres froides

DAUPHINÉ

Chalon/Saône

Mâcon

Valence

francoprovençal

Bourguignon

LYON

lyonnais

St Etienne

Roanne

forez

Vichy

Auvergnat

SALE(M) 'salt', for example, *a* was retained as it was in Provençal, but later became *ò*, thus giving *sò* 'salt', *pòla* 'spade' and *pòre* 'father'. But in certain conditions, for example after *th*, *a* developed into *e* as in *'thevra* 'goat'.

Some features distinguish Francoprovençal both from Provençal and French: *balma*, meaning 'cave', has kept the *l* sound in the name of the *Col de Balme*, which is above Chamonix, compared with *Sainte-Baume* in Provence and *Baume-les-Dames* in Franche-Comté. This -*l*- subsequently became -*r*-, as, for example, in *tharfò* 'to heat' from the Latin CAL(E)FACERE.

Like Provençal, Francoprovençal has preserved the unstressed final vowels that French has lost, although it still retains a trace of them in the written -*e*: *'nouva* 'neuve', *'nouvo* 'neuf', *'nouve* 'neuves', *i 'pourton* 'ils portent'. But Francoprovençal has not kept the same vowels as Provençal: Provençal has changed -*a* into -*o* (*la 'nostro* 'la nôtre'), while Francoprovençal has kept the -*a* (la *'noutra*).*

THE OÏL *AREA*

It is in the *oïl* area that dialects suffered most from the invasive expansion of one among their number, Francien, which was originally spoken only in the Parisian region. (See *Paris begins to stir*, p. 53.) Thus, the number of people who speak a dialect has declined more irreversibly over the centuries in the *oïl* area than anywhere else in France. Being closer to the dominant dialect of the Île-de-France, the other *oïl* dialects were in a way infiltrated by the latter, leading to rather confused situations in many places, where the people often did not know themselves if they were speaking patois or French.

This is the case in Saintonge, for example, where the inhabitants, unsure of how to describe the unique language they speak, are reluctant to call it French but do not see it as a patois. As a result, they often refer to it as 'broken French'.[152] As for the inhabitants of Haute-Bretagne, in addition to the expression 'broken French', they use phrases such as 'deformed French' or 'abbreviated French'. And where their dialect has words that are different from the standard French equivalents, they call their own word a 'nickname' (*surnom*), a 'misnomer' (*dénommé, faux nommé*) or the 'quaint name' (*nom baroque*) and the French word becomes the 'right word'.[153] In Picardy you can also hear the expression 'mangled French' (*français écrasé*).[154]

---

* I would like to thank André Martinet for writing this section on Francoprovençal.

105

Oïl dialect divisions

The dialects which survive in the *oïl* area can, roughly speaking, be divided into four or five main groups:

- in the north, *Picard*, *Walloon* (which extends into Belgium) and *Haut-Normand*;
- in the east, *Romance Lorrain*, *Bourguignon* and *Bourbonnais*, with *Franc-comtois* being a transitional dialect with the Francoprovençal area;
- in the centre, *Francien* (the dialect of the Île-de-France), *Orléanais*, *Berrichon*, and *Champenois*, which extends to the border with Belgium;
- in the west, *Bas-Normand*, *Gallo*, *Mayennais*, *Manceau*, *Angevin* and *Tourangeau*. All of these dialects are quite close to Francien. *Anglo-Normand* belongs to this western group: it is still spoken in Jersey, Guernsey and Sark (by 10,000 inhabitants out of 75,000 in Jersey, by 10,000 out of 52,000 in Guernsey and by 60 out of the 120 people of truly Sark origin);[155]
- further south, *Poitevin* and *Saintongeais* are, by contrast, transitional dialects with the *oc* area.

It would be a tedious task to list the features which allow us to say that the dialects shown on the map on p. 107 exist. Instead, we shall try to make things a bit more concrete by taking just a few of them and pointing out one characteristic which stands out.

What are the *oïl* dialects like?

Of the *oïl* dialects, those in the north and east are most clearly different from the one which became French. In the Middle Ages, *Picard* seemed to be a serious rival to *Francien* with a real chance of becoming the common language, since it was then one of the languages of diplomacy in the north and enjoyed considerable literary prestige in the thirteenth and fourteenth centuries. (See tables pp. 57, 58.)

Without wishing to describe Picard in relation to French, it is amusing to note that, on one point at least, the two dialects seem to enjoy contradicting one another: for Picard says *canter*, *keval*, *canchon* and *vaque* where French says *chanter*, *cheval*, *chanson* and *vache*, but where French has *cerf* and *cité*, Picard says *cherf* and *chité*.[156] (See table p. 108.)

The western dialects were originally very close to Francien and must have diverged from it quite late. Moreover, it is very difficult to separate them out from one another since the facts overlap to such a large extent. One curious feature to note is the retention in the Gallo region (especially in the north of Côtes d'Armor, Ille-et-Vilaine and Morbihan) of a series of plurals which differ from the singular in the final vowel. Just as French has

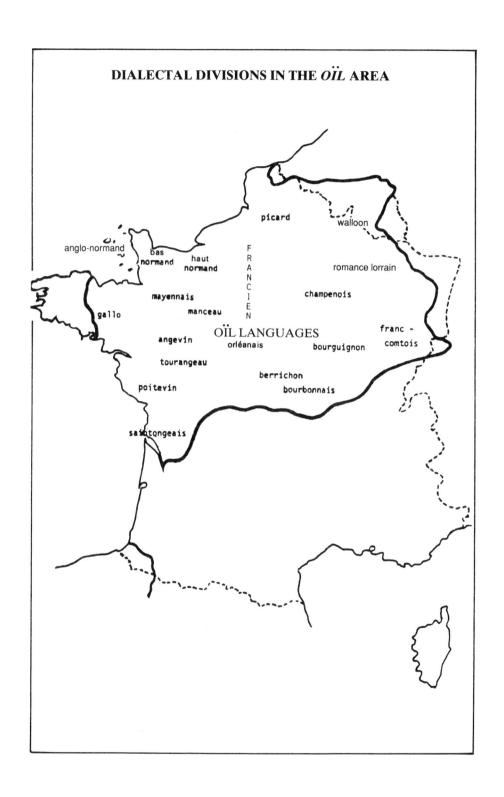

DIALECTAL DIVISIONS IN THE *OÏL* AREA

picard

walloon

anglo-normand

bas
normand

haut
normand

F
R
A
N
C
I
E
N

romance lorrain

mayennais

manceau

champenois

gallo

OÏL LANGUAGES

angevin

orléanais

bourguignon

franc -
comtois

tourangeau

berrichon

poitevin

bourbonnais

saintongeais

A LITTLE BIT OF PICARD

Le P'tit Quinquin

Canchon dormoire	*Berceuse*
Dors, min p'tit quinquin*	*Dors, mon tout petit,*
Min p'tit pouchin,	*Mon p'tit poussin,*
Min gros rojin.	*Mon gros raisin.*[1]
Tu m' f'ras du chagrin	*Tu m'f'ras du chagrin*
Si te n' dors point qu'à d'main.	*Si tu n'dors point (jus)qu'à d'main.*

1. A term of endearment (a hypocorism) like 'mon poussin, mon lapin'.

---

cheval-chevaux, so for words such as *ruisseau, copeau, couteau, oiseau, agneau, pourceau*, etc. these dialects have a singular in -*è* and a plural in -*yaou*: for 'oiseau' they have one *oisè* and several *oisyaou*, and so on. The singular of 'poulet' is the same as in French, but the plural is also in -*yaou*.[157]

These few examples make us aware of certain regularities which have been preserved in the dialects and often make French, by comparison, look like the exception and the realm of the random.

WHAT DOES THE FUTURE HOLD FOR THE DIALECTS?

A new direction for the regional languages

The information given in the previous sections was intended to put some phonic 'flesh' on terms such as *patois* and *dialect*. But we should not be deceived by the apparent simplicity of the facts presented: local peculiarities have in many cases been overlaid by the forms of the dominant language, French, which are heard every day of the week. As a result, people who were bilingual gradually become monolingual without realising it.

Dialects do not always die in the same way. In some regions the local language has slowly been contaminated, which may lead to a Frenchified dialect and then a dialecticised French and finally to a regional form of French. This has happened with the *oïl* languages that were closest to French such as *Gallo* and *Tourangeau*.

In other regions, there are people who speak the patois until the day they die (Forez, Haute-Loire,[158] the *oc* dialects and the non-Romance language regions), with no intermediate stage of a more or less Frenchified patois. The Channel Islands (Jersey, Guernsey and Sark) would seem to be an example of this.[159] In the *oïl* zone this is the case in regions where the patois is furthest from French. In Burgundy the two solutions 'cohabit': the

---

* I would like to thank Anne Lefebvre and Fernand Carton for their help in translating *Le P'tit Quinquin*.

patois is still spoken with no confusion in Morvan, whereas in the north of Nièvre people no longer distinguish between the patois and French.[160]

Those who speak only a dialect are nowadays rare pearls whom the linguists point out to one another, provoking interest and envy because they all feel a kind of affection and admiration for such people who have preserved linguistic riches of inestimable value.

Amongst bilinguals who speak French and the patois, and whose numbers are declining by the day, the dialect has assumed a different function nowadays. Instead of being used purely for the spontaneous communication of everyday needs, – a role which is now naturally fulfilled by French – the patois becomes an object of study, almost a cult, as well as a way of asserting one's identity. And in that, perhaps, lies its hope of surviving, as the language of affectivity and a sign of belonging to a restricted community and a particular place.

Finally, both for the bilinguals and for the majority of French people who never had the opportunity to learn a dialect, there remains French. The diversity of the former dialects lives on to some extent in the varied and sometimes unexpected forms of regional French.

3

FRENCH IN FRANCE
Regional varieties

DIVERSITY AND GEOGRAPHY

There is no such thing as 'the' French language

In order to guarantee the predominance of one language 'unique and indivisible' in one Republic 'unique and indivisible', the French Revolution had proclaimed the need to abolish the patois. Grammarians from the seventeenth century onwards and schools from the nineteenth century onwards tried to impose observance of the rules of a single French language, with forms that had been fixed once and for all, forms that were often difficult to remember and which were the object of inexplicable admiration even in their wildest irregularities. All these attempts at unification culminated in the spread of French to the entire country and to the strict regulation of the written language.

The oral language that is heard and spoken every day is less docile and has preserved some degree of diversity both in vocabulary and pronunciation, even though each individual is convinced that he or she is speaking the same French as their next door neighbour because they have no difficulty in understanding one another. However, you only have to keep your ears open to realise that there is not *one* French language but *several* varieties of French: and then you begin to spot appreciable differences, even in a milieu which you might have thought was homogeneous, amongst educated Parisians, for example.

The emperor's got no clothes

Dictionaries of French pronunciation have always given a single pronunciation for each word, usually the one used by the author. André Martinet and myself provided a new perspective on the problem, when five years of work led to the publication in 1973 of the *Dictionnaire de la prononciation française dans son usage réel*:[161] for the first time we were striking a blow in a dictionary against the myth of the uniformity of French pronunciation, and we were doing so for almost one word in five. And yet the seventeen people whose pronunciation was described in this dictionary were all of a good (not to say high) level of education, which made it seem even more scandalous that there should be variations in the pronunciation of the very people who, in theory, set the norm. What is more, we had taken the precaution of using evidence only from informants who, in many cases were born in the provinces, but who had lived in the capital for a long enough time to blur their most obvious peculiarities, the vestiges of habits acquired during childhood in their native province. If living for such a long time in Paris had not eliminated the differences we found in this small group of informants, we should not be surprised to find far more when we extend the analysis to the country as a whole. It is this diversity of regional French that we shall now examine.

The regional diversity of French

We should first of all explain what we mean by the regional diversity of French, because it must not be confused with the diversity of the patois.

Let us recall that the patois are the forms taken by spoken Latin in the different regions and that over the centuries these patois lived alongside French, which was finally learnt and spoken by the entire population, who became bilingual patois-French speakers.

Thus, even though in reality there is some inevitable overlapping, we should take care to distinguish between:

– the *patois*, which are *not* French. The question of their diversity was discussed in the previous chapter;
– the *French which is taught* and which is a kind of ideal entity which everybody has their own idea about but which nobody speaks and which, by definition, cannot have diversity;
– finally, the *varieties of French* in everyday life. It really is true that each individual preserves for a long time the peculiarities of the language they learnt in the circle and the region where they lived. These peculiarities vary from one place to another.

First, a spot of geography

We must always stress the utmost importance in France of linguistic geography, because inhabitants of Toulouse or Strasbourg rather than Paris can be spotted as soon as they open their mouths, although we cannot always identify the social circle they belong to. A top banker from Paris speaks, and especially pronounces, French differently from one of his colleagues from Toulouse or Alsace, although the pronunciation of each one of them very closely resembles that of their humblest employee who comes from the same region as themselves.

Remember that the dialectal fragmentation of Latin took place on French soil before the spread of French and that its mark has lasted for centuries: the existence of this long past enables us to understand why we must turn first to the geographical framework to consider the variety of usages of the language.

The differences that we can see relating to age, social circle, level of education, or the communicative situation always appear to strengthen or weaken features first identified on the regional level.

Putting Paris in its place

Thus, describing French in its contemporary diversity means first of all taking account of the geographical factor, but also – whether we like it or not – becoming aware of the part played by the language spoken in Paris, where most of the economic, political and cultural activities of the entire country are concentrated. Whether they live in Paris or the provinces, whether they are workers or farmers, intellectuals or artists, and whether they like it or not, all modern French people are influenced by the capital.

The phenomenon is an old one. We have already seen how, since the tenth century with the election of Hugh Capet as King of France in 987 – just a thousand years ago – Paris grew steadily more important, on the political level, of course, but also on the linguistic level. And today Paris more than ever takes pride of place as the city where people from the six corners of the Hexagon and the four corners of the world meet and communicate in French, each with their own regional peculiarities: in this sort of melting-pot various usages of French live side by side, mingling and mutually influencing one another.

The result of all these contacts is that, for French, the most representative of the dynamic usages is not the provincial who has stayed at home, nor Parisians by birth who are themselves marked by their 'province', but that hybrid creature: the 'Parisian by adoption', whom one linguist has, without fear of paradox, called the 'provincial Parisian'. These typical Parisians come to speak a language which is difficult to identify on the regional level, to the extent that we can consider their French usage to be 'average': born of the amalgam of different contributions imported from everywhere into the Parisian crucible, they are both entirely Parisian and the entire provinces.

To the great regret of many French people, this situation, which smooths the corners and blurs the differences, does of course run the risk of leading, at some point in the future, to a kind of insipid uniformity replacing what was, even recently, the charming individuality of each of the French-speaking provinces. However, in spite of the 'steamroller' effect of the media, which constantly reflect and amplify the language of the typical Parisian, that day has not yet arrived. There is still diversity and we can see it first in the choice of words.

DIVERSITY OF VOCABULARY

Using rags for napkins

I know an old couple who live in Paris but who come from the provinces (and are therefore 'typical Parisians'). They use two different words for 'bolster': when the wife points to what she calls the *traversin*, the husband calls it *polochon*, and that after more than thirty years of married life.

Another Parisian by adoption, who arrived from his native Savoie a long time ago, still uses the word *lavette* for what Parisians call a *gant de toilette*, and who would only use a *lavette* to wash the dishes. In Brest, the same *lavette* becomes a *vadrouille*.

On the other hand, the word *linge*, which is used in Paris to refer to all household items made of cloth, is used only to mean *serviette de toilette* in Savoie. In this French usage, if you wish to be more precise, you would say *linge de toilette* rather than *serviette de toilette*.

In Provence, the word *torchon* means not only a dishcloth but also an *essuie-main* and a *serviette*. In such a situation it is impossible not to think of the saying 'mélanger les torchons avec les serviettes'.

A trip round the kitchen

Although the French, like other nationalities, normally adapt their vocabulary to the circles they are living in, when it comes to the kitchen they tend to cling to the words they learnt in childhood and which they never subsequently modify. I once heard a man who had been living in Paris for a long time but who had spent his childhood in Savoie (another typical Parisian) ask his wife, who was born in the south-west, where the *pôche* was. To which, without the slightest hesitation and with no mistake, she answered: 'La *louche*? Elle est dans le *poêlon*.' I am not sure if people from less southerly regions would have understood that the *louche* was in the *casserole*.

Still in the kitchen, I heard a woman in Nice talk about the *potager* to mean not the vegetable garden but the place where the stove stood. Even more curious is the fact that what most people refer to as the *cuisinière* is often called a *gazinière* in some regions, even when it does not work on gas.

I have also heard somebody born in Tunisia but relocated to Marseille use the word *plat* for a flat plate. The word *assiette*, she explained, could only be used to refer to a *hollow* plate, and if she wanted to refer to a *plat de service* she would use the phrase *grand plat*.

Another peculiarity of people from Tunisia, and one which invariably makes Parisians smile, is that the word they use for *taking* crockery out of the cupboard is *tirer* (just as others use the expression *tirer les marrons du feu*).

Staying in the kitchen, most people know that the fish bought under the name of *colin* in Paris is a *merlu* in the south and that *bar* and *loup* on the one hand and *lotte* and *baudroie* on the other are simply different names for the same fish, with some being used in the north and the others in the south.

Supper in one's slippers? Beware!

You have to be careful. If you are invited to dinner or supper, with no further detail, you can't be sure what is meant: in Paris *dîner* is the evening meal, but there are many regions where it is the midday meal and the evening meal is called *souper*. Since in Paris *souper* is taken much later in the evening, usually after a visit to the theatre or cinema, there could well be a few missed invitations!

Finally, when people talk to me of *chaussons*, I personally take the word to mean 'little knitted bootees for babies who cannot yet walk', but for most of the people around me the word means 'woollen slippers with a covered heel'. When they want to talk about what I call *chaussons*, they use the word *bottons*. And I always have to make something of an effort to accept their usage, which for me is bizarre. It is true that when it comes to language it is always other people who seem to be deviating from the norm.

Linguistic surveys

Using words like *potager, dîner* and *botton* can obviously lead to minor misunderstandings. They can also be an indicator which allows you to guess where somebody comes from or allows the speaker to use it as a sign that they belong to the same linguistic community.

There has been an increase over the past few years in research into peculiarities specific to various regions,[162] with some recent local studies of vocabulary.[163] Three such studies published between 1983 and 1987 on towns quite close together – Vourey near Grenoble,[164] Gap[165] and Lyon (and its surrounding area)[166] – give a measure of the vitality of certain regionalisms and the extent to which they have spread beyond their place of origin.

114

Lyon has given France its *mâchons* but kept its *cuchons*

Several hundred words were recorded in this quite restricted geographical area, but few of them appear in all three surveys.

Take the example of *cuchon*. The word originally meant a 'pile of hay' but now means only 'a pile of, a lot of' in phrases like *on voit un cuchon de voitures dans le parc* or *il y a un cuchon de bois derrière la maison*. It is still used frequently in the three towns of Gap, Vourey and Lyon, even by fifteen-year-olds, but the original meaning of 'pile of hay' is heard only in the country.[167]

The *mâchon*, which originally meant a good or copious meal in Lyon, is known and used in the Dauphiné but seems not to be known in Gap. The people I questioned in Paris had heard the word but thought it meant the opposite: a light snack. This is also the meaning which young people in Lyon give it nowadays.

The word *cuchon*, for its part, does not seem to have crossed the northern borders of the Lyonnais, but just how far south has it travelled? In other words, what is the size of the region covered by this regional word? These are the questions that future linguistic research will have to answer.

Get off my foot!

Although regional French contains features which never existed in the patois, we can agree with the dialectologist Gaston Tuaillon who said that regional French is what is left of the dialect after it has disappeared. But we should hasten to add that some regionalisms can become standard French. (See table p. 116.)

In the region of Grenoble, shopkeepers offer to *ployer* everything you buy from them, which makes people from other regions smile, especially if the offer is to *ployer* a slab of butter, a litre of milk or a kilo of nuts. This use of the word *ployer* for *envelopper* seems quite to be specific to the Grenoble region.[168]

Do you know the meaning of the word *agassin*? Originally it meant a 'corn on the foot' in the Dauphinois dialect. Now it means 'foot' in the regional French of Grenoble, whilst it has kept its initial meaning of 'corn' in Gap. In Lyon, young people hardly know the word any more, or if they do it is with the meaning of 'foot ache'. However, the word has spread somewhat beyond its region of origin and is well known to fans of detective novels: the author Frédéric Dard, who himself comes from the Dauphiné, uses the word several times in the San Antonio series with the meaning of 'foot'.[169] However, the word *agassin* is not in very wide use and belongs to a familiar style.

In a more literary register, we can think of the phrase used by Descartes

A FEW OLD DEBTS THAT FRENCH OWES TO THE REGIONAL LANGUAGES

Try and guess what dialects the following words come from. They have been classified according to their dialectal origin: Alsacien, Breton, Catalan, western *oïl* dialects, Gascon, Languedocien, Limousin, Lorrain, Lyonnais, Normand, Picard-Walloon, Provençal, Savoyard and the dialect of the Val d'Aoste.

There are some signs that should put you on the right track. Look and think before turning to the answers at the bottom of the example.

1	2	4	7	9
abeille	bouquet	flapi	bijou	beurre
aïoli	brioche	guignol	biniou	chope
anchois	câble	jacasser	darne	poêle
aubade	crabe	moutard	dolmen	
auberge	crevette	ronchonner	goéland	10
badaud	égrillard		goémon	choucroute
barque	enliser	5		frichti
brume	falaise	alpage	8	quiche
cadenas	flâner	avalanche	boulanger	turne
cambrioler	garer	chalet	caboche	
casserole	(se) gausser	crétin	cauchemar	11
cigale	girouette	(se) fâcher	cingler	chabichou
daurade	grésiller	luge	coron	jabot
esquinter	harpon	mélèze	écaille	
goujat	houle		escarbille	12
jarre	marécage	6	estaminet	barrique
langouste	masure	cagibi	grisou	cadet
muscade	pieuvre	califourchon	hagard	
ortolan	potin	crachin	houille	13
rascasse	quille	dupe	houlette	espadrille
salade	ricaner	gaspiller	rémoulade	galère
tortue	varech	lessive		
troubadour		margoulin		14
truffe	3	mitonner		cassoulet
	piolet	palourde		causse

1: Provençal – 2: Normand – 3: Val d'Aoste – 4: Lyonnais – 5: Savoyard – 6: Western *oïl* dialects – 7: Breton – 8: Picard-Walloon – 9: Lorrain - 10: Alsacien – 11: Limousin – 12: Gascon – 13: Catalan – 14: Languedocien

---

who, during a journey in Germany, 'méditait dans son *poêle*': you may think it rather strange that he should have crawled into his stove to meditate until you discover that at that time the word referred to a 'room equipped with a stove'. And we can find this same meaning in the Romance dialects of Lorraine.[170]

Dialect words in standard French

If you consult specialised works, you will be surprised to discover that a given word which you thought was pure French in origin is actually a dialect loan word. A few random examples:

nouns – *avalanche, barque, boulanger, carlingue, casserole, cauchemar, flaque, glacier*, etc.
verbs – *brusquer, cambrioler, fâcher, se gausser, larguer, maquiller, mitonner, vadrouiller*, etc.
adjectives – *crétin, dupe, égrillard, faraud, gai, mièvre*, etc.

All these words and many more besides (Pierre Guiraud has recorded 1,200),[171] have enriched the French language over the centuries. Each dialect has made its own contribution, but the prize seems to go to words from Provençal. In the table on p. 116 you will find only a few dozen of these 1,200 dialect words which we so gaily assume to be pure French.

Do you *tourner* or *touiller* your lettuce?

There are some people who *touillent* their lettuce, others who *brassent* it, and yet others who simply *tournent* it. You can also *fatiguer* it or even *terbouler* it.

Having a linguist's curiosity, I carried out a regional survey between 1974 and 1978 in an attempt to measure the degree of diversity in the usage of some familiar French words and map their geographical distribution.[172] The survey covered a hundred people in all those parts of Europe where French is spoken.

The harvest was far better than I had hoped for: for the action of tossing lettuce we found no fewer than sixteen verbs. It should be added that some people gave several answers, but there was not one term on which there was unanimity.

These are the verbs:

– *tourner* came top in more than a third of responses;
– *brasser, mélanger* and *remuer* are used a great deal;
– *touiller* is less frequent, quoted by 10 per cent of respondents;
– *fatiguer, mêler*, and *retourner* are rare;
– *ensaucer, faire, malaxer, mouer, préparer, soulever, terbouler* and *virer* are each used only by one informant.

As you can see, there is a vast choice of words to describe this simple action, and the one most commonly used is not the most amusing.

The words recorded in this and more recent surveys have been entered on the map on p. 119. You may find it amusing to compare your own experience with the data on the map, which certainly have no claim to having exhausted the subject.

What do you wash the floor with?

To wash the floor, French people use a kind of cloth which is most commonly called a *serpillière* nowadays, but most French people will no doubt know other words to describe the object, words such as *wassingue* and *cinse*, but also *loque, panosse*, and even *faubert* or *guenille*.

Here, the survey shows even more contrasted results: we recorded twenty-one different terms, but there was an overall winner in *serpillière*, which had a clear majority. After which, but very far behind, came: *wassingue, cinse, torchon, panosse, chiffon, loque, toile, lave-pont, pièce* and *patte*. But the most curious words were those proposed each by just one person, words such as *emballage, emballe, faubert, gaguchar*, (un) *laplace, guenille, peille, drap de maison, pouques* and *loque à reloqueter*.

We further noted something that we might have expected, namely that in a given region, for example Champagne, only the oldest people use the word *loque*, either on its own or in competition with *serpillière*, whilst the youngest know only the word *serpillière*. In this way we can see the word *serpillière*, as it passes down the generations, gradually taking over from the various regional forms. (See map p. 120.)

DIVERSITY OF GRAMMAR

Ça a eu payé!

Let's take a look at grammar now. Most French people will know the comic sketch by entertainer Fernand Raynaud 'La vigne, ça a eu payé, mais ça ne paye plus' with its verbal form *ça a eu payé*, known as the 'double compound past tense'. This form is the only one in French grammar for which there are no clearly defined rules of usage. And yet French speakers always give a categorical answer to questions such as: 'Would you use a form like:

– *Quand il a eu mangé ce gâteau*, il s'est senti mal,

or like:

– *Il a eu coupé, ce couteau*,

and do they seem correct to you?'

Ask the question of any French person you know and you will find that many educated people use this grammatical form with a clear conscience, both in speech and writing in the firm conviction that it is the only correct one, whereas other equally educated people with an equally strong

DO YOU TOURNER OR TOUILLER YOUR LETTUCE?

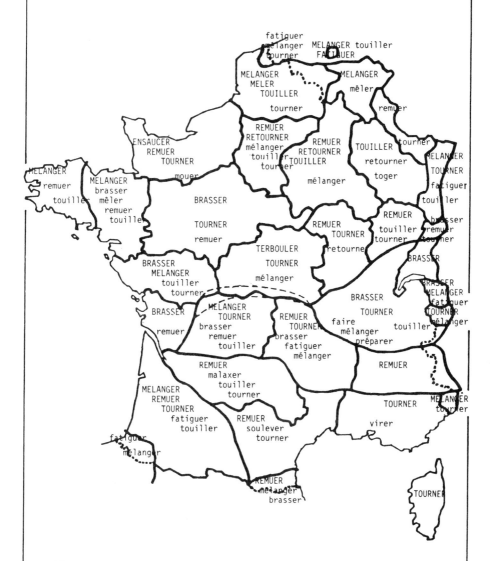

The map above was the result of a survey of natives of different regions. The words in UPPER CASE represent the word which the informants listed as being the only one they ever used, while words in lower case compete with other words.

Spot the terms you are familiar with and, where possible, add others of your own.

DO YOU MOP THE FLOOR WITH A SERPILLIÈRE OR A WASSINGUE?

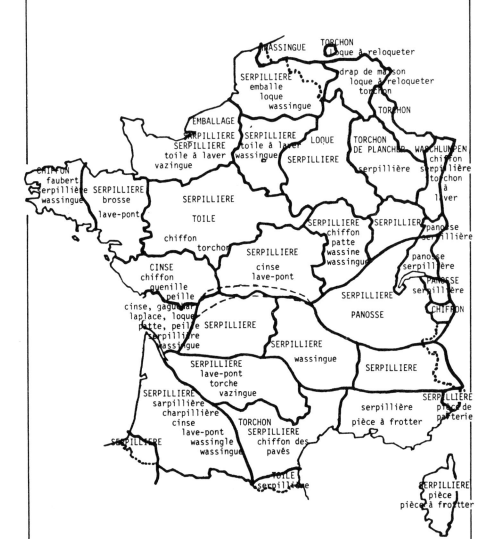

Nowadays, *serpillière* is the most frequently found word, but there are still at least twenty other words used to describe the same object. The distribution shown on the map was established by a survey carried out in the late 1970s.

The words in UPPER CASE represent the word which the informant listed as being the only one they ever used, while words in lower case compete with other words.

Do you know all the words you can see on this map? Can you find any others?

conviction of being right refuse to use it and declare just as forcibly that such forms are incorrect and totally deviant. Other people, such as myself, consider them to be highly useful but cannot bring themselves to use them.

Who is to be believed? Grammars and dictionaries display the same differences of opinion. These double compound forms are quoted in Grevisse's *Le bon usage* (p. 1297, 12th edition), whilst pointing out, however, that they belong rather to the spoken language. Joseph Hanse, in his *Nouveau dictionnaire des difficultés du français moderne* gives an example of the double compound past tense in a letter written by Mme de Sévigné in 1672. But although this book details the various forms of the compound past, many other dictionaries and grammars have nothing to say about them, as if they did not exist.

'Fans' of the double compound past tense

What is the situation on the ground? An informal survey[173] conducted during the regional survey mentioned earlier revealed that these forms are more frequent and widespread in the *oc* and Francoprovençal areas, where the double compound past is used both in subordinate clauses (quand il *a eu mangé*, il s'est senti mal) and main clauses (elle les *a eu mises*, ces chaussures). In the *oïl* area it is found only in the first usage, in other words only in subordinate clauses, and even then not everywhere. (See map p. 122.)

A similar survey carried out by researchers from the University of Lausanne revealed that the majority of Swiss people use the double compound past tense in both subordinate and main clauses.[174]

These regional groupings based on grammatical preferences, together with the remark made at the beginning of this chapter on the divergent views of people of the same level of education, do seem to demonstrate that geography plays the most important role in determining the diversity of usages in French.

Those who believe that the double compound past tense is a perfectly natural usage are not far from thinking that those who do *not* use it are ignoramuses who are depriving themselves of the subtle distinctions that French conjugation offers them. But the latter should take heart from the fact that observing and listening to French speakers shows that they get by very well using different means. Instead of saying '*Quand il a eu mangé* du gâteau, il s'est senti mal', they say '*Une fois qu'*il a mangé . . . ' or '*Après avoir* mangé . . . ', which allows them to indicate the proper chronology of events in relation to one another using different forms. Perhaps that is why the double compound past tense is neither completely condemned nor completely recommended as the norm.

USE OF THE DOUBLE COMPOUND PAST TENSE

To form a *double compound past tense* you add an extra auxiliary to an already compound past tense. From the compound past *quand il a payé* you get the double compound past *quand il a eu payé*.

Quite paradoxically, both those who use the form and those who do not are all convinced that they are adhering to the norm.

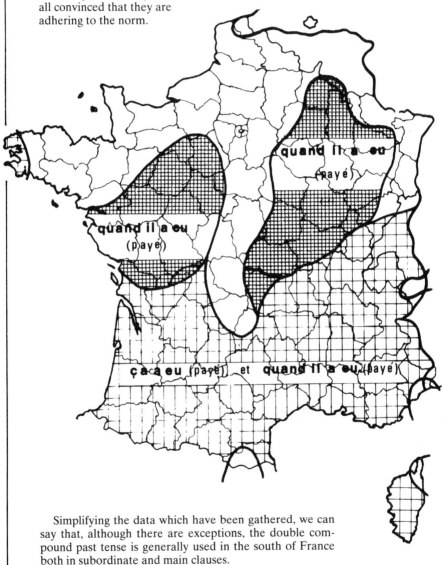

Simplifying the data which have been gathered, we can say that, although there are exceptions, the double compound past tense is generally used in the south of France both in subordinate and main clauses.

The north of France is divided between those who never use it and those who accept it only in a subordinate clause.

DIVERSITY OF PRONUNCIATION

Don't confuse *accent* with *pronunciation*

With pronunciation we have a completely different problem. The very first words a person utters betray what is commonly called 'the accent', described in quite impressionistic and metaphorical terms as *pointu*, harsh, drawling, working-class, or, somewhat more precisely, as Parisian, southern, north-eastern (*chtimi*), 'pied-noir', etc.

We should point out immediately that the word 'accent' is not here being used with the meaning linguists give the word, since for them *accent* is the stress placed on a syllable, which is pronounced with more force, more length or at a higher pitch, than the rest of the word. Depending on the language, the positioning of the accent may be pertinent, as in English or Italian, or not pertinent, as in French where any syllable in the word may be emphasised according to the speaker's mood without changing the meaning of the word.

You can never be too suspicious of words like *accent* which seem to mean the same thing to all users of a language, but which have a more technical, precise and restricted meaning for the specialists. They can be a source of misunderstanding.

I know of the misfortunes of a journalist who wanted to find out about 'accents', in other words (as *he* thought) the different ways in which different people pronounce the same words, with particular reference to the 'Parisian accent'. He made use of the computer at the Maison des Sciences de l'Homme in Paris. Since the computer had been programmed with the meaning which the specialists give the word, he had the unpleasant surprise of finding not what he was looking for but definitions such as 'acoustic indicators of segmental elements', 'sub-glottal pressure, the correlate to dynamic foregrounding' or even 'prosodic facts and discreet units'. Totally at sea in such technical documentation, where even the titles were meaningless to him, he must have wondered why linguists, whose job it was after all, had made no study of what he called 'accent'. What he did not know was that to access the plentiful literature on the subject, he had to look up not *Accent* but *Variety in pronunciation*, *Phonological diversity* or *Regional pronunciation*.

Un grand pain rond

The four vowels that you hear in the title of this section *un grand pain rond* are called nasal vowels because in order to articulate them, some air has to pass through the nose. In this respect, French is something of an exception amongst European languages because it is alone with Portuguese and Polish in having nasal vowels distinct from oral vowels

123

(so called because all the air passes through the mouth).

In French, *grand* has a distinct nasal vowel because it can be contrasted with *gras* which has an oral vowel. Similarly, *pain* can be distinguished by its nasal vowel from *paix* with an oral vowel, and the same is true of *rond* and *rôt*. This distinction between nasal and oral vowels is made by all French speakers, but the number of nasal vowels varies with the individual.[175] (See *The thirteen basic vowels*, p. 164.)

Three or four nasal vowels?

Some people do indeed distinguish between four different nasal vowels, those in *un grand pain rond*, but such people are increasingly thin on the ground, since there has been a very widespread tendency for several generations to pronounce the vowel in *un* and the vowel in *pain* in the same way, a trend which can be explained in part by the infrequent occurrence of the vowel *un* in French vocabulary. (See table p. 125.) The coming together of the vowel *un* with the vowel in *pain* should in theory cause few problems of comprehension, but the context does not always disambiguate between *brin* and *brun*, *Alain* and *alun*, *empreint* and *emprunt*, *intolérant* and *un tolérant*, etc.

At the time of writing (January 1987), I have just had confirmation of this watching a news item on TF1 about the *Festival du Film Fantastique* in Avoriaz. The actress Sabine Azéma, who pronounces *un* like *in*, realised the ambiguity of what she had just said because, having said of a film director 'C'est *in* tolérant', she added: 'Je veux dire qu'il est tolérant.' And she was right to do so because everybody had understood *intolérant* and not *un tolérant*. I have no idea what the birthplace is of this actress who makes a distinction between only *three* nasal vowels, but in doing so we can say that she is following a fairly general trend and one which is becoming more and more widespread.

However, there are still somewhat archaic people (like me, but also like most of those who live south of the Loire as well as many French speakers outside France) who quite naturally and effortlessly use *four* nasal vowels. Am I bid any more? Is it possible to have more?

Five nasal vowels

Well, yes, in fact, it is. There are no limits to the subtleties of French pronunciation. There are people who distinguish between *five* different nasal vowels: the ones heard in *un*, *grand*, *rond*, *pain*, and *pin*. The distinction between *pain* and *pin* is usually one of length, with *pain* being longer than *pin* (less frequently there may be a difference of timbre). This same distinction is found in other words, for example *vin* and *vingt*, *faim* and *fin*, etc.

THE PHONEME *UN* BEFORE ITS COMPLETE DISAPPEARANCE

Theoretically, the vowels in *brin* and *brun* are not pronounced in the same way, but there is an increasing number of people, especially in the Paris region, who do pronounce them in the same way, with both words sounding like *brin*. Before the vowel *un* disappears completely from usage in French, here is a list – which is not far from being exhaustive – of some sixty words where you can still hear it in certain regions.

Pronunciation 'un' or 'in'		*Various pronunciations*
alun	lundi	acupuncteur
brûle-parfum	munster	acupuncture
brun	nerprun	bunker (Ger.)
bungalow	nuncupation	dumping (Eng.)
chacun	parfum	dundee (Eng.)
commun	pétun	funky (Eng.)
défunt	quelqu'un	jumping (Eng.)
défunte	remprunter	jungle (Eng.)
embrun	tribun	junker (Ger.)
emprunt	tungstate	junte (Sp.)
emprunter	tungstène	lunch (Eng.)
emprunteur	tungstique	luncher (Eng./Fr.)
emprunteuse	tungstite	muntjac (Jav./Eng.)
falun	un	pacfung (Ch./Eng.)
humble	unciforme	punch (Eng.)
importun	unciné	puncheur (Eng./Fr.)
inopportun	unguéal	punk (Eng.)
(à) jeun	unguifère	punkette (Eng./Fr.)
lumbago	unguis	rhumb (Du.)
		shunt (Eng.)
		shunter (Eng./Fr.)
		zérumbet (Pers.)

As you can see from the map (p. 126), these pronunciations were recorded in Champagne (Aube and Haute-Marne) and in Centre (Indres) for the *oïl* area, in Ain for Francoprovençal, and in Tarn for the *oc* area.

Six nasal vowels

We have found even better than five, but only in the *oïl* zone (Orne, Eure-et-Loir, Cher). The person recorded in Orne added to the preceding distinctions a difference in pronunciation between the vowel in *vent* (short) and the final vowel in *avant*, *parents* (long). A man who was a near-centenarian from Eure-et-Loir distinguished all plurals by a long nasal vowel. As for the sexagenarian recorded in Cher near Sancerre, he made no difference between the vowels of *brin* and *brun*. He had three timbres for the nasal vowels, but each timbre was pronounced long in the plural

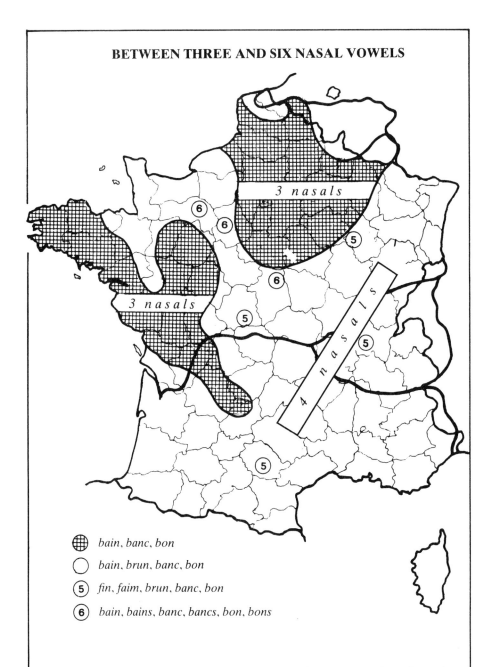

BETWEEN THREE AND SIX NASAL VOWELS

3 nasals

3 nasals

4 nasals

⊞ *bain, banc, bon*

◯ *bain, brun, banc, bon*

⑤ *fin, faim, brun, banc, bon*

⑥ *bain, bains, banc, bancs, bon, bons*

Not all French speakers distinguish between the same number of nasal vowels: three vowels (*bain, banc, bon*), four vowels (the same three plus *brun*), but there are also people who distinguish between five, and even six.

and short in the singular. He also had the peculiarity that with the word *lapins* he pronounced the final nasal vowel not only long but, as he put it himself, 'as if the word ended in -*ng*'.

Nasal vowels in the south

This pronunciation used by our informant from Cher for plurals of the *lapins* type is reminiscent of the pronunciation that French people identify as southern and which may be transcribed by -*ng*: 'Tu *vieng*, il est *brung*, c'est *bong*, un *frang*', etc. It should be noted however that the value of this pronunciation in the south is different since it accompanies *all* nasal vowels and the difference in pronunciation causes no change in meaning (in the south, 'un *lapin*' and 'des *lapins*' are both pronounced with -*ng* at the end of the word), whereas in the usage of our informant from Cher only the plural takes -*ng*. And that feature allows him to indicate a difference of meaning.

How do speakers react to such diversity?

These differences in pronunciation, which sometimes indicate a difference in meaning for the speaker, usually go unnoticed by the hearer. Or rather, they always think it is just an 'accent' (in the everyday meaning of the word, not in the meaning of stressed syllable), and that this 'accent' comes in addition to the 'real' word without changing its meaning, like the southern nasals. As a result, the hearer disregards it in oral communication with other people. A part of the message transmitted may thus be lost on the interlocutor, who re-establishes it more or less successfully from the context and the situation.

In this way, each individual thinks it is 'the other' who has an 'accent' and does not speak 'proper' French. The Parisian who only distinguishes between three nasal vowels is blamed by a southerner for confusing *brin* and *brun* or for pronouncing *franc* almost like *front*, and the latter is considered 'comical' because he adds an -*ng* to words ending in a nasal vowel.

And yet, in spite of differences which may become a hindrance to understanding, the French language remains an instrument of communication which works.

127

4

FRENCH OUTSIDE FRANCE
The status of French and international diversity

THE SITUATION OF FRENCH

How far will the decline go?

The days have long gone when French could take pride in having the international position it enjoyed for centuries. Since the inter-war period,[176] no one any longer disputes that English takes first place, with French coming in a very distant second.

Faced with a situation which seemed to call for a reaction, General de Gaulle set up the Haut Comité de la Langue Française in 1966, a body with direct links to the Prime Minister's office, given the aim of defending and spreading the French language.

Now, once more, cries of alarm are going up, as is witnessed by the very title of the review *Qui-vive International*,[177] and solutions are being proposed 'to keep the French language alive'.[178] This is a 'vast programme' as General de Gaulle would have said, especially since English has been almost the only language used in world scientific research since the 1950s.

A language unloved in international congresses

Even when international congresses take place in France, communication is more and more rarely in French, especially in the fields of physics, chemistry and astronautics.

The situation is less catastrophic in the social sciences, but international congresses where most contributions are in French are considered a rarity. Curiously enough, one such case is the annual colloquia of the Société Internationale de Linguistique Fonctionnelle.[179] But this association of linguists, which has held congresses every year since 1974 in various European, African and American countries, expressly allows all languages at its meetings and publishes its circulars in three languages (French, English and the language of the host nation). In spite of that, more than 90 per cent of contributions have always been made and published spontaneously in French. That, however, is an exception, and it has to be admitted that French is becoming increasingly difficult to export.

And yet . . .

The golden age of French

It should be remembered that as early as the Middle Ages French was being exported beyond the borders of France – and to England first of all with William the Conqueror. It was in French that Marco Polo, in the thirteenth century, dictated the tale of his adventures in the Far East. From the sixteenth century onwards, it was again French which gradually replaced Latin, until then the international language, in the realms of philosophy, medicine, banking and big business. It then became the language of diplomacy and high society in every country in Europe. It also became the language *par excellence* of science and technology.[180] In the seventeenth century the German Leibniz wrote most of his works in French, and at the end of the eighteenth century the Italian Casanova also wrote his *Mémoires* in French. Until the end of the First World War French was to remain the only diplomatic language in use in all European states.[181]

During the seventeenth century French had also launched itself across the seas in conquest of distant lands in America and the Indian Ocean, then in Oceania in the eighteenth century, and finally to a large part of Africa in the nineteenth century.

The last expansions date from the beginning of the twentieth century with the arrival of French colonisers in Togo and Cameroon, and Belgian colonisers in Rwanda and Burundi. (See table pp. 130–1.)

French – coming a good second

For several centuries French was recognised as the universal language, to the extent that foreign monarchs invited French writers of great repute to their court (Descartes and Queen Christina of Sweden, Voltaire and Frederick the Great of Prussia), but now it takes a very distant second place to English in that role. French people might reflect with some bitterness on the prophetic pronouncement of the English philosopher David Hume who said in 1767: 'Let the French draw vanity from the present expansion of their language. Our solid and flourishing American establishments . . . promise to give the English language superior stability and durability.'[182]

However, French remains one of the official working languages of the great international organisations[183] such as: the United Nations Organisation in New York where more than a third of the delegates representing 159 nations at the General Assembly use French; NATO in

Between the seventeenth and twentieth centuries, the French language was transported to the four corners of the earth in countries which have now for the most part achieved independence but where some sections of the population still speak it.

Arrival of the first French people	*Present situation*
Seventeenth century	
1604 Canada	Independent since 1931
1610 St-Pierre-et-Miquelon	TOM since 1946, DOM since 1976
1635 Martinique and Guadeloupe	DOM since 1946
1637 Guyana	DOM since 1946
1638 Senegal	Independent since 1963
1643 Madagascar	Independent since 1960
1662 Newfoundland	Canadian since 1949
1663 Reunion (ex-Bourbon Isle)	DOM since 1946
1674 Pondicherry	Indian since 1954
1686 Chandernagore	Indian since 1951
1697 Haïti	Independent since 1804
1699 Louisiana	American since 1812
Eighteenth century	
1715 Mauritius (ex Ile-de-France)	(GB 1810) Independent since 1968
1721 Mahe	Indian since 1956
1738 Kārikāl	Indian since 1954
1742 Seychelles (GB 1794)	Independent since 1975
1759 Yanam	Indian since 1954
Nineteenth century	
1830 Algeria	Independent since 1962
1837 Guinea	Independent since 1960
1841 Comoros	Independent since 1974
except for Mayotte	French territory community since 1976
1842 Tahiti (Fr. Polynesia)	TOM since 1946
1853 New Caledonia	TOM since 1946
1855 Mauritania	Independent since 1960
1860 Lebanon (Fr. mandate 1920)	Independent since 1943
1860 Syria (Fr. mandate 1920)	Independent since 1946
1863 Kampuchea (ex-Cambodia)	Independent since 1953
1867 Cochin China	Vietnam since 1949
1880 Congo	Independent since 1960
1880 Marchesas and Tuamotu	TOM since 1946
1881 Tunisia	Independent since 1956
1881 Gambier (Fr. Polynesia)	TOM since 1946
1882 Zaire (ex-Belgian Congo)	Independent since 1960
1883 Annam	Vietnam since 1954
1883 Benin (ex-Dahomey)	Independent since 1960
1885 Tonkin	Vietnam since 1954
1886 Wallis and Futuna	TOM since 1959
1889 Central African Republic	Independent since 1960
1889 Gabon	Independent since 1960
1893 Ivory Coast	Independent since 1960
1893 Laos	Independent since 1975

1895	Mali	Independent since 1960
1896	Burkina Faso (ex-Upper Volta)	Independent since 1960

Twentieth century

1900	Niger	Independent since 1960
1900	Chad	Independent since 1960
1911	Cameroon	Independent since 1960
1912	Morocco	Independent since 1956
1919	Burundi (ex-Belg. colony)	Independent since 1962
1919	Togo	Independent since 1960
1922	Vanuatu (ex-New Hebrides)	Independent since 1980
1923	Rwanda (ex-Belg. colony)	Independent since 1962

TOM = Territoire d'Outre-Mer; DOM = Département d'Outre-Mer.
Taken from *Dictionnaire universel des noms propres*, Paris, Le Robert.

Brussels and Luxembourg; UNESCO (United Nations Educational, Scientific and Cultural Organisation) in Paris.

Together with English and Arabic, it is also one of the languages of the Islamic Conference and the Arab League. Finally, as Jacques Chirac reminded us recently, French is the official language of the Olympic Games and, together with Latin, remains the diplomatic language of the Vatican.

French has suffered a considerable decline but it has not disappeared. Its international situation is precarious but not completely desperate. Thierry de Beaucé, former director of cultural affairs at the Quai d'Orsay, is determinedly optimistic about the spread of French around the world.[184]

French in other languages

A very recent sign of the survival – or of the renewal – of the cultural prestige of French in America was the release in 1986 of a cassette entitled *Culturally Speaking* (Forrest Production, Beverly Hills) which gives a list of words and expressions from European languages which can be used to give a more 'cultural' veneer to the English written and spoken in the United States. Of the five languages appearing on the cassette, French, with sixty-six words or phrases, comes well before Italian (twenty-six), Latin (nineteen), German (seventeen) and Yiddish (fourteen).

Many French words and phrases can also be heard in conversations conducted in German, Italian, Spanish, Portuguese and many other languages. In most cases they are words in common usage, even among people who do not speak French and do not even know that the words in question are French.

Usually, these French words used in foreign languages have taken on a particular restricted meaning in the host language. In Portuguese, for example, *mise* has the very precise meaning of 'to have a (hair) set' at the hairdresser's; in Italian *champignons* refers only to 'cultivated mushrooms', with *funghi* remaining the generic term; and in Spanish a *nécessaire*

131

FRENCH IN ENGLISH
(a few examples)

The following words are not only French. They are also used in English:

à la mode	femme fatale
beau	(c'est) magnifique
(le) beau monde	laissez faire (*sic*)
(très) chic	malaise
comme ci, comme ça	pièce de résistance
coup d'État	pied-à-terre
the crème de la crème	qui sait?
déjà vu	repartee (*sic*)
double entendre (*sic*)	savoir-faire
(par) excellence	tête-à-tête
fait accompli	tour de force
faux pas	vis-à-vis (the . . .)
	voilà

can only be a 'travelling bag'. You will find a few examples of these words which have passed into common usage in other languages in the tables above and on pages 133–5.

Thus, although it is in decline as a language of international communication, French is managing to lead some kind of parallel life in foreign languages.

French is still spoken outside France

Although French is no longer in first place as an international language, it is still used as the standard language to varying degrees both in Europe and on the other continents.

A map of the 'Francophone' world (p. 136) shows that French is present on the five continents. However, you can never be too careful with maps like this, which are far from easy to interpret, since we have to distinguish between countries where French is the official language and is in effect spoken by the majority of the inhabitants (Québec), from those countries where French is an official language but is hardly used by the population (black Africa). And then you have to find the very special situation where French is not the official language but is very widely used by the inhabitants (North Africa).

Just how many francophones are there in the world?

Whatever the country (with the possible exception of Canada), there is nothing more difficult than to find statistics which reveal the reality of linguistic usage. We can never be quite sure whether the number of

FRENCH IN GERMAN
(a few examples)

The following words are not only French. They are also used in German:

a propos (*sic*)
bonbon
boutique
cache-nez
calembour
canaille
carnet de passage (à la douane)
carte blanche
chacun à son goût
chagrin
chaise longue
châle
champignons (de Paris)
chef
chignon
cordon-bleu

cravate
croissants
dame
déjà vu
galant homme
gourmand
mode
pardon!
parfum
porte-monnaie
s'il vous plaît
soldat
trottoir
voilà
voyeur

(List compiled with the help of Dagi and Wolfgang Rolf.)

FRENCH IN ITALIAN
(a few examples)

The following words are not only French. They are also used in Italian:

à la page
bigné 'chou à la crème'
boutique
(pasta) brisé (*sic*)
cachet (le médicament)
champignons 'champignons de Paris'
charlotte (la pâtisserie)
chic
console 'meuble pour tourne-disque'
(uovo) à la coque
coup de foudre
crème de la crème
croissants 'brioches'
défilé (de mode)
dernier cri
dessert
en passant
et voilà
esprit (de finesse)

grandeur
gratin (sens culinaire)
(della) haute
laisser-aller
laisser faire
maître (à penser)
marrons glacés
mousse (l'entremets)
pain carré 'pain de mie'
paltó 'gros manteau'
papillon 'nœud papillon'
pardon
parure (de bijoux)
pour cause
puré (*sic*) 'purée'
robe-manteau
soubrette 'girl de music-hall'
toilette
vinaigrette

(List compiled with the help of Anna Capelli.)

FRENCH IN PORTUGUESE
(a few examples)

The following words are not only French. They are also used in Portuguese:

à vol d'oiseau	mise 'mise en plis'
bâton 'rouge à lèvres'	
beige	(palitos) de la reine 'biscuits à la cuiller'
camionnete (*sic*)	paquete 'paquebot'
champignons 'champignons de Paris'	passe vite 'presse-purée'
	pneu
chantilly 'crème Chantilly'	ralenti (pour une voiture)
capot (de voiture)	raquete (*sic*) 'raquette'
chef (de cuisine)	salão 'salon'
chic	soutien 'soutien-gorge'
chofer (*sic*) 'chauffeur'	tablier 'tableau de bord'
crêpes	tarte
fauteuil	toilette (les vêtements)
flan	

(List compiled with the help of Danièle and Gérard Castello Lopes.)

---

francophones given for a particular country refers:

– only to those who do in fact speak French every day;
– to those who can speak it but normally use another language;
– to those who understand it without really being able to speak it.

In a book on the French language published in 1986, the author puts the number of francophones in the whole world at 140 million,[185] and some estimates are even more optimistic, rising as high as 200 million or even 300 million. Such figures could only be reached by counting all those who are potential francophones because French is the official language in their country rather than those for whom French is the language of everyday use. But only the latter are of interest to us. The following estimates, obtained by grouping scattered data together,[186] will give us some idea:

10 million in Europe (not counting France);
15 million in North Africa and the Middle East;
10 million in the Americas (Canada, United States, West Indies);
 7 million in black Africa;
 4 million in the rest of the world (Indian Ocean, Asia, Oceania).

Adding in the 62 million inhabitants of France gives us a total of around 100 million true 'francophones'. But these figures are difficult to verify and clearly open to dispute.

134

FRENCH IN SPANISH
(a few examples)

The following words are not only French. They are also used in Spanish:

arriviste	croissants
bébé	entrecot (*sic*)
bidé (*sic*) (appareil sanitaire)	fular (*sic*) 'foulard'
bonbons 'petits chocolats'	foie gras 'n'importe quel pâté'
bricolage	garage
bulevar (*sic*) 'boulevard, galerie marchande'	menage 'ménage'
	mousse (l'entremets)
buqué (*sic*) 'bouquet'	nécessaire 'mallette de toilette'
bureau (le meuble)	parqué (*sic*) 'parquet'
capo (*sic*) 'capot de voiture'	prêt-à-porter
carnet 'papiers d'identité'	ralenti (d'une voiture)
cassette (de magnétophone)	reprise (pour une voiture)
chalet 'villa'	restaurant
chemilaco 'chemise Lacoste'	(patatas) soufflées 'pommes dauphine'
chiffonnier (le meuble)	toilette
chofer (*sic*) 'chauffeur'	

Other French expressions found in Chilean Spanish:

atelier (d'artiste, d'architecte)	rouge 'rouge à lèvres'
beige	(papas) soufflées 'pommes dauphine'
boutique	(vino) tchambré (*sic*) 'chambré
buffet (le meuble)	tchantilly (*sic*) 'crème Chantilly'
(menta) frappé (*sic*) 'avec des glaçons	tchic (*sic*) 'chic'
garage	tchofer (*sic*) 'chauffeur'

(List compiled with the help of Ana Maria and Koldo de Viar, Julia Arnáiz, Rodrigo and Yvonne Medina.)

A survey of the French-speaking world outside France

Let us, then, forget precise figures and take a rapid bird's eye view of the countries where French is spoken. Later on we shall come back and take a closer look at the characteristics of the French spoken in some of them. (See p. 139 *et seq.*)

As you can see from the map 'French in the world' (p. 136), French as a language of everyday use in Europe extends beyond the borders of France to Belgium (pp. 139–41), the Grand Duchy of Luxembourg, Switzerland and a small part of Italy (pp. 141–4).

In *Luxembourg*, French enjoys long-standing prestige since, from the Middle Ages, its rulers were often Walloons married to French princesses. French replaced German as the official language in 1946. However, Luxembourgers are usually trilingual, and their everyday family conversations are in the local dialect, which is Germanic.[187]

In *Italy*, French was for centuries the language spoken in the Val

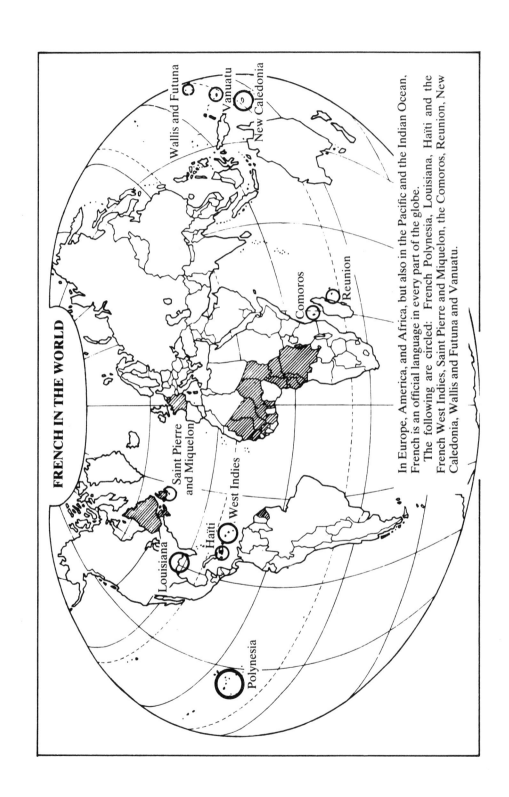

FRENCH IN THE WORLD

Wallis and Futuna

Vanuatu

New Caledonia

Reunion

Comoros

Saint Pierre
and Miquelon

West Indies

Haiti

Louisiana

Polynesia

In Europe, America, and Africa, but also in the Pacific and the Indian Ocean, French is an official language in every part of the globe. The following are circled: French Polynesia, Louisiana, Haiti and the French West Indies, Saint Pierre and Miquelon, the Comoros, Reunion, New Caledonia, Wallis and Futuna and Vanuatu.

d'Aoste, as also in the Duchy of Savoie, which also took in a part of Piedmont. It was even declared the official written language in Savoy in 1536, three years before it was in France (edict of Villers-Cotterêts, 1539).[188] Savoie was finally annexed to France in 1860, but the valleys of Piedmont, known as 'Vaudois', and the Val d'Aoste remain under Italian control. The constitutional law of 1948, which made French once again, together with Italian, an official language for the Val d'Aoste alone, was unfortunately never really put into force. Consequently, only old people and a handful of militant francophones still cling to a French which is increasingly being italianised.[189]

The Channel Islands (Jersey, Guernsey and Sark), the remains of the ancient Duchy of Normandy, still enjoy a special status authorising the use of French, although it is the language of administration (together with English) only on Jersey.

In *North America*, outside the tiny islands of Saint-Pierre-et-Miquelon, French is spoken daily in Canada by numbers which vary according to the region (pp. 142–8, 149). There are also French-speaking communities in the United States: in Louisiana (p. 148), in Missouri, in the high valley of the Mississippi, in the village of Frenchville in Pennsylvania, and in New England (Vermont, Maine, Rhode Island, New Hampshire, Massachusetts and Connecticut)[190] on the east coast.

In the *West Indies*, in addition to the French West Indies (Martinique, Guadeloupe and dependencies) (p. 148–51), which are DOMs (Départements d'Outre-Mer), the Republic of Haïti, which has been independent since 1804, has kept French as its only official language.[191] It should be remembered that after the Second World War it was probably the vote cast by Haïti which led to French being accepted, by a majority of one, as a working language at the United Nations. Still in the West Indies, there are two more small francophone communities in the American Virgin Islands, both in Saint Thomas.

In *South America*, French Guyana became a Département d'Outre-Mer in 1946, after being a colony since the middle of the nineteenth century.

In *Africa*, in the eighteen countries where French is an official language (either on its own or with other languages) the vast majority of people are not francophone. By contrast, in the three countries of the Maghreb (Morocco, Algeria, Tunisia), French is not an official language but it is understood and spoken by a considerable section of the population. (See p. 151–8.)

In the *Middle East*, Lebanon deserves a special mention. Since the nineteenth century most of the inhabitants of Beirut have spoken fluent French, taught in many private schools. Among the former pupils of the French Jesuit fathers are *all* the presidents of the Lebanese republic, dozens of ministers and hundreds of members of parliament and top civil servants.[192] It is remarkable that French should have retained such prestige in this country even though the French mandate lasted for only twenty-three years, from 1920 to 1943. English has been gradually gaining ground over the last twenty years, but more as the language of banking and trade,[193] whereas French still seems to be the language of culture.

In the *Indian Ocean*, French has remained the language of the intellectual élite of Madagascar long after independence (1960) and it was calculated that in 1975 some 20 per cent of Madagascans knew French.[194] However, in 1972 in the high plains there were violent demonstrations against French, branded as the 'language of slavery', whilst at the same time the inhabitants of the coastal regions were marching for the opposite cause to the tune of the *Marseillaise*.[195]

The *Comoros* to the north of Madagascar consist of four main islands which became *Territoires d'Outre-Mer* in 1958. Only Mayotte voted to remain French after the 1974 referendum. It uses French as the language of foreign relations but very few of its people speak it.

Of the small islands around Madagascar, only Reunion, formerly the *Île Bourbon*, is a *Département d'Outre-Mer* (since 1946). It is also the oldest island occupied by the French, having been taken over in the seventeenth century. Although no statistics are available, it is estimated that slightly over a quarter of the populations speak French.[196]

In neighbouring Mauritius, formerly the *Île de France*, and the much more northerly Seychelles, although English has become the official language, French has maintained an important position in the life of the natives and enjoys a degree of social prestige.[197]

In *Asia*, there are no more than vestiges of French to be found in the former trading posts of India, but the situation is slightly different in the countries of former French Indo-China, where seventy-five years of colonisation made a section of the population genuinely bilingual and where, in spite of a steady decline which began thirty years ago, French still has prestige for the intellectual élites. This prestige survives especially in Laos and Kampuchea (former Cambodia), but in Vietnam French has ceased completely to be a common language in higher education. Furthermore, since 1970 there has been an increasingly noticeable advance in the use of English in daily life.[198]

In *Oceania*, French is found in three groups of islands: on the one hand in two overseas territories, New Caledonia and French Polynesia, which includes the Marquesas Islands, the Gambier Islands, the Tuamotu Islands, the Austral Seamounts and the Society Islands (Tahiti), and on the other hand in a former Franco-British condominium, the New Hebrides, which became the independent state of Vanuatu in 1980.

In New Caledonia, French is both the official language and the main common language, whereas it is in roughly equal use with Tahitian in Polynesia and with English in Vanuatu.[199]

To the north-east of New Caledonia, the Wallis and Futuna Islands, which were placed under French protectorate between 1887 and 1959, are now *Territoire d'Outre-Mer* in quite an unusual situation, since each island still has its own monarch.

THE DIVERSITY OF FRENCH OUTSIDE FRANCE

We shall take a slightly closer look at some varieties of French spoken outside France, as we did for the regional varieties of French spoken in France: in Belgium, Switzerland, Canada, Louisiana, the West Indies and Africa.

FRENCH IN BELGIUM

Flemish and French

Founded in 1830, Belgium has, since the Middle Ages, been cut in two by a horizontal linguistic frontier stretching from Verviers to Courtrai, with the Flemish region and its Germanic language to the north and the Walloon region with its Romance language to the south. The situation is particularly complex nowadays because the French language of the Île-de-France spread not only to Wallonia but also to the aristocracy in Flanders in the Middle Ages. As a result, French very rapidly became the language of religion and administration as well as the language of culture and writing throughout the land. Attempts were made in the fourteenth century to oust French, but with little success since the middle classes were also gradually becoming frenchified, and in the middle of the eighteenth century French became the language of all town dwellers both in Flanders and elsewhere.[200]

Today, as can be seen from the map on p. 140, French is the standard language of the entire Walloon region and there is the important French-speaking enclave of Brussels in Flanders.

What is Belgian French like?

The Belgian 'accent' is easily identifiable, but it is difficult to give a single description of it because different parts of the country have different pronunciations. However, Jacques Pohl[201] has managed to summarise in six main points the features which allow us to recognise it:

- the general distinction between the vowels of *brin* and *brun*;
- the retention of the distinction between the *a* of *patte* and the *a* of *pâte*, by a difference of length and not of timbre;
- the opposition of a short and a long vowel in words such as *aimé/aimée*, *cri/crie*, *nu/nue*, *bout/boue*;

139

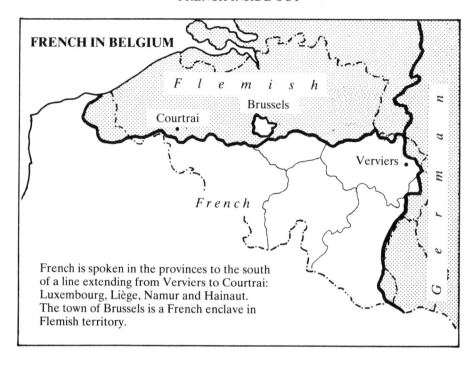

FRENCH IN BELGIUM

F l e m i s h

Brussels

Courtrai

G e r m a n

Verviers

F r e n c h

French is spoken in the provinces to the south
of a line extending from Verviers to Courtrai:
Luxembourg, Liège, Namur and Hainaut.
The town of Brussels is a French enclave in
Flemish territory.

- articulating as two syllables words such as *lion, buée, nouer*;
- pronouncing the vowel *u* in *huit* and *enfuir* like the French *ou*;
- the tendency of voiced final consonants (as in *Serbe, perde, douze, marge*) to become unvoiced so that they have the same sound as *serpe, perte, douce, marche.*

Less widespread but still quite common, especially in the working classes in Brussels, are other characteristics such as the difference in pronunciation between *bouleau* and *boulot, maux* and *mots*, (cha)*peau* and *pot*, as well as the nasalisation of vowels in front of a nasal consonant (for example, *même* pronounced as if it were written *minme*).

None of these features, which often preserve ancient forms, is specific to Belgium, and they are to be found in one or another region of France. It is their constancy and frequency which makes them characteristic of the Belgian 'accent'.

From the lexical point of view, specifically Belgian words abound. A far from complete and highly subjective sample can be found in the table entitled 'A small French-French lexis' (Belgium) on p. 141.

A SMALL FRENCH–FRENCH LEXIS[202]
(Belgium)

ajoute (feminine noun)	'ajout'
auditoire	'salle de cours'
avoir le temps long	's'ennuyer d'attendre'
bonbon	'biscuit sec'
brosser un cours	'sécher un cours'
calepin	'cartable'
carte-vue	'carte postale illustrée'
chicon	'endive'
drache	'pluie battante'
dracher	'pleuvoir à verse'
drap	'serviette de toilette'
farde	'dossier, chemise'
femme à journée	'femme de ménage'
filet américain	'steak tartare'
fricassée	'omelette au lard'
légumier	'marchand de légumes'
nonante	'quatre-vingt-dix'
octante	'quatre-vingts'
pain français	'baguette'
pâté	'petit gâteau à la crème'
pistolet	'petit pain rond'
pli	'raie' (des cheveux)
pralines	'chocolats'
quartier	'petit appartement'
savoir	'pouvoir'
septante	'soixante-dix'
tapis-plain	'moquette'
tomber faible	's'évanouir'
torchon	'serpillière'

FRENCH IN FRENCH-SPEAKING SWITZERLAND

Three official languages

Swiss French, which is an official language on an equal footing with Italian and German, is not very different from the French spoken in the neighbouring regions of France (Franche-Comté, Bourgogne, Savoie): the political frontier between Switzerland and France is not a linguistic frontier. Furthermore, French enjoys considerable prestige among the élites of German-speaking Switzerland, who know French far better than the inhabitants of French-speaking Switzerland know German.[203]

The French spoken in Switzerland

Amongst the characteristics which Swiss French shares with the eastern regions of France and part of Belgium, we can quote the pronunciation of an open vowel (like that in *port*) at the end of words such as *pot*, *mot*, *sabot* and *abricot*, which also allows these regions to distinguish, as in French-speaking Belgium, between *pot* and *peau*, *mot* and *maux*, the final vowel of *sabot* and that of *beau*, the final vowel of *abricot* and that of *artichaut*, etc.

More specifically Swiss are certain lexical items such as *panosse* for 'serpillière' (see map p. 120), *relaver* for 'faire la vaisselle', *poutser* for 'nettoyer, faire le ménage' or *lavette* for 'gant de toilette'. (See *débarbouillette* in Canada, p. 149.) Can it be sheer coincidence that this totally random selection of items concerns one of the qualities for which the Swiss are most noted: cleanliness.

You will see from the table below that specifically Swiss vocabulary extends to far more domains.

A SMALL FRENCH–FRENCH LEXIS
(French-speaking Switzerland)

panosse	'serpillière'
poutser	'nettoyer énergiquement'
cheni	'désordre, objet sans valeur, petites saletés'
lavette	'carré de tissu-éponge pour se laver'
cornet	'sac en papier'
gâteau aux pruneaux	'tarte aux quetsches'
galetas	'grenier'
septante	'soixante-dix'
huitante	'quatre-vingts'
nonante	'quatre-vingt dix'
une crevée	1. 'une grande quantité'
	2. 'une grosse bévue'
pôche, pochon	'louche'
dévaloir	'vide-ordures'
foehn	'sèche-cheveux'
s'encoubler	's'empêtrer'
livret	'table de multiplication'
tâches	'devoirs (pour l'école)'
fourrer un livre	'recouvrir un livre (pour le protéger)'
se mettre à la chotte	'se mettre à l'abri'
donner une bonne-main	'donner un pourboire'
réduire ses vieux souliers	'ranger ses vieilles chaussures'

You can see from the map opposite that in Switzerland, French is spoken to the west of a line which goes from Basle to Sion, in the Cantons of Geneva, Vaud and Neuchâtel, in the western half of the Valais and of the canton of Fribourg, as well as in the Bernese Jura, which has recently separated from the canton of Berne.

In Italy, French is an official language in the Val d'Aoste and is still spoken in Vaudois valleys of Piedmont.

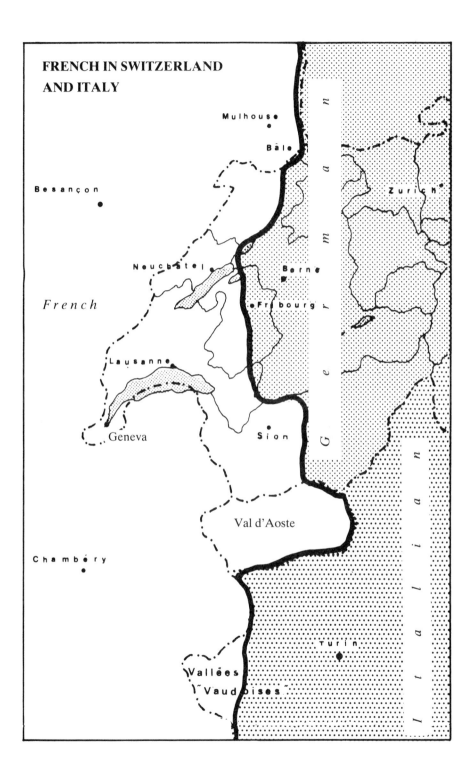

FRENCH IN SWITZERLAND
AND ITALY

Mulhouse

Bâle

Besançon

Zurich

French

Neuchâtel

Berne

Fribourg

Lausanne

Geneva

Sion

Val d'Aoste

Chambéry

Turin

Vallées
Vaudoises

G   e   r   m   a   n

I   t   a   l   i   a   n

FRENCH IN CANADA

Six million francophones

French was introduced into Canada in the seventeenth century and the proportion of people of French origin varies according to the region:[204] the French presence is very low in the western provinces, constitutes the overwhelming majority in Québec, and is characterised in the east by a linguistic usage especially worthy of attention; that of the Acadians.

In the case of Canada, we must be careful not to confuse the ethnic French population with those who still speak French on a daily basis, because although the percentages are roughly the same in Québec (80 per cent of ethnic French origin and 82.5 per cent speaking French in the home), they diverge quite considerably in the other regions, where English has gradually supplanted French, especially in the younger generations. In New Brunswick in 1981, almost 36 per cent of the population, 251,000 people, were of French origin but no more than 216,000 (only 31 per cent of the population) had kept French as their language of everyday use. In Nova Scotia, where the vast majority of inhabitants are anglophones, out of 8.5 per cent of French origin there are now only 2.9 per cent who speak French every day. In the western provinces, the percentages of Canadians who speak French at home are 3.8 per cent in Ontario and 3 per cent in Manitoba (about 363,000 people in all) and less than 1 per cent for the other provinces (less than 62,000 people). (Source: Statistiques du Canada 1981.)

For Canada as a whole, one of the few countries where linguistic statistics are accurate, it is calculated that there are six million 'true' francophones, of which just over five million live in the province of Québec. (See map p. 145.)

The Acadians, a people with no geography

The problem of the survival of the French language is especially acute for the Acadians: these descendants of the first French to arrive in America, from Poitou, Aunis and Saintonge, had settled in around 1604 along the coasts of what is now Nova Scotia.

Although united by their history and language,[205] the Acadians have no geographical location: there is no point looking for Acadia on a map of Canada because you will not find it. Even young Acadians, when questioned in a survey conducted in 1977, could not agree among themselves on the boundaries of Acadia.[206]

Nowadays there are Acadians but no Acadia, and even the origin of the word remains obscure. There are those who believe that the name of Acadia is the one Champlain mistakenly gave to the shores of what is now Nova Scotia, confusing it with *Arcadia*, the name given a hundred years

144

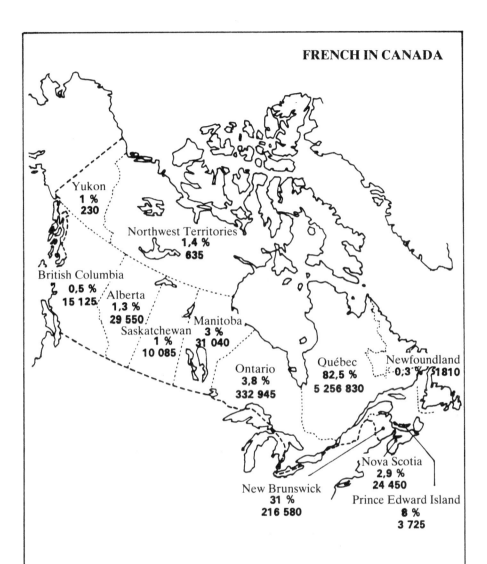

FRENCH IN CANADA

Yukon
1 %
230

Northwest Territories
1,4 %
635

British Columbia
0,5 %
15 125

Alberta
1,3 %
29 550

Saskatchewan
1 %
10 085

Manitoba
3 %
31 040

Ontario
3,8 %
332 945

Québec
82,5 %
5 256 830

Newfoundland
0,3 % 1810

Nova Scotia
2,9 %
24 450

New Brunswick
31 %
216 580

Prince Edward Island
8 %
3 725

The percentage of people speaking French at home in relation to the total population of the province is shown for each province, as well as the number of people represented by that percentage.

(Source: Statistiques du Canada, 1981.)

previously to the coasts of Virginia because of the good life they seemed to offer. Another theory claims that it is, in fact, a name of Indian origin, since there are place-names such as *Tracadie* (New Brunswick) and *Shubenacadie* (Nova Scotia) which have the same suffix. We would then have, for *Acadia*, the choice between a word from the Indian Micmac language meaning 'campsite' and another Indian word from the Malecite language meaning 'fertile land'. Whatever the case, it is a word which, in spite of their geographical dispersion, unites the Acadians, whose history contains some dramatic episodes.

The 'Great Upheaval'

It was in 1755, one and a half centuries after their arrival, that the Acadians suffered what they call the 'Great Upheaval', which is also the blackest period of their history.

After being the object of conflict between France and England up to 1670, what was then called 'Acadia' (in other words, what is now Nova Scotia) remained French from 1670 until 1713, when it passed under English domination. But the Acadians, who had always wished to remain neutral in the disputes which set the English against the French, refused to give an oath of allegiance to the King of England.[207] Deemed undesirables by the British government, they were deported in 1755: forcibly embarked on forty-six boats gathered at Grand-Pré, a great number of them of them were to be scattered through several regions of what is now the United States. Many perished at sea, but some finally settled in Louisiana after a detour via Santo Domingo: these are the ones called the *Cajuns* or *Cadjins*, which represents the approximate local pronunciation of the word *Acadiens*. (See p. 148.) Others, with the assistance of the Indians, took refuge in the forests of present-day New Brunswick, while others were sent to England or shipped back to France.

It was not until a century later that the world became aware of this entire tragic event when the American poet Henry Longfellow wrote a long poem of 1,400 lines retracing the sad story of Evangeline Bellefontaine, a young woman of Grand-Pré who is cruelly separated from her fiancé by deportation and spends the rest of her life looking for him. She finally finds him again in Philadelphia, but it is too late: they are both very old and he is dying. Through the story of Evangeline, this long poem, translated into fifteen languages, acquainted the entire world with the existence of the Acadians.

This people, devoted to its past and its religion, has taken as its national anthem the hymn *Ave maris stella*, and as its flag, the French tricolour with the five-pointed star of the Virgin Mary in the blue stripe.[208] These inhabitants of a land which has disappeared have been able, in spite of their tribulations, to keep alive the language of their forebears, which only goes to prove that, in the words of Antonine Maillet: 'To be an Acadian is to be the descendant of somebody, not to occupy a land.'

French in Quebec

Compared with the turbulent history of the Acadians, the history of the people who colonised the valley of the Saint Lawrence starting from Québec, Trois Rivières and Montréal to create *Nouvelle France* or *Canada* seems smoother and more fortunate: within a century the various populations had managed to join up by a process of constant settlement.[209] The increase in the number of francophones then proceeded at a regular rate, rising tenfold between 1760 (65,000) and 1851 (670,000), and then again by almost ten between 1851 and the middle of the twentieth century (5,000,000 in Québec in 1971).

It was in 1763, fifty years after Acadia, that Canada in its turn became an English colony. At that time, a quarter of the population of Québec was anglophone, and Montréal was to remain predominantly anglophone until 1871. Since then, Montréal has become the second largest French-speaking city in the world, after Paris and on a par with Brussels. For its part, the city of Québec is now almost entirely francophone.

Ptsi-z-infin and grin-minmin

When you disembark at Québec, you are struck by pronunciations such as *ptsi-z-infin et grin-minmin* ('petits-enfants et grand-maman'), and to begin with you may have some difficulty identifying words like *banc*, *gant*, and *vent* which are pronounced as a Parisian would pronounce *bain*, *gain*, and *vin* but with different timbres. You quickly become used to this difference, as you do to hearing *p'tit* pronounced *p'tsi*.

The reason for this well-known characteristic of the French spoken in Canada lies in what the linguists call in their jargon the assibilation of occlusives (assi*b*ilation and not assi*m*ilation). This means pronouncing *t* (in (par)*ti*, *tiens*, *tuer*) as *ts* and *d* (in *dis*, *dieu*, *du*, *duel*) as *dz*.[210] The phenomenon is found in Québec and, to a lesser extent, in Ontario,[211] but does not affect the Acadians.[212] The latter, for their part, have the peculiarity of pronouncing *guerre* or *curé* as if these words were written *djerre* or *tchuré*, and, of course, they pronounce *Acadien* as *Acadjin*. (See the *Cadjins* or *Cajuns* of Louisiana p. 148.)

However, generally speaking, all the francophones of Canada have common features of pronunciation,[213] with the exception of the Acadians, whose turbulent history has left them isolated and who have thus preserved specific archaisms: for example, pronouncing the vowel in *pomme* as *ou* (remember the quarrel of the 'ou-ists' in France in the seventeenth century). (See p. 71.)

As far as the lexis is concerned, the differences between provinces are far less noticeable, and in the table entitled 'A small French–French lexis' (Canada) (see p. 149) you will find a certain number of words which may lead to confusion in Europe but which are all understood throughout Canada. This lexis will provide unambiguous understanding of the sentences presented at the end of the list.*

FRENCH IN LOUISIANA

Three language varieties in addition to English

Founded in 1682, Louisiana, so called in honour of Louis XIV, remained French for only eighty years. After an Anglo-Spanish interlude, it was ceded to the Americans in 1803 by Buonaparte for the sum of fifteen million dollars. The first immigrants saw their numbers swollen by the arrival of the Acadians in 1755 (the *Cajuns* or *Cadjins*), and, in addition to the new influx of refugees from France after the Revolution, the French-speaking population of Louisiana was increased even further by a large number of black slaves from the West Indies.

These three types of settlement explain the three varieties of language that exist in Louisiana:[214]

- colonial French, also called *old creole French* (New Orleans and the plantations along the Mississippi). This language has preserved long vowels in speech and also has a written form;
- Acadian (or *cajun*), only in the spoken form. It is the most widespread variety and resembles the French spoken by the Acadians in Canada;
- *black creole* (or *Louisiana creole*), also called *gumbo French* or *courima-vini*. It is not French but a creole close to the West Indian creole and it is spoken mainly in the south of the State.

In 1869, English became the official language and French disappeared almost completely from the curriculum until 1968. At that time French acquired the status of official language and Louisiana set up a Council of the Development of French in Louisiana (CODOFIL). But today, in spite of the attempts made by CODOFIL, it seems that the French language continues to decline (some 300,000 francophones) and that only old people still use it and keep it alive.[215]

FRENCH IN THE WEST INDIES AND GUYANA

Creole and French

Overseas departments just like Guyana, the French West Indies consist of Martinique and Guadeloupe with its dependencies: Îles des Saintes, Marie-Galante, La Désirade, Saint-Barthélémy and the French part of Saint-

* I am grateful to Catherine Philipponneau, lecturer at the University of Moncton, for sending me all the documents relating to the Acadians and their language.

A SMALL FRENCH–FRENCH LEXIS
(French-speaking Canada)

amarrer[xx](ses chaussures)	'attacher' (ses chaussures)
appareiller[xx] (la terre)	'préparer la terre pour les semailles'
(s')*appareiller*[xx]	's'habiller'
assez	'très, beaucoup'
bleuets	'myrtilles'
boucane	'fumée'
cabaret	'plateau (de service)'
cartable	'classeur'
casher (un chèque)	'toucher' (un chèque)
champlure	'robinet'
charrue	'chasse-neige'
chavirer[xx] (un seau)	'renverser' (un seau)
(se) *chavirer*[xx]	'se faire du souci, devenir fou'
chialer	'maugréer, râler'
chaussette	'pantoufle'
couverte	'couverture' (de lit)
débarbouillette	'gant de toilette' (petite pièce de tissu)
escousse, secousse[x], *élan*[xx]	'moment, laps de temps'
espérer[xx]	'attendre'
filière	'classeur métallique'
grand bord[xx]	'salle de séjour'
gréements[xx]	'les meubles'
gréyer (la table)	'mettre' (la table)
(se) *gréyer*, (se) *dégreyer*[xx]	's'habiller', 'se déshabiller'
hardes[xx]	'vêtements' (non péjoratif)
(le) *large*[xx]	'la grande forêt'
ligne à linge	'corde à linge'
linge	'vêtements' (extérieurs)
magasiner, faire son magasinage	'faire ses courses, ses achats'
(se) *mâter*[xx]	'se cabrer'
mitaine	'moufle'
(un) *mousse*	'un petit garçon'
pas mal	'assez'
(c'est) *pas pire*	'(c'est) très bien'
patenter, patenteur	'bricoler, bricoleur'
pêcher[xx] (du gibier)	'prendre' (du gibier)
peindre	'peindre (un tableau)'
peinturer	'peindre (un mur)'
platte	'ennuyeux'
portrait	'photographie'
(n'avoir plus que la) *ralingue*	'être maigre comme un clou'
sacoche	'sac de dame'
tabagie[x]	'bureau de tabac'
virer de bord[xx]	's'en retourner'
virer (la terre)[xx]	'retourner (la terre)'

[x] term used mainly in Quebec. [xx] term used mainly by Acadians.

A FEW SENTENCES HEARD IN CANADA

Ils sont allés à l'hôtel pour une petite secousse.
   'Ils sont allés à l'hôtel un petit moment.'
A matin, le postillon était chaud, il était encore sur la brosse.
   'Le matin, le facteur était ivre, il avait encore pris une cuite.'
Elle plume des patates pour le dîner.
   'Elle épluche des pommes de terre pour le déjeuner.'
Elle est en famille, elle va accoucher ben vite.
   'Elle est enceinte, elle va accoucher très vite.'
Sa mère lui a donné une belle catin pour sa fête.
   'Sa mère lui a donné une belle poupée pour son anniversaire.'
Au magasin général, ils ont du butin à la verge.
   'Au magasin général, ils ont du tissu au mètre' (la verge = 0.91 metres).
Il est parti dans les bois chercher des cocottes et il s'est écarté.
   'Il est parti dans les bois chercher des pommes de pin et s'est égaré.'
Y a un char qu'a fessé un p'tit suisse.
   'Il y a une voiture qui a heurté un petit écureuil gris.'
Le téléphone n'a pas dérougi.
   'Le téléphone n'a pas cessé (de sonner).'
Elle braillait à chaudes larmes.
   'Elle pleurait à chaudes larmes.'
Conseils à la gardienne:
   '1. *donner la bouteille au bébé*;
   2. *lui faire faire son rapport*;
   3. *l'emmener se promener en carrosse.'*
Conseils à la dame qui garde les enfants:
   '1. donner le biberon au bébé;
   2. lui faire faire son rot;
   3. l'emmener se promener dans son landau.'

Martin. Obviously, French is the official language and it is understood by most of the population.

However, as in Guyana, Reunion, Haïti and Mauritius, the language of common usage is usually the creole, which is a language formed in the seventeenth century as a result of contacts between colonisers speaking French and slaves speaking various African languages. These slaves had been gathered together on the western coasts of Africa before being shipped to the colonies. The French creoles are not garbled or simplified French but languages in their own right and completely distinct from French. West Indians and Guyanans are thus generally creole–French bilinguals.

A few characteristics of French in the West Indies

If you ask somebody from metropolitan France to describe the French spoken in the West Indies, he or she will usually say that West Indians do not pronounce the *r* in words like *roue, terre, porte*, etc. This impression is false because the consonant is usually there but pronounced so weakly at the back of the mouth that it is difficult to hear. If you listen carefully, you will realise that *roue* is in no way confused with *houe*, nor *terre* with *taie, porte* with *pote*, etc. Here as with Canada, it takes only a few moments to establish the correspondences between these usages of French and those which metropolitan French people are accustomed to.

From the point of view of lexis, some expressions are only slightly surprising for the visitor from France disembarking in the West Indies: thus 'un conducteur au volant de son *transport en commun*' instead of 'au volant de son autobus', or 'la farine a *pris fin*' to say there is none left. It takes somewhat longer to realise that the word *linges* actually refers to outer garments and that a child who is said to be *vorace* is simply greedy. Other words, such as *zouc* 'la fête', *zouquer* 'danser' or *tébé* 'fou', which are completely unknown outside the West Indies, will cause real problems of communication.*

FRENCH IN AFRICA

French-speaking Africa

Francophone African countries occupy a good half of the land area of Africa, from Mauritania in the west to Chad in the east and Zaire, Rwanda and Burundi in the south. In all these countries, with the exception of Senegal where the French influence dates back to the seventeenth century, French was introduced only in the nineteenth century in the colonial era. It was initially spread by the army,[216] so that, for example, in the Central African Republic and in Chad there exists a 'military French' which is also called 'français tirailleur' or 'français tiraillou' and which developed in particular during the two world wars. Nowadays, it has given way to 'le français des écoles'.[217] (See the map of French in Africa, p. 152.)

African French

There is not *one* kind of French spoken in Africa, just as there is not *one* kind of French in France, but all the varieties of French spoken in Africa do have one point in common: nowadays it is a 'school' French, in other words almost always learnt at school and not in the family. As a result, each of the many African languages leaves its own mark on the French spoken in the region.

An extreme example is represented by the following sentence, where we see manifested in French a phenomenon specific to Bantu, a language in

---

* I am grateful to Danielle Saada for her help.

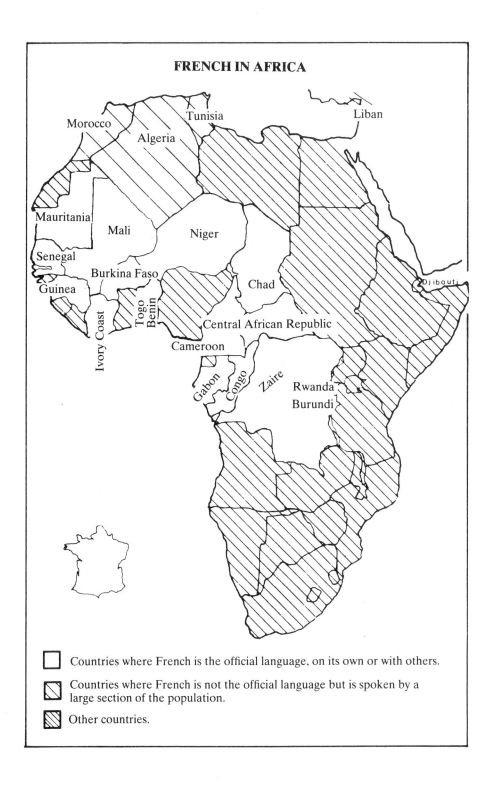

FRENCH IN AFRICA

Morocco
Tunisia
Liban
Algeria
Mauritania
Mali
Niger
Senegal
Burkina Faso
Chad
Guinea
Djibouti
Togo
Benin
Ivory Coast
Central African Republic
Cameroon
Gabon
Congo
Zaïre
Rwanda
Burundi

☐ Countries where French is the official language, on its own or with others.

▨ Countries where French is not the official language but is spoken by a
large section of the population.

▨ Other countries.

which the rules of grammatical agreement affect all the words in the sentence:

Nous voulons des hôpit*aux* pour les hommes et des hôpit*ales* pour les femmes, des écoles norm*ales* pour les jeunes filles et des écoles norm*aux* pour les jeunes gens. Enf*in* et enf*ine*, nous demandons la création de tribun*ales* dans la brousse comme il y a des tribun*aux* dans les centres urbains.[218]

The table on p. 154 entitled 'A small French–French lexis' (black Africa) contains, as well as local meanings of French words (*ambiance*, *vidange*, etc.), examples of local lexical creations which conform completely with traditional processes of word formation in French (*essencerie*, *boyesse*, etc.).

Surveys on the numbers of French speakers in Africa all show that, although the élite speaks an excellent and sometimes polished French, the rest of the population hardly speaks it at all: between 5 and 10 per cent depending on the country.[219]

French does not play the same role in every country, however. In Zaire,[220] French above all is *read* (more than 80 per cent of books, magazines and newspapers are written in French) and, of course, *heard* (films, television and radio games). However, it is not truly a lingua franca in this country in the sense of being an instrument of communication between peoples who do not speak the same mother tongue.[221]

In the Ivory Coast, by contrast (and especially in Abidjan), French is used on all social occasions,[222] and can therefore be considered an important lingua franca.

In other countries, such as Togo, Benin,[223] the Central African Republic or Chad,[224] it never is. It should be remembered that in the last two countries French was an unknown language until the beginning of the twentieth century.

French in North Africa

The French have been present in the three countries of the Maghreb for different lengths of time: 132 years in Algeria (1830 – colony, then department – 1962), seventy-five years in Tunisia (1881 – protectorate – 1956) and forty-four years in Morocco (1912 – protectorate – 1956). In these three countries the great period of French immigration lasted until the First World War, but a large number of French people who settled in Tunisia and Morocco arrived there from Algeria, which goes some way towards explaining why a certain number of French expressions are common to the three countries of North Africa.

There were as many Italians as there were French people in Tunisia before independence, but they all spoke French as well. By contrast, there have always been far fewer other foreign nationals in Morocco than there

A SMALL FRENCH–FRENCH LEXIS
(black Africa)[225]

ambiance	'fête' (Zaire)
ambianceur	'celui qui fait la fête, fêtard' (Zaire)
arachides	'cacahuètes' (Zaire)
(en) *arbre*	'(en) bois; (Rwanda and Burundi)
(faire la) *bouche*	'se vanter'
(serrer la) *bouche*	'refuser de dire la vérité'
boyesse	'domestique de sexe féminin' (Rwanda and Burundi)
boyerie	'logement réservé aux domestiques' (Rwanda and Burundi)
cadavéré	'fainéant, fatigué' (Niger)
chaîne	'fermeture à glissière' (Niger)
deuxième bureau	'maîtresse, amante' (Zaire, Central African Rep.)
(cher) *dit*	'(cher) ami' (Zaire)
essencerie	'poste à essence' (Senegal)
fringueur, sapeur	'qui soigne son aspect vestimentaire' (Congo, Niger)
gâté	'abîmé' (Cameroon, Ivory Coast, Mali, Senegal, Zaire)
grassir	'grossir (pour une femme enceinte)' (Cameroon)
grossir	'grossir, prendre du poids' (Cameroon)
grigriser	'jeter un sort' (Niger)
gros mots	'grands mots, mots savants' (Zaire)
marabouter	'jeter un sort' (whole of West Africa)
mouiller (un cours)	'sécher (un cours)' (Niger)
(avoir des) *serpents*	'avoir des coliques' (Rwanda and Burundi)
(il) *tombe*	'il pleut' (Rwanda and Burundi)
torcher	'éclairer avec une lampe électrique' (Cameroon, Ivory Coast, Central African Rep.)
vidanges	'bouteilles vides' (Zaire)

have been French. Foreigners in Algeria – especially Spaniards but also Italians and Maltese – were naturalised more or less automatically by the law of 1889. Before that, in 1870, autochthonous Jews had been able to acquire French nationality thanks to the Crémieux decree.[226] They were the first beneficiaries of the French educational establishments, whereas Muslims began to attend French schools only from the beginning of the twentieth century.

Nonetheless, as far as Algeria is concerned, we can say that by that time, and especially after 1930, French had already taken hold everywhere.[227] That means that unlike the rest of French-speaking Africa, French took its place in the lives of the people mainly by means of oral communication and not through school. It is equally significant that this was also the date after which the French in Algeria no longer felt the need to learn Arabic.

After independence, every effort was made to institute wholesale arabicisation of education in all three countries of the Maghreb, but there was a more marked decline of French in Algeria than in Tunisia, for example, where President Bourguiba, while proclaiming that Arabic was the national language, was also, with President Leopold Sedar Senghor of Senegal, one of the most ardent defenders of an international organisation for the French language. In Morocco, after a period of intense arabicisation, the government decided in 1958 that it would be more reasonable to restore French to equal status with Arabic, although the latter remained the only official language.

Today, in spite of the inevitable advance of English, French continues to have a privileged status in the three countries of the Maghreb. French sits side by side with Arabic on road and street signs and in all public places. French is taught in all three countries from the third year of primary school (between ten and twenty hours a week).[228]

In secondary education French is the compulsory second language and some subjects, such as mathematics, science and technology, are taught only in French. A survey carried out in Tunisia in 1970 on a hundred children at the end of secondary education showed that in 35 per cent of cases every member of the family spoke French, but the figure rose to 56 per cent if only brothers and sisters were counted. The same survey revealed that there was a preference for French when communicating with officialdom and that children in the playground communicated in both languages, normally mixing French and Arabic in the same sentence.[229] Another survey shows that in every case French is spoken, to varying degrees of correctness, by everybody with a school education in Tunisia.[230]

The femininity of the French 'r'

There is a curious feature of the pronunciation of French in North Africa which divides the population according to sex: the men usually pronounce the French r 'rolled [r] and with the tip of the tongue, as in Italian (and as in France in Molière's time), whereas the women pronounce it at the back of the throat' in the Parisian style [ʁ]. (See the diagrams on p. 173.)

Neither of these pronunciations presents any difficulty for people whose mother tongue is Arabic since in that language both consonants exist and are even used to distinguish between different words. So, for example, the verb meaning 'to send' and the verb meaning 'to get washed' are distinguished by the presence of a rolled r in /jarsəl/ 'he sends' and a French-style r in /jaʁsəl/ 'he gets washed'. Arabic speakers therefore have no particular reason to pronounce the French r in one way rather than the other. Why, then, should there be a difference between men and women on this point?

The explanation[231] can be found in the fact that soldiers and the first teachers in the early years of colonisation pronounced the rolled r. Since at that time only men learnt French, they were also the only ones to learn and pass on that particular pronunciation. When, much later, girls learnt

155

French, it was with teachers who pronounced the *r* at the back of the throat in the French fashion. They are now the ones who spread the norm of the non-rolled *r* and that must to some extent explain why the idea has taken hold that the non-rolled *r* is a characteristic of women.

A survey carried out in Algeria in 1983[232] has confirmed that all women with a school education under the age of forty pronounce *r* at the back of the throat in the French style whereas men are torn between the fear of appearing effeminate and the desire to conform to the scholarly norm.

Before French there was the *sabir*

Another factor must be taken into account in explaining the existence of the rolled *r* in North Africa in the early years of colonisation. Before the French arrived, there was already a language which used the rolled *r* and which served as a language of transaction and negotiation between Europeans and the Arabic-speaking population. This language, called a *lingua franca* or *sabir*, combined Italian, Spanish, Portuguese and Arabic words in a syntax reduced to the bare minimum. It played its role perfectly in commercial exchanges, but had the peculiarity that each party to the exchange thought it was the language of the other person. General Faidherbe noted this in 1884: 'What is curious is that when they use this language the trooper is convinced that he is speaking Arabic and the Arab is convinced that he is speaking French.'[233]

This language was very widespread in North Africa and also in the Near East, and when, in 1834, Gérard de Nerval wanted to make himself understood in Lebanon, where French was only just beginning to be spoken, he used the *sabir* or *lingua franca*. In fact, even though they may not know it, many people have come into contact with *sabir* in *Le Bourgeois gentilhomme* (Act IV, Scene v) in which Molière mischievously makes Monsieur Jourdain think that it is Turkish. (See table p. 157.)

And the Pieds-Noirs?

Under colonisation the peoples of the Maghreb did not learn French only at school. They spoke it every day with the European colonisers, the French of North Africa whose language was a special kind of regional variety.

When the Pieds-Noirs – a name given originally only to the Algerian French but later also to those from Tunisia and Morocco – returned to France in the 1960s, their voluble dialect with its singing intonations became better known. To get some idea of it, you only have to listen to the songs of Enrico Macias, the sketches of Guy Bedos or Michel Boujenah, some of the films of Roger Hanin or the comedy *La famille Hernandez*.

MOLIÈRE'S GRAND TURK WASN'T SPEAKING TURKISH

The language in this passage from *Le Bourgeois gentilhomme* is not an invention of Molière, who was using the *sabir*, a simplified language formed from Spanish, Italian and Arabic words which was used for a long time as the language of commerce between all the countries around the Mediterranean. It was also called *lingua franca*.

Sabir	*Translation*
Se te sabir,	Si toi savoir,
Te respondir;	Toi répondre;
Se non sabir,	Si toi pas savoir,
Tazir, tazir.	Te taire, te taire.
Mi star Mufti.	Moi être Mufti.
Ti qui star ti?	Toi, qui être toi?
Non intendir:	Toi pas comprendre:
Tazir, tazir.	Te taire, te taire.

Molière, *Le Bourgeois gentilhomme*, Act IV, Scene v

A SMALL FRENCH–FRENCH LEXIS
(North Africa)

à la baballah	'à la hâte, n'importe comment'[x]
(faire des) *balbizes*	'faire des choses insignifiantes, inutiles et même un peu bêtes'[x]
le *cachoune*	'la cachette'
caillasse	'caillou'
la *chkoumoune*	'le mauvais œil, la poisse'
crier (quelqu'un)	'gronder, engueuler (quelqu'un)'
(je vais) *m'étendre*	'(je vais) me reposer, m'allonger'
estagnon	'bidon d'huile d'olive'[x]
fatigué	'malade'
hlou	'sympathique'
un *kif*	'un plaisir'
kifer	'prendre son pied'
un *kifiste*	'un bon vivant'
mabrouk	'félicitations'
par force	'bien entendu'
(laver le) *par-terre*	'(laver le) sol, le carrelage'
rasra, rasratique	'angoisse, angoissant'
rkik	'peu sympathique, antipathique'
rognonnade	'longe de veau'[xx]
shra	'demeuré, un peu fou'
tchatcher, faire la tchatche	'bavarder, tailler une bavette'[xx]

[x] used mainly in Tunisia.   [xx] used mainly in Algeria.

The table entitled 'A small French–French lexis' (North Africa) (p. 157) contains a few examples of this vocabulary, some items of which have passed into standard French.

5

WHAT IS FRENCH?
Specificity and structure

WHAT IS A LANGUAGE?

The paradox of languages

Diversity of usage, of which only a few aspects have been covered in the preceding pages, is not specific to French. All languages have varieties: a Bavarian does not speak like a Prussian, an English man or woman does not speak like an American or an Australian, nor do they speak like the Scots or the Irish, an Egyptian does not speak like a Moroccan, and a Chinese from Peking does not speak like a Chinese from Hong Kong. And yet linguists themselves do not hesitate to talk about English, German, Arabic or Chinese as if it were a single entity, as if they had forgotten the diversity.

The reason for this is that they have managed to identify a common base behind this diversity which is acknowledged as being inherent in any language. If an English person and an American person manage to understand one another it is doubtless because the diversity can be overcome. Whether it be English, French or any other tongue, a language appears to be an instrument of communication which is entirely original and full of contradictions, being at one and the same time *diverse*, since individuals each use it in their own way and according to their own needs, and necessarily a *unity* for each individual to be able to understand another.

It can be seen then that communication is the central preoccupation of the linguists: their first concern is to establish as precisely as possible those elements which enable communication by the use of languages, which are instruments specifically adapted to this function.

The sounds and words of French

To analyse the sounds and the words of French and understand how they become a system, you have to be willing to work with a number of linguistic concepts which will be briefly explained below. Try not to be put off

159

WHAT IS A LANGUAGE?

Here, summed up in a brief definition in which each word counts, are the features which are indispensable to defining a language:

> A *language* is an instrument of communication by which human experience is analysed, differently in each community, into units endowed with a semantic content and a phonic form, the *monemes*; this form is in turn articulated into distinctive and successive units, the *phonemes*, of which there are a determinate number in each language, and whose nature and mutual relationships also differ from one language to another.
>
> André Martinet

by a small number of rare but indispensable technical terms, and just take the next few pages at a gentle pace.

Words and monemes: the first articulation

To communicate orally, we use what most people call words but which the linguists more accurately call *monemes*. These linguistic units have a spoken form (for example, the French word *fil*) and a meaning (in this case, 'long, fine strand of textile material').

You must not, however, make the mistake of assuming that a moneme always corresponds to a word: in *un grand jardin* there are indeed three monemes and three words (*un* + *grand* + *jardin*), whilst in *un jardinet* there are only two words but, yet again, three monemes ('un' + 'jardin' + 'petit' by means of the diminutive *-et*). A single word can also contain several *monemes*. Thus, in a verbal form like *aimerions* there are three monemes: the moneme 'aimer', the moneme 'conditional' and the moneme 'first person plural'. That is why linguists are somewhat suspicious of the concept *word*, which is clearly identifiable in the written form but somewhat vague in the spoken language, and why they prefer the term *moneme* (which, in some other schools of linguistics, is called *morpheme*, *seme*, etc.).

Monemes, then, are two-sided units:
- a *phonic* side, made up of the sequence of sounds used to pronounce it;
- a *semantic* side, which is the meaning.

We say they are units of meaning. In French, *clé, jardin* and *fil* are units of meaning or *monemes*.

The second articulation: the phonemes

The phonic part of these units of meaning is in turn articulated into elements of a completely different kind, the *phonemes*, units which have only one side, the phonic, with no semantic counterpart. This phonic side appears most clearly when you hear a foreign word without understanding it.

In addition, phonemes have a different function from that of monemes. Their function is not to *signify* but to make *distinctive*: in *fil*, the *f*, the *i* and the *l* have no meaning. But *f* is distinctive in French because it allows us to distinguish *fil* (with an *f*) from *mil* (with an *m*), *vil* (with a *v*), and so on. Likewise, the *i* is distinctive because it allows us to distinguish *fil* from *fol* (with an *o*), *foule* (with *ou*), and so on. And finally the *l* is distinctive because *fil* refers to something different from *figue* (with a *g*) and *fine* (with an *n*).

You will have realised that in *foule* there are only three phonemes (as there are also in *figue* and *fine*), because it is important not to confuse phonemes, which are *distinctive* sounds, with the letters of the alphabet, which are only a rough written representation of them.

We will say that *fil*, *mil*, *vil*, *foule*, *figue*, *fine*, etc. are French *monemes*, while *f*, *m*, *v*, *o*, *ou*, *g*, and *n* are French *phonemes*.

The above is simply a practical application to the French language of the definition of a language given by André Martinet in his *Éléments de linguistique générale*, and it is from this definition that all the principles of functional linguistics flow. (See the example entitled 'What is a language?' on p. 160.)

The 'hard core' of language

The amateur of the French language who has, through the meritorious reading of the preceding chapters, acquired an acute awareness of the multiplicity of forms of French, may now be wondering why the linguists are always itching to complicate life by going in search of the most aberrant forms of French in the tangle of its varieties. Such a reader would no doubt like to be on more solid ground and simply want to be told what the essentials of the language are, in other words on the one hand the basic sounds, the *phonemes*, which are used to form the words (or more precisely the *monemes*), and on the other hand the words themselves, their forms, origins, meanings and combinations.

Well, here at last is the 'hard core' of the language: first the *phonemes* (the sounds) (pp. 162–74) and then the *monemes* (the words), which are in turn described according to their phonic form (pp. 174–80), their graphic form (p. 180), and finally the meanings they carry (pp. 190–205).

THE SOUNDS OF FRENCH

Sounds and letters

As a rule, we all of us write a lot less than we speak. And yet if you ask French people to describe the form of a French word, they will spontaneously give you its written form (even if some of the letters exist only in writing and are never pronounced).

The fact is that the written language has acquired such importance in the history of French that it takes considerable effort to think of the spoken language independently of its written form. And yet in the history of all languages the spoken form has always come before writing, and writing is merely a more or less faithful transposition of the spoken form.

If you want to understand how the French language functions, you should not begin by studying its written form, which is far from being an exact replica. We shall therefore put off problems related to orthography to the next chapter and simply remind ourselves that we must resist the temptation to confuse the sound (in speech) with the letter (in writing): although the word *fil* does indeed consist of three sounds and three letters, the same is not true of *riz* (three letters, two sounds) or *eau* (three letters, only one sound). In what follows, therefore, the terms consonant and vowel will always refer to pronunciation and never to the written letters.

The eighteen basic consonants of French

To form French monemes we make use of *eighteen basic consonants*, the sixteen found at the beginning of the following words:

pain	*fin*	*teint*	*sein*	*chim(panzé)*	*Quint*
bain	*vin*	*daim*	*zinc*	*geint*	*gain*
main		*nain*			

lin rein

and three other consonants: the one found, for example, at the beginning of *yeux* (or *hiatus*) and at the end of *paille* (pronounced like the *y* in *foyer*), the one found at the end of *living* (pronounced as in English), and the one at the end of *vigne*.

The final consonant of *paille*, *veille*, *pille*, *nouille*, etc. (remember that we are talking about pronunciation and not writing) is accepted as French without discussion. The second, more recent, is something of an intruder: it is the sound used at the end of words such as *parking*, *camping* and *lifting*, which are supposedly borrowed from English.

What, the English might well ask, is a *lifting*?

However, we must nowadays agree to incorporate this consonant into the system of French sounds. Every survey[234] in every region shows that until the middle of this century this English phoneme, spelt *ng*, was rendered in French either by the French sound *gn* (as in *vigne*) or the sound *n* (as in *copine*). But if you listen to how people pronounce such words as *parking* or *meeting* nowadays, you will hear a consonant very close to the one we have already noted among southern French speakers following nasal vowels ('le *paing*, c'est très *bong*'). In other words, Modern French now has an extra end consonant: alongside the consonants at the end of *tétine* and *intime* there is final consonant in *lifting* which is perfectly distinct from the other two.

What most French people may not know is that this last word, in spite of appearances, is not really an English word at all. It cannot possibly have been borrowed from English because no English person knows it with this meaning. It is a French creation made by using the ending *-ing*, which has become a French suffix used to form new words. An English-speaking linguist[235] quoting this French form *lifting* in an article written in English felt the need to give an English translation of it in brackets (*face lift*), thereby showing that the term *lifting* on its own was incomprehensible to English speakers. But *lifting* is not the only example. Other French inventions, such as *footing*, *caravaning* and the very recent *zapping* also turn out to be pure products of the French language. Is this to be welcomed or regretted? We shall see later that this new sound fits perfectly well into the traditional system of French consonants.

Putting *niais* and *brugnon* in the same *panier*

The French sound system has thus been enriched by an extra consonant which the phoneticians call a *velar nasal*: *nasal* because in pronunciation some air passes through the nose (as with *m* and *n*), and *velar* because it is pronounced by pressing the back of the tongue against the soft palate or velum (as with the consonants in *Quint* and *gain*). At the same time, however, another nasal consonant which was until recently very much alive is tending nowadays to fall into disuse, especially among young people: the *palatal nasal*, which some people still pronounce in words like *brugnon*, *accompagné* and at the end of *trogne*, is becoming increasingly confused with the sequence *-ni-* found in *niais*, *union* or *panier*. That is why this palatal nasal does not appear in the table of the eighteen basic French consonants.

The thirteen basic vowels

One of the most striking features of French, and one which is a source of difficulty for foreigners learning the language, is the richness of its vowel system. Not content with distinguishing between the ten *oral* vowels in:

lit	*lu*	*loup*
thé	*jeûne*	*paume*
taie	*jeune*	*pomme*
	fa	

it also has at least three *nasal* vowels:

front

frein

franc

That gives a total of thirteen basic vowels, in other words more than twice the number of vowels in Spanish, which has only five (corresponding to the five vowels of the Latin alphabet).

To these we could also add another *oral* vowel, the one in *pâte* and *mâle*, but this vowel is losing ground in modern usage because it is tending increasingly to become confused with the vowel in *patte* and *malle*.

Finally, we could add the long vowel of *maître*, which some people pronounce differently from the short vowel in *mètre*, but the tendency to confuse these two vowels – the long and the short – is even more advanced.

The list of nasal vowels could be completed by including the vowel of *brun*, but as we have already seen (*Three or four nasal vowels?*, p. 124), the modern tendency is to confuse the vowels of *brin* and *brun*, which reduces the number of basic nasal vowels to three.

An audible 'mute *e*'

There is a vowel we have so far said nothing about, even though it plays a large part in the teaching of French pronunciation: it is the vowel known traditionally as the 'mute *e*', which is the name usually given to both the *e* in *melon* or *tenir* (where its pronunciation is optional) and the *e* in *frelon* or *dehors* (where it is obligatory).

Since the pronunciation of this vowel, when it is pronounced, is increasingly the same as the vowel in *feu* or *peur*, it is not necessary nowadays to include it in the table of the French vowel system as a phoneme distinct from /ø/ or /œ/.

In summary, we can say that the basic system of distinctive sounds – or phonemes – in French consists of thirty-one units: eighteen consonants, ten oral vowels and three nasal vowels, which combine to make all the words of the language possible.

THE PHONEMES OF FRENCH

The consonants

	bilabials	labiodentals	dentals	sibilants	fricatives	velars
unvoiced	p	f	t	s	ʃ	k
	pain	*fin*	*teint*	*sein*	*chim*(panzé)	*Quint*
voiced	b	v	d	z	ʒ	g
	bain	*vin*	*daim*	*zinc*	*geint*	*gain*
nasals	m		n			ŋ
	main		*nain*			(parki)*ng*

	j	l	r
	y(aourt)	*lin*	*rein*
	semi-	apical	uvular
	vowel	lateral	spirant

The vowels

oral			nasal	
i	y	u		
lit	*lu*	*loup*		
			ẽ	õ
			frein	*front*
e	ø	o		
thé	*jeûne*	*paume*		
			(œ̃)	ã
			(*brun*)	*franc*
(ε:)	ε	œ	ɔ	
maître	*taie*	*jeune*	*pomme*	
	a	(ɑ)		
	patte	(*pâte*)		

The phonemes in brackets (the vowels of *pâte*, *maître* and *brun*) are nowadays in the process of disappearing. The nasal palatal /ɲ/ of *vigne* has not been shown on the table of consonants because nowadays it is usually replaced by [n+j] as in *panier*.

The sounds represented in writing by *u* in *nuit* and by *ou* in *oui*, called semi-vowels because they do not form a syllable, are to be classed with the phonemes *u* and *ou* heard in *pus* or *pou*.

Why lay the sounds out in tabular form?

You will probably have noticed that the words containing the phonemes included in the basic list (*pain*, *fin*, *teint*, etc. for the consonants, *lit*, *lu*, *loup*, etc. for the vowels) are set out in a certain order in the table of French phonemes. This layout is not random: it is an attempt to emphasise the links between the phonic elements of French. (See table above.)[236]

What the vertical columns represent

Pain, *bain* and *main* have been placed in the same vertical column because their initial consonants are pronounced with the same organs and at the same point in the vocal channel: they are all three pronounced by bringing the lips together – they are *bilabials*. In the next column, *fin* and *vin* are pronounced by placing the upper teeth against the lower lip – they are *labiodentals*. In the third column, *teint*, *daim* and *nain* are pronounced with the tip of the tongue against the upper teeth – they are *dentals*, and so on.

The final consonant of *parking* thus finds its place quite naturally in the table of French consonants at the intersection of the horizontal line *main*, *nain* (because it is a nasal) and the vertical column *Quint*, *gain* (because these three consonants /k, g, ŋ/ are all pronounced at the back of the mouth.

The table is, in fact, representational art

Looking at the French consonant system as it is represented in books on phonology using the signs of the International Phonetic Alphabet:

$$
\begin{array}{cccccc}
p & f & t & s & \int & k \\
b & v & d & z & 3 & g \\
m & & n & & & \eta \\
\hline
& & j & & l & r
\end{array}
$$

one has the impression of being in the presence of pure abstraction, but nothing could be further from the truth. In fact, it is basically a representational table barely masking below the surface the outline of the vocal organs from the outside in: lips, teeth, hard palate, soft palate, uvula . . . (See the diagram on p. 167.)

What the horizontal lines represent

The horizontal lines group together phonemes with an articulatory feature in common, with the first two lines representing *oral* consonants.

What distinguishes the series of consonants on the first line (*pain*, *fin*, *teint*, *sein*, *chim*(panzé), *Quint*) from those on the second line (*bain*, *vin*, *daim*, *zin(c)*, *geint*, *gain*) can be demonstrated by putting your fingers on your Adam's apple and pronouncing one after the other but without pronouncing the vowel that comes after them the *p* of *pain* and then the *b* of *bain*, the *f* of *fin* and then the *v* of *vin* and so on. The small vibrations that you feel in your finger tips for *b*, *v*, etc. are produced by the air passing between two small folds of flesh, called the *vocal cords*, which are situated at the level of the larynx inside the windpipe. They vibrate when *b*, *v*, *d*,

166

PHONATORY APPARATUS

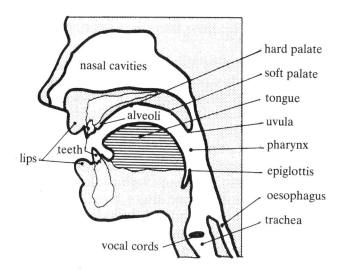

nasal cavities

hard palate
soft palate
tongue
uvula
pharynx
epiglottis
oesophagus
trachea

alveoli

teeth
lips

vocal cords

ARTICULATION OF THE MAIN FRENCH CONSONANTS

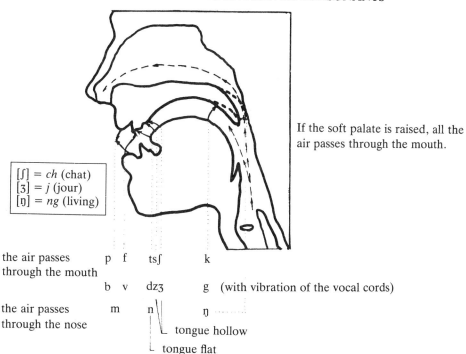

If the soft palate is raised, all the air passes through the mouth.

[ʃ] = *ch* (chat)
[ʒ] = *j* (jour)
[ŋ] = *ng* (living)

the air passes through the mouth   p   f   tsʃ   k

     b   v   dzʒ   g   (with vibration of the vocal cords)

the air passes through the nose   m   n   ŋ

tongue hollow

tongue flat

To make the diagram easier to read, the articulation of the palatals /ɲ/ and /j/, the lateral /l/ and the uvular /r/ [ʁ] has not been shown.

etc. are being pronounced. We say they are the *voiced* consonants, while the consonants *p, f, t*, etc. are called *unvoiced* or *voiceless* because they are pronounced without vibration of the vocal cords.

The terms used by French phoneticians for this phenomenon (*sonore* for voiced and *sourd* for unvoiced) are not the best of choices. *Sourd* also means 'muted' and yet *p, f*, and *s* are quite 'strong' consonants pronounced with considerable muscular tension, whilst *sonore* also means 'resonant' and yet the consonants *b, v* and *d* are more relaxed and 'softer' sounds.

The line *main, nain,* (park)*ing* contains the *nasal* consonants (some of the air passes through the nose), whereas with the initial consonants of the first two lines (*pain, fin* . . . and *bain, vin* . . .), all the air passes through the mouth.

r, l and *ill* are out on a limb

The six voiced, the six unvoiced and the three nasal consonants are thus linked to one another by common articulatory features, with each one of them sharing at least one feature with at least one of the other consonants, a fact which is brought out clearly by the layout of the phonemes in the table.

If the consonants /l/, /r/ and /j/ have not been included in this table, it is because they share no distinctive feature with the other consonants. The consonant in *lin* is the only one in which the air passes along the sides of the tongue. We call it a *lateral*. The consonant in *paille* is the only one to be slightly palatalised: we call it a *palatal semi-vowel*. As for the consonant in *rein*, its mode of articulation, frequently uvular, varies considerably between regions and has been pronounced differently at different times in history, but it has no feature in common with other consonants in the table.

It is comparisons of this type which have allowed linguists to establish that each of the sounds in the table are distinctive units in French.

Not every sound is a phoneme: the various kinds of French 'r'

The preceding analysis may have explained why it is that linguists are so anxious not to confuse sounds with phonemes, because although every phoneme is manifested as a sound, the opposite is not true: not every sound attested in a language is necessarily a phoneme.

If you hear the word *riz* pronounced in the modern Parisian manner, with the consonant *r* articulated against the uvula at the back of the mouth (linguists call it a *uvular frictionless continuant*), or as it was pronounced in Molière's time, in other words by rolling the tip of the tongue (called an *apical vibrant*), the message you get will still be about a 'grass used as a basic foodstuff in many countries, especially in the Far East'. And yet the two pronunciations of the *r* have a very different sound even to the untrained ear of the non-specialist. Nonetheless, no linguist will consider them to be two different phonemes in French, because, whether it is

168

pronounced with a *uvular frictionless continuant* or an *apical vibrant*, the word that is heard will still evoke the same reality: RICE. The different pronunciations will simply give information on the urban or rural origin of the speaker.

Matters would be very different indeed if, instead of pronouncing an *apical vibrant*, the speaker used another consonant, such as an *apical lateral*, in other words an *l*, which is quite close to it. If this second consonant were used, a different meaning would be intended, the meaning of *lit*, 'an item of furniture covered with a mattress on which one can stretch out and go to sleep'. In this case we are no longer talking about mere nuances of pronunciation which allow us to identify the person speaking or guess what region they come from, but of something absolutely fundamental from the linguistic point of view, since replacing the consonant *r* by the consonant *l* enables us to go from the meaning of 'riz' to the meaning of 'lit' and so to modify the message. It is on such differences which are pertinent for communication that linguists base their identification of the basic sounds of a given language and which they call its *phonemes*.

How do we determine the 'hard core'?

We have seen that only some people nowadays distinguish between the vowels of *brin* and *brun*. We say they distinguish between *two* phonemes where others know only *one*.

Similarly, an inhabitant of Cher (see p. 125) who distinguishes between *lapins* (with a nasal vowel followed by a final *-ng*) and *lapin* (with just a nasal vowel) has one more nasal vowel than southerners who tack a consonantal appendix *-ng* on to all final nasal vowels without distinction, which thus prevents them from using the feature to signal a difference in meaning.

We have also seen that there are still some people who distinguish between the vowels of *patte* and *pâte*, whilst others do not, some people (but not all) who pronounce *saule* differently from *sole*. There are also some people (but not all) who distinguish between *sole* and *sol*. This means that people who speak French do not all have the same number or the same set of phonemes.

In such circumstances you might be wondering what criteria we chose to select the phonemes of the basic system, the 'hard core', of French. The choice was guided by observation of the most recent French usages.

Current trends

Surveys conducted over the last fifty years[237] on the pronunciation of French both inside and outside France have all demonstrated a fairly clear and gradual convergence on a phonological system very close to the one which has developed in the crucible that is Paris, while benefiting from contributions from other regions where French is spoken. This confirms the hypothesis that André Martinet and myself made when, in the *Dictionnaire de la prononciation française dans son usage réel*, we chose to describe the pronunciation of seventeen educated people living in the Paris area, but with provincial ties, as representative of a usage which could be taken to be a kind of average of all the various usages of French.

The method of investigation

Before this average can be arrived at, one still has to begin with distinctions that each member of the community makes. In order to rapidly emphasise the phonological distinctions that a given individual makes, different questionnaires were devised using word pairs differing from one another by only one sound, such as *faim/vin*, *pomme/paume*, *mettre/maître*, etc., what the linguists call *minimal pairs*.

The first phonological questionnaire was created by André Martinet,[238] who used it on 400 officers in a prison camp in 1941. I myself have devised a certain number of them.

One of them, in a disguised form, is presented in the table on p. 171 under the title: 'Aunt Riboulet's recipes'. This text is to all appearances about cooking recipes, but in fact it contains words intended to bring out the potential phonological distinctions that a reader may make. Alongside words which allow us to spot the essential distinctions common to the entire population, I have added, not always with much conviction, certain words which might still display historically attested phonemes that have nowadays disappeared in most cases.

From the few experiments that I have undertaken to measure the validity of this little test, I have been able to discover that some French people today still make unsuspected distinctions. Such is the case, for example, of a young Parisian woman, who was twenty seven years old in 1982 and who made a distinction in pronunciation between *fin* and *faim*. Following her reading of 'Aunt Riboulet's recipes', which worked as a kind of litmus test, this young woman explained that she gave a different pronunciation to the final vowels of *crétin* and *certain*, of *pin* and *pain*; she then provided an entire list of words which showed that these really were two distinct phonemes for her. And yet, according to historians of the language, this distinction, although formerly very widespread, has not existed in Paris for centuries.

AUNT RIBOULET'S RECIPES

This text conceals a test to find out what sound system a person uses. It contains what phonologists call *minimal pairs* (see p. 170) such as *jeune/jeûne, pomme/paume* and *brin/brun*.

Even somebody who is not a professional linguist could easily discover many more, but the ability to recognise these almost homonymous pairs will obviously depend on the pronunciation of the person involved. Thus *brin/brun* is not a minimal pair for a young Parisian but is for a southerner. By contrast, *pomme/paume* will be a minimal pair in Paris but not in the south.

Je ne sais pas si je vais me rappeler une des fameuses recettes de ma tante, celle qui était née à Cognac, qui s'était mariée avec un médecin de Maubeuge et qui travaillait rue de la Palx. Quand elle était jeune, je l'ai souvent vue venir installer sa tente sur le terrain de camping qu'elle avait loué près du parking de la mairie. Dans son foyer, tout était prévu car c'était la reine des cuisinières, l'atmosphère était gaie, ses menus attiraient des nuées d'invités, mais une fois toutes les six semaines, ma foi, elle pratiquait le jeûne. Ses recettes, qui enthousiasmaient ses amis, sont assez farfelues, essayez-les si ça vous tente, ou si ça vous chante.

Avec un couteau pointu, elle taillait de grosses rouelles de porc dans le filet, mais vous pouvez aussi mettre un bon morceau de veau, avec un os. Il ne serait pas sot d'utiliser à la rigueur de l'agneau de bonne race, mais c'est plus coûteux. On fait macérer la viande crue, émincée en petits carrés, pendant des heures sous le vasistas, ouvert à cause de la buée, dans une assiette creuse, avec de l'huile, des feuilles de vigne, quelques pommes avec leur peau, ou pelées ou passées au mixer, du citron vert, des grains de pavot et du curcuma – c'est une poudre jaune qu'on trouve facilement parmi les produits exotiques, entre les baies de poivre rose et l'épice aux cinq parfums. Mettez aussi du sel et du piment des îles. N'en mettez pas des tas, ça va piquer! Vous appuyez bien avec la paume de la main, pour que la viande soit bien imprégnée. Mais surtout, il ne faut pas l'égoutter.

Faites cuire ensuite les échalotes hachées dans un bon verre de vin sec, genre muscadet ou bourgogne blanc, jusqu'à ce que le liquide soit complètement évaporé. Je sais qu'elle faisait revenir le tout sur le gaz, mais je ne saurais dire combien de temps elle laissait sa viande mijoter lentement sur le feu baissé. Si, par hasard, la viande est trop desséchée, ne soyez pas malheureux, vous pouvez augmenter l'onctuosité en ajoutant une tasse de lait, à condition de ne pas la noyer. L'ensemble doit être d'un beau ton brun, pas trop foncé. Vingt minutes avant la fin, pour obtenir une sauce bien liée, on met de la crème – au moins un pot – un bouquet d'estragon frais et deux brins de persil. Elle allait le cueillir dehors, même quand il y avait de la boue sur le sol, et le rapportait dans un drôle de petit panier en mauvais état. Elle déposait ensuite sa casserole sur le bout du buffet, à côté de la bibliothèque, dans le living. Elle la plaçait assez haut pour que le chat n'y pose pas les pattes et ne fasse pas de taches, mais chacun pouvait aller humer le plat. Avant de le goûter, elle attendait toujours la fin, ma tata. Faites en autant, si vous n'avez pas trop faim.

Ma tante accompagnait ce plat de champignons sautés ou en beignets, de céleri cru ou d'une jardinière de légumes, d'artichauts violets de Bretagne au beurre fondu ou en soufflé, ou, faute de légumes frais, tout simplement de riz ou même de pâtes, si ce n'était pas une noce ou un jour de fête.

Essayez cette recette. On vous prendra pour un maître. Moi, je l'ai faite au mois de juillet dernier, et j'ai eu du succès. Si vous n'avez pas tout retenu, n'ayez pas honte, je vous l'écrirai et je vous faciliterai la tâche en vous donnant aussi celle de la dorade farcie de crabe et de sole, celle de l'aileron de requin à la nage, du pâté de lion au cresson, de la terrine de renne aux oignons ou enfin celle de l'antilope en daube.

Mais oui, c'est vrai, je le peux!

Language changes

We can see from this that phonetic development often follows totally unexpected paths, to the surprise even of the professional historians of French.

As for the non-specialists, they cannot for the life of them see how a language can change, even if it seems perfectly obvious to them when they consider the language at a remove of several centuries. In fact, everything seems to conspire to cover up the tracks, especially when the language under consideration is French.

On the one hand, the idea people normally have of French is based on the written language. Now, this written form has long since been codified, regulated and stabilised. Therefore, it has apparently not changed. On the other hand, when, in spite of everything we become aware that certain developments have indeed taken place, we have to make a great effort to accept that a language can change without ceasing to function, since, after all, people have continued to communicate and understand one another throughout the whole period.

So let's see if we can find in literature some traces of the spoken language of earlier times.

How French was pronounced at the time of Molière

Let us take another look at *Le Bourgeois gentilhomme* and pay some attention to the lesson given by the philosophy master, because, in explaining to Monsieur Jourdain what the consonants and vowels of French are, he is giving us a veritable description of pronunciation in the seventeenth century. Especially revealing are the details he gives on the articulation of the *d* and the *r*, which were not pronounced then as they are today.

The philosophy master states quite precisely that the *d* is pronounced 'by tapping the tip of the tongue above the upper teeth', in other words rather like the same consonant in modern English, whereas in French nowadays it is more normally pronounced by placing the tongue against, not above, the upper teeth.

The pronunciation of the *r* was even more remote from the one we can hear nowadays, at least in the towns. Molière goes into great detail: it is pronounced 'by raising the tongue to the palate so that, being brushed by the air expelled with force, it yields to it and constantly returns to the same position, making a kind of trembling'. You may perhaps have recognised in this description not the very weak consonant that most French people now pronounce at the back of the mouth – the *uvular frictionless continuant* [ʁ] to be precise – but a consonant in which the tip of the raised tongue repeatedly and rapidly strikes against the front palate, as in Italian and

THE PRONUNCIATION OF 'R'

Nowadays	In Molière's time
The back of the tongue is brought loosely against the uvula and lets the air pass in a continuous stream.	The sound was pronounced not at the back of the mouth but the front, by repeated slight tappings of the tongue above the upper teeth.

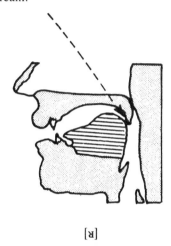

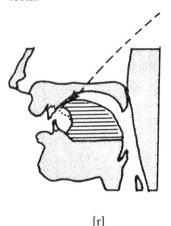

[ʁ]

[r]

Pronunciation of /r/ in Paris nowadays

Pronunciation of /r/ in Molière's time

(uvular frictionless continuant)

(apical vibrant)

Spanish, and also like the rolled *r* which can still frequently be heard in many rural areas, but more rarely in the towns. (See the diagram above.)

This scene from *Le Bourgeois gentilhomme* becomes much more amusing, but this time without the actors realising it, when the actor playing the part of the philosophy master does not realise that, while attempting to describe an *r* rolled on the tip of the tongue, he is actually pronouncing it as he normally does at the back of the mouth. But professional phoneticians are the only ones to enjoy the laughter supplement produced by this involuntary comic effect.

Mec and *mac*

Re-reading Molière confirms then that the *r* was still rolled on the tip of the tongue in the seventeenth century. Closer to our own times we can find

173

evidence, in sound this time, in the films of the 1930s, of forms of pronunciation that have disappeared.

Fifty years ago there was a very clear distinction in Paris between the *a* of *patte*, pronounced very much to the front of the mouth, quite close to *è*, and the *â* of *pâte*, pronounced very much to the back, close to the *o* of *col*. There was at the time a song which began with the words: 'Nuit de Chine, nuit câline, nuit d'amour . . .'. When you hear it nowadays on an old record, you have the impression that the singer is saying not *nuit câline* but *nuit colline*, so back and rounded is her *â*.

In another song from the beginning of the century, Bruant makes *tertre* rhyme with *Montmartre*, which he pronounced *Montmertre*.

Another trace of these former pronunciations which has survived in contemporary usage is the slang word *mec* which is now part of the familiar language of young people. The word is an abbreviation of *maquereau*. So the word *mec* keeps alive the former pronunciation of this word, which was quite close to *mèquereau*. Nowadays, the word *mec* has taken on the more general meaning of 'person of the male sex' and is distinct from *mac*, a new abbreviation of *maquereau* which has kept its initial meaning of 'pimp'. So although both words have the same etymology, we can say that all *macs* are *mecs* but not all *mecs* are necessarily *macs*.

THE FORM OF WORDS

Words and monemes

Let us first recall that the minimal significant units which enable us to communicate are not words but monemes, which is a more precise concept (see the table on p. 160 entitled 'What is a language?'): in the word *fillette* there are two units of meaning, one which obviously corresponds to the meaning 'girl' and the other, manifested by the suffix *-ette*, corresponding to the meaning 'small'. The word *fillette* thus combines two monemes, exactly as there are two separate monemes in *petite fille*, with the separation of the two monemes appearing clearly only in the written form. But let us, for the time being, stick with the spoken form.

The appearance of French words

If you compare French to most other Romance languages, including the dialects of France, what strikes you most is the phonetic 'erosion' the Latin forms underwent to give Modern French vocabulary. The word *foie*, for example, contains only three phonemes in French, whereas in Spanish it has five (*higado*) and in Italian six (*fegato*), two languages in which the consonants of Latin have left perfectly audible traces. In French it takes mental gymnastics to recover the lost consonants, and even that does not

174

always work. You can manage it, for example, for a word like *croire* by thinking of compounds like *crédible* or *crédule*, which were borrowed at a later date from Latin with their original *d* (CREDERE). In *lier* and *nier*, it is a *g* that we have to restore: it can be found in *ligature* and *négation*. But with a word like *oie* we have no means in the lexical inventory of French of rediscovering the *c* of the Latin AUCA, whereas it is still there in the Italian *oca*.

All of which leads us to believe that it must be simpler for a French person to understand Italian than for an Italian to understand French. Because French has *crédible* and *crédule* alongside *croire*, French people can guess without too much effort that the Italian word *credere* means 'croire', whereas French words by contrast provide too few indications to allow an Italian listener to guess what consonant (or vowel) has gone missing. It might be a *d* as in *croire* (Ital. *credere*) or *foi* (Ital. *fede*), but it could also be a *t* as in *roue* (Ital. *ruota*), a *g* as in *tuile* (Ital. *tegola*), or a *q* as in *eau* (Ital. *acqua*), and so on.

French, a language of puns

One of the most important consequences of this highly 'advanced' phonetic development of French for the functioning of the language today is the particularly large number of *homophones*, words with different meanings but which are pronounced in the same way and can therefore not be distinguished by the ear. The series most usually quoted is *sain, saint, sein, ceint, seing, cin(q)*, but there are many others: *ver, vert, vers, ver(re), vair – saut, seau, sot, sceau – temps, tant, taon, tan – nid, ni, nie – roux, roue – trop, trot –* and, for verbs of the first conjugation, the series *aimez, aimer, aimé, aimée*. The list of such homophones is inexhaustible.

This is not a cause for rejoicing if you look at it strictly from the point of view of communication, since what is said by a speaker may be interpreted in several different ways by the listener (even though more often than not the context will tell us unambiguously whether the conversation is about a *sein* or a *saint*, a *saut* or *sot*, *temps* or a *taon*).

On the other hand, however, what expressive possibilities are offered by these ambiguities! What seemed to be an inconvenience then becomes a virtue which writers and poets have made abundant use of for stylistic purposes and which all users of the language are tempted to use for playing with words. Which of us has not at some time or other made use of similarities of sounds conveying different meanings to attempt the occasional pun?

The French language even seems to be *made* for such an exercise, which, on reflection, deserves more consideration than the scorn with which it is usually greeted. It does, after all, require considerable mental agility and some degree of imagination, as well as a good knowledge of the French language. And I have always wondered why, when people have enjoyed themselves playing with words in this way, they usually apologise for making a 'bad' pun. Why 'bad'?

People invariably quote Victor Hugo, who said that 'the pun is the droppings of the spirit on the wing'. But why not quote Valéry? When he advised: 'Entre deux mots, il faut toujours choisir le moindre', he was not above making a pun by playing on the phonic ambiguities of the French language.

The reader may take pleasure in discovering (or re-discovering) in the table on p. 177 other more or less successful, and above all more or less conscious, examples of such plays on words, which seem so typically French when you consider that, for a series of words such as *sain, saint, sein, ceint, cin(q)*, which are pronounced in the same way in French, Italian has forms which make puns completely impossible: *sano, santo, seno, cinto, cinque*. The same would be true of Spanish or Portuguese.

The artful definitions of the crossword puzzles

Crossword clues also take advantage of the plasticity of French vocabulary to play on words and their different phonic or graphic forms. The following are a few definitions which are amusing (especially if read out loud). It should be noted that, even though they may make the crossword solver smile, they offer scant help in finding a solution:

'état de grasse'	=	*obésité*
'objet d'arrhes'	=	*acompte*
'gros maux'	=	*calamités*
'cheik en blanc'	=	*émir*

(Examples taken from Jean Delacour, *Dictionnaire des mots d'esprit*, Paris, 1976)

Different forms with the same meaning

The puns and crossword clues just quoted are based on a property of French that the same sound form, for example the sound [so], can have different meanings, such as 'seau', 'saut', 'sot', etc. Conversely, there are many instances in French vocabulary where the opposite is true and it is the same *meaning* that can be represented by different forms.

In the following twelve words: *aveugle, binocle, monocle, oculaire, oculiste, œil, œillade, œillère, œillet, ophtalmie, ophtalmologiste* and *zieuter*, the same meaning 'eye' is found in six different forms, represented by: *-eugle, -ocle, ocul-, œil-, ophtalm-* and *zieu-*. In this case, in the jargon of the linguists we are dealing with *formal* or *morphological variants* of the same moneme 'œil'.

The wide variety of these forms corresponding to the same meaning is

A FEW PUNS
(intended or otherwise)

Since the *pun* is a play on words based on homonymy, in other words on words having the same sound but different meanings, French is the language *par excellence* of the pun because its particularly advanced phonetic development has left it with many such homonyms.

Entre deux mots, il faut choisir le moindre

(Paul Valéry)

Et le désir s'accroît quand l'effet se recule

(Corneille, *Polyeucte*, I, i, 42)

On s'enlace – Puis un jour – On s'en lasse – C'est l'amour

(Victorien Sardou)

(A coquette who is no spring chicken, simpering to a young man)
– Méfiez-vous, jeune homme, je suis rusée!
– Oh! Madame, c'est un 'r' que vous vous donnez.

(Stendhal, *Correspondance*)

(Elle) Il me faut, disons le mot, cinquante mille francs . . .
(Lui) Par mois?
(Elle) Par vous ou par un autre!

(Sacha Guitry)

Dans ces meubles laqués. rideaux et dais moroses,
Danse, aime, bleu laquais, ris d'oser des mots roses!

(Alphonse Allais)

. . . Mais le bébé, il sait pas,
il sait pas à quel sein se dévouer;
pour lui, c'est la mère à boire . . .
Elle était bonne pour moi, ma mère,
c'était une mère veilleuse.

(Marc Favreau, alias SOL, *Les Œufs limpides*)

. . . les poules sortirent du poulailler (*text dictated . . .*)
dès qu'on leur avait ouvert la porte . . .

. . . les poules sortirent du poulailler (. . . *text written down*)
des cons leur avaient ouvert la porte . . .

(Extract from an anonymous collection of gaffes)

---

not an isolated example in French, where derivation occurs in two different ways: by popular or by learned formation. In the above list, *œil*, *œillade*, *œillère*, *œillet* and *zieuter* are from the ordinary French *œil (or yeux),* whilst *oculiste*, *oculaire*, *monocle*, *binocle* and even *aveugle* are learned words formed directly from the Latin OCULU(S), and *opthalmie*, *ophtalmologiste* are borrowed directly from the Greek OPHTALMOS.

This is one of the original features of French, in which learned words formed, or re-formed, from Latin and Greek constantly mingle with popular formations. This peculiarity explains to some extent the wealth and the complexity of French morphology.

Latin and Greek formations

Borrowing from Latin took place from a very early stage, since it was Latin which served as a model and the main source of lexical renewal from the times of Charlemagne: words such as *figure*, *virginité*, *trinité*, and *vérité*, or *calice*, *candélabre*, *céleste*, *adultère*, *église*, *maculer*, *miracle*, *nature*, *question*, etc. were all borrowed from Latin before the fourteenth century. At that time it was frequently religious vocabulary that was borrowed, but there were also *aromatiser*, *basilic*, *élément*, *occident*, *orient*, *administrer*, *clarifier*, etc., which are of more common usage.

For vocabulary of Greek origin, the borrowing was made either directly or via classical Latin, which had itself borrowed from Greek: *académie*, *emblème*, *épiderme*, *épithète*, *agate*, *apathie*, *archipel*, *athée*, etc., all examples from the sixteenth century.[239]

The situation today

The habit of drawing on Greco-Latin sources is, then, an old one, and the French language has in this respect become quite dogmatic, to the point of rejecting in many cases any derivation from an existing French word. Could we imagine the language coining new words from *nœud*, *loi*, *nain* or *jeu* without going back to the Latin (*nodosité*, *légiférer*, *nanisme*, and *ludique*)?

For words ending in a vowel, popular formations are arrived at by the simple insertion of a *t*:[240] *abri* gives *abriter* and *chapeau* gives *chapeauter*; *café* gives *cafetière*, just as *tabac* gives *tabatière*. The case of *tabac* is an interesting one since *tabatière* contains a *t* where we would have expected the final consonant of the written form to appear; and, indeed, the form *tabaquière* did exist at one time, but it was later reshaped by analogy with the other derivations with *t*. The case of *sirop* giving *siroter* is exactly the same and testifies to being a popular formation, whereas *sirupeux*, derived from the same word, is a learned formation.

Learned formations do not always look learned

Learned and popular formations constantly mingle in the daily language, and, anodyne as they seem, the words *fraternel*, *sécurité*, *fragile* and *frigide* are no longer felt to be learned formations alongside the words *frère*, *sûr*, *frêle* and *froid*, which are by contrast the product of a normal development from Latin to French. The habit has become so strong that nowadays the French quite naturally derive *vocal* from *voix*, *lacté* from *lait*, *céleste* from

FRENCH BETWEEN LATIN AND GREEK

We often talk of the Greco-Latin origin of scientific vocabulary. The same meaning can be rendered by different prefixes, one borrowed from Latin and the other from Greek: AQUA- and HYDRO-, SUPER- and ÉPI-, ÉQUI- and ISO-, etc.

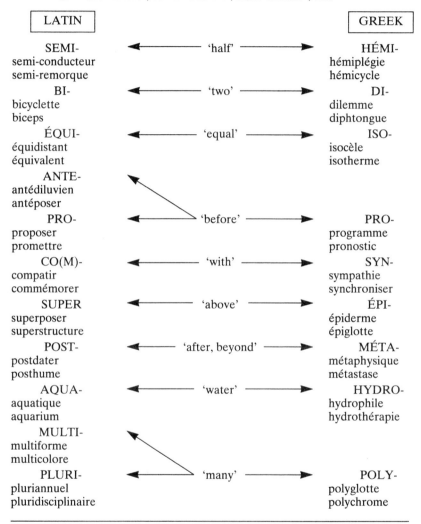

LATIN		GREEK
SEMI- semi-conducteur semi-remorque	⟵ 'half' ⟶	HÉMI- hémiplégie hémicycle
BI- bicyclette biceps	⟵ 'two' ⟶	DI- dilemme diphtongue
ÉQUI- équidistant équivalent	⟵ 'equal' ⟶	ISO- isocèle isotherme
ANTE- antédiluvien antéposer		
PRO- proposer promettre	⟵ 'before' ⟶	PRO- programme pronostic
CO(M)- compatir commémorer	⟵ 'with' ⟶	SYN- sympathie synchroniser
SUPER superposer superstructure	⟵ 'above' ⟶	ÉPI- épiderme épiglotte
POST- postdater posthume	⟵ 'after, beyond' ⟶	MÉTA- métaphysique métastase
AQUA- aquatique aquarium	⟵ 'water' ⟶	HYDRO- hydrophile hydrothérapie
MULTI- multiforme multicolore		
PLURI- pluriannuel pluridisciplinaire	⟵ 'many' ⟶	POLY- polyglotte polychrome

ciel and *maritime* from *mer*, using not the French root but the root of Latin origin.

It is true that in these cases it is difficult to see what else could be done, but what about the next example? For the noun *charité*, the adjective that comes to mind is *charitable*, and yet in recent times the French have taken to referring not to 'œuvres de charité' or 'bonnes œuvres' but to 'organisations *caritatives*', as if this use of the learned term added an extra dose of respectability to these good works.

In a similar vein, the French now more readily refer to a person as *mature* (a word which certainly goes back to the Latin MATURA(M) but is in fact a more recent borrowing from English) rather than calling them *mûre*, an adjective which in theory is a synonym but which the French now prefer to use to describe fruit and vegetables.

The form of words is elastic

In addition to phonetic development, which has reduced the three syllables of the Latin CREDERE to the one syllable of *croire* and the two syllables of ROTA to the one syllable *roue*, there exists another kind of development which affects the length of linguistic utterances: the *chemin de fer métropolitain* was first reduced to *métropolitain* and then to *métro*. Similarly, *voiture automobile* became *automobile* and then *auto*.

These developments are accounted for in information theory, which establishes a relationship between the frequency of a linguistic utterance and its 'cost', which, roughly speaking, means its length: the more an expression is used, the less information it gives, which leads to less effort being made to utter and memorise it. This explains the transition from a long form like *voiture automobile* to the short form *auto*.

You must not, however, imagine that the fate of words is to have ever shorter forms. The history of the word *cinématographe* offers a good illustration of the ability of words to be shortened and lengthened by frequency of use. The invention of the Lumière brothers proved so successful that it led in a very short space of time to the reduced form *cinéma*. The pastime then became so popular that the word was shortened even further to *ciné* (or, for some people, *cinoche*). People went to the *ciné* until the arrival of television began to empty cinema houses everywhere. As the word became less frequent, so its length increased, and people now say they are going to the *cinéma*, once more giving the word a 'cost' more suited to its new frequency of use.

THE WRITTEN WORD

Relegating the spoken language to second place

In the previous chapters we have attempted to bring out the features which characterise spoken French, so giving priority to a form of the language which by a long tradition has been relegated to a position far behind the written form. The prestige attached to the written language goes back to the Middle Ages, to the time when the French language, alongside Latin, had in its turn become a language that was written.

The written language certainly enjoys prestige, but so does its diabolical counterpart, orthography, which comes for many people to mean the language itself.

Like a phoenix arising from the ashes

French orthography has had a bizarre life. For centuries, it borrowed from Latin clothes that were too big for the slimmed-down forms of words that had been wasted away by phonetic development (see *The form of words*, p. 174).

After suffering from the inadequacy of the Latin alphabet to represent the new sounds of French, the spelling of words was then complicated in an attempt to remedy this state of affairs, and in particular to enable distinctions to be made between homophones with different meanings. It has thus gradually developed into the French spelling we know today: tyrannical and often incoherent.

And yet it still has its admirers even now, people who adore what they call its subtleties, but it also has its detractors, who put forward reforms to abolish what they call its aberrations. (See the table p. 182.)

From this battle the existing orthography seems to emerge victorious, since it is still there, immutable and intransigent. Since it has been a compulsory subject at school, the martyrs to it have become legion, and since 1985 it has also had its champions.

Spelling championships

At the very time when it has been discovered that French people no longer know how to spell, the recent success of 'spelling championships' gives an unexpected lie to those who thought people had lost interest in it.

In 1985, the magazine *Lire*, on the initiative of Bernard Pivot, organised the first spelling championships. It was already quite remarkable that over 50,000 people were prepared to pay twenty-five francs for the right to take part in the eliminating heats, but the fact that over five million television viewers sat down to watch the results of the 1986 championships on 6 December of that year completely changes the public image of spelling. More precisely, the figures published by Médiamétrie[241] showed a television audience for the final dictation of more than 1,200,000 people (aged fifteen and over): 700,000 men and 500,000 women, most of them under the age of fifty. They probably all did the dictation, which seems to have lost its image as a punishment and become an entertainment which people play with the same enthusiasm they bring to the television game show 'Les chiffres et les lettres', popular in Britain under the name of 'Countdown'. There is no escaping the facts: spelling is a crowd puller.

AN ANTHOLOGY OF SPELLING CHAOS

The French claim to be Cartesians, and yet what are we to say about their attachment to the oddities of their spelling system, just a few examples of which are to be found below?

The same spelling can be pronounced in different ways:

ch-	[k-]	*ch*iromancien, *ch*oléra	[ʃ-]	*ch*irurgien, *ch*ômage
-qu-	[-k-]	équ*ilibre, équ*arisseur	[-kɥ-]	équ*ilatéral, équ*ateur
oi-	[o-]	*oi*gnon	[-wa-]	m*oi*gnon
-at	[-a]	célib*at*, grab*at*	[-at]	m*at*
-ac	[-a]	tab*ac*, estom*ac*	[-ak]	l*ac*, ham*ac*
-emme	[-am]	f*emme*	[-ɛ]	g*emme*
-am	[-ã]	Ad*am*	[-am]	macad*am*
-et	[-ɛ]	carn*et*, robin*et*	[-ɛt]	n*et*
-er	[-e]	défi*er*, ram*er*	[-ɛr]	fi*er*, am*er*
mon-	[-ø-]	m*on*sieur	[-õ-]	m*on*seigneur
-ieur	[-ø]	monsi*eur*	[-œr]	ri*eur*
-is	[-i]	rad*is*	[-is]	jad*is*
-il	[-i]	gent*il*, fus*il*, out*il*	[-il]	c*il*, ex*il*, prof*il*
-ix	[-i]	crucif*ix*	[-iks]	phén*ix*
-ill-	[-ij-]	f*ill*e, s*ill*age	[-il-]	v*ill*e, v*ill*age
-ils	[-il]	des f*ils* (de fer)	[-is]	des f*ils* (de famille)
-guille	[-gij]	ang*uille*	[-gɥij]	aig*uille*
-baye	[-bɛi]	abb*aye*	[-baj]	cob*aye*
-oya-	[-ɔja-]	g*oya*ve	[-waja-]	v*oya*ge
-tient	[-si]	qui balbu*tient*	[-tjɛ̃]	qui entre*tient*
-vent	[-v]	qui cou*vent*	[-vã-]	au cou*vent*
-tions	[-sjõ]	des por*tions*	[-tjõ]	nous por*tions*

Different spellings for the same pronunciation:

the phoneme /s/		*the phoneme /ã/*		*the phoneme /ɛ̃/*	
s	in *sale*	*an*	in *tant*	*en*	in *moyen*
ss	in *caisse*	*am*	in *camp*	*ein*	in *sein*
ç	in *français*	*ean*	in *Jean*	*ain*	in *sain*
sc	in *sceau*	*en*	in *cent*	*aim*	in *daim*
t	in *inertie*	*em*	in *temps*	*in*	in *brin*
c	in *cité*	*aen*	in *Caen*	*im*	in *timbre*
		aon	in *paon*	*yn*	in *syncope*
				ym	in *thym*

The results, however, were less brilliant. The quite exceptional 1985 semi-finalist distinguished himself by producing a faultless dictation, but the 1986 champion made one and a half mistakes, and the last candidate out of the 117 finalists in 1986 to be given a placing made more than fifteen mistakes (the average number of mistakes for all finalists was seven).[242] We must assume, therefore, that the average French person would have made more than twenty mistakes.

In love with one's own executioner

How can we explain this infatuation with an entertainment which must ultimately bring so little gratification? After all, the majority of the participants by the end of the test could do no more than note their degree of incompetence: making *only* ten or fifteen mistakes in a thirty-five line text ranked them just good average! It would seem that some schoolchildren made more than fifty mistakes, and yet in spite of that a rapid survey revealed that even these young people are scarcely in favour of reforming the spelling system even though it penalises them. So what do they find so fascinating about it?

More generally, how is it possible at one and the same time to consider that spelling should be compulsory and indispensable for schoolchildren whilst accepting as perfectly ordinary that adults in every walk of life should make a total of twenty mistakes in a one-page dictation?

Is this masochism, or do these ardent fans of spelling who respect and adore their own executioner have a taste for the paradoxical? There is no answer to these questions, but one thing alone is certain: none of the recent plans for reform,[243] from the most anodyne to the most daring, will succeed, because public opinion is too divided on this needlessly complicated system of spelling. (See the table on p. 184.)

The golden age of orthography

And yet in Old French things had started out quite well. In spite of the inadequacy of the twenty three letters of the old Latin alphabet (with no distinction between *v* and *u* or *i* and *j*) to represent all the new sounds of the nascent French language, the written form did manage more or less to match the pronunciation: for 'mer' they wrote *mer*, for 'clair' they wrote *cler* and for 'hier' they wrote *ier*.

Writing at that time was almost phonetic, but there were still some difficulties in finding graphic equivalents for the new French sounds. However, we must assume that the minstrels and the poets were reasonably content with it since they knew their texts almost by heart and so had no need to do a proper reading of them.

The great change

Things went bad for spelling in the thirteenth century. The written language was transformed when it was handed over from the poets to the lawyers and their clerks, who were more demanding when it came to the unequivocal identification of written terms which had to be properly read and understood. The graphic forms put on padding and length, and above all they moved increasingly away from the pronunciation of the words.

FOR AND AGAINST SPELLING

Sainte-Beuve	'Spelling is the beginning of literature.'
Alain	'Spelling (. . .) is a form of politeness (. . .). You must dress according to custom, speak not shout, write according to the spelling.'
Colette	'I adore words with a complicated spelling.'
Vialatte	'Spelling is always too simple. It would be as well to make its rules more complicated. . . . When you are in love with the language, you love its difficulties. You love it as it is, like your grandmother with her wrinkles and her warts.'
Théophraste	'What interest is there in simplifying spelling just because young cretins cannot be taught it?'
	(*Les Lettres françaises*, 6 January 1966)
Martinet	'The existence in their language of a grammatical spelling is a terrible handicap for French speakers. If the time they devote to learning it, and so often to no avail, were put to use for other things, a Frenchman would no longer be that gentleman who is ignorant of geography and bad at mental arithmetic.'
Vendryes	'. . . a conventional system set up from start to finish by the determination of a handful of jumped-up scholars.'
Valéry	'The absurdity of our spelling, which is in truth one of the most comical fabrications in the world, is well known. It is an imperious and imperative collection of a large number of etymological mistakes which have been artificially fixed by inexplicable decisions.'
Brunot	'. . . a parasitical plant . . .'
Catach	'French spelling . . . is a mere two centuries behind the times.'
Blanche-Benveniste and Chervel	
	'. . . the spelling cannot be improved upon: since it is a deep-seated disease it can only be eradicated.'

On the walls of the Sorbonne in 1968: 'Spelling is a mandarin.'

Hier replaced *ier*; what had been written *vint* (for 'twenty') was now spelt *vingt*, with the *g* from the Latin VIGINTI restored.

In the Latin alphabet that was used to write French there was no distinction between u and v or i and j, and a French form like *feue* for 'fève', for example, was ambiguous because *v* was the initial form and *u* the internal form for the same letter. On the other hand, the vowel *u* was also written as *u* inside the word and *v* at the beginning.

The absence of accents added to the confusion: the form *feue* could be understood to mean either 'fève' or 'feue' (the feminine of *feu* 'deceased'). So to remove these ambiguities an etymological consonant was added. In the new spelling, the presence of the *b* in *febue* indicated that the letter *u* should not be read as the vowel *u* but the consonant *v*, corresponding to the B of the Latin FABA. Traces of this habit can still be found in the surname *Lefèvre*, which can still be found with the spelling *Lefebvre* or

SPELLING THROUGH THE CENTURIES[246]

12th century	Latin alphabet (23 letters). All written letters corresponded to sounds: *fame* 'femme', *abe* 'abbé', *cler* 'clair'.
13th–15th centuries	To make texts, at that time all manuscript, more legible, unpronounced consonants were added: *debuoir* for 'devoir', *adiouter* for 'ajouter'. Also, *doi* becomes *doigt*, *vile* becomes *huile*, and so on.
16th century	Introduction of the consonants *j* and *v* into written texts. A system of accents on vowels developed by the printers allows superfluous consonants to be eliminated: *école* replaces *eschole*. But orthography as such does not exist. Distinction between *u* and *v*, *i* and *j* to distinguish the vocalic value from the consonantal value. It is not yet codified and several spellings are accepted. The new forms of spelling are adopted more rapidly in Holland and Flanders than in France.
17th century	Orthography becomes the art of writing words according to an accepted model. *-ois* was written for *étois*, *François*, but it was pronounced *-ais*.
18th century	The new orthography triumphs. The use of *é* spreads. The *è* is definitively adopted for words like *succès*, *après* in place of *succes*, *apres*. *-ais* is also adopted for *étais*, *Français* (thanks to Voltaire). Internal consonants disappear: *mesme* becomes *même*, *teste* becomes *tête*, etc. A few slip through the net: *baptême*, *sculpteur*, *dompter*, *cheptel*, etc. The norm of the day is the average practice of the printers. The third edition of the *Dictionnaire de l'Académie* (1740) is the basis of modern spelling, but it takes on a prescriptive role with the sixth edition (1835).
19th century	This edition returns to an etymological spelling, putting back previously suppressed consonants and introducing Greek consonants: *analise* reverts to *analyse* and *misantrope* to *misanthrope*. The birth of grammatical spelling: variation of nouns and adjectives by gender and number, conjugation of the verb and agreement phenomena. Spelling becomes compulsory both in the administration and in the universities. In 1878, the Academy agrees to a twenty-sixth letter: *w* (seventh edition).
20th century	Successive proposals for reform meet with no success. *The Dictionnaire de l'Académie* is no longer used by the printers.

Lefébure, where the *b* is a reminder of the в in the Latin FABER 'blacksmith'.

The confusion between the two letters u and v gave rise to the Christian name *Louis*, which is only one of the two possible readings of (C)LOVIS. This name of Germanic origin was also spelt CLOUIS with an initial *c* which was already weak at the time of the Merovingians and which later disappeared completely.[244]

For the same reasons they wrote *adiouter* (based on the Latin ADJUXTARE 'to add') to indicate by the presence of the *d* that the *i* here represented the consonant *j*. Following the same path, *temps* (Latin TEMPUS) replaced *tems*, and consonants which were never pronounced began to appear in many written words.

You will have noticed that in order to avoid confusing the reader we have made a distinction in the Latin words between the v and the u and the ɪ and the ɪ. But if we were to follow the Roman habit, we would be using the same letter for both u and v and for ɪ and ɪ.

The preoccupation with etymology can also be seen in the writing of the number six which had previously been written with a final *s* (*sis*) and which at this time took an *x* instead on the model of the Latin SEX 'six'. The same fate by analogy lay in store for *dis*, which became *dix*, and all eyes were modestly averted from the fact that *dix* comes from DECE(M) and not DEX.[245]

The abundance of unpronounced letters in the official spellings and in administrative documents caused the malicious gossips to claim that, in addition to their concern to restore the Latin etymologies in order to remove ambiguity, the clerks had another, much more materialistic, aim: like Balzac and Alexandre Dumas in a later century, they were paid by the line.

In fact, many other reasons can be found for this invasion of apparently useless letters, beginning with *legibility*. An initial *h* was added to words like *vile*, *vit*, and *vis* from the thirteenth century onwards, giving *hvile*, *hvit*, *hvis*, so that *vile* 'huile' could be distinguished from *vile* 'ville', *vit* '8' from *vit* 'il vit', or *vis* 'porte' from *vis* 'visage'. Similarly, the *p* added to *lou* not only recalled its Latin origin LUPU(M) but also avoided confusion with *lon* 'l'on' which, if hastily written *by hand*, could not be distinguished from *lou* 'loup'.

It was also to improve legibility that the upstrokes and downstrokes on letters became longer; *un* and *malin* were written *ung* and *maling*; the final *s* of the plural after *e* (pronounced *é*) was written *-ez* (les *bontez*); the final *i* became *y* (*luy*, *celuy*, *vrai*), etc.

As well as greater legibility, there was the *need to distinguish* different words by the use of different written forms. This, for example, may justify the incoherence of *dix* (with an *x* modelled on *six*) by the need to make a distinction between *dix* '10' and *dis* from the verb *dire*. Similarly, in the written form *doigt* could no longer be confused with *doit* from the verb 'devoir', and there could be no confusion between *sain*, *sein*, *saint*, *ceing* or *cin(q)*.

Reformers and traditionalists

Since that time the written form of words has been changed again, torn between the etymologists in love with the past, who took the spelling further and further away from the pronunciation, and the phoneticians, who wanted to do the opposite and bring the two closer together. (See table p. 185.)

Nowadays the French labour under the false impression that this spelling, which nobody dares touch any more, has been fixed for a very long time. The illusion is maintained by the works of the classical authors, who were republished in the nineteenth century with modern spelling. And yet one only has to consult the first edition of *Le Bourgeois gentilhomme*, for example, to see that there is an *s* in *maistre*, that *luy* and *vray* have a final *y* and that *savoir* was still written with its old spelling *sçavoir*. (See table containing the extract from the original text of *Le Bourgeois gentilhomme*, p. 188.)

The *chausse-trap(p)es** of French spelling

And the result of all this? A spelling so difficult that even the most experienced writer and the most learned academic are never sure of themselves. At any time, they might find themselves consulting the dictionary to check

- accents: *zone* but *cône*, *traiter* but *traîner*, *avènement* but *événement* . . .
- double consonants: *siffler* but *persifler*, *charrue* but *chariot*, *savonner* but *époumoner*, *rognonnade* but *oignonade* . . .
- endings: *quincaillier* but *écailler* . . .
- hyphens: *tout à fait* but *c'est-à-dire*, *contrepoison* but *contre-plaqué* . . .
- compound noun plurals: *des gardes-pêche*** but *des garde-robes* and *des garde-manger* . . .
- subtle distinctions between words such as *le fabricant* and *en fabriquant*, expressions such as *un travail fatigant* and *un homme se fatiguant*, derivatives such as *blocage* (from *bloquer*) and *truquage* (from *truquer*), etc.
- and also perhaps the traps which are so well known since Mérimée's

* The spelling of *chausse-trap(p)e* is still controversial because of a recent change of opinion by the Académie (see note p. 223) even though it had decided in committee on 30 November 1961 that the word would be spelt with -*pp*- in the ninth edition of its *Dictionnaire* (1986 *et seq.*). Today we find *chausse-trape* in the *Petit Larousse*, the *Petit Robert*, the *Lexis* and the *Dictionnaire des difficultés de la langue française* (Larousse). The reader is given the choice between *chausse-trape* and *chausse-trappe* in the *Quillet-Flammarion* and *Bordas* dictionaries as well as in Grevisse's *Le Bon Usage* (Duculot). Only Hanse, in the *Nouveau dictionnaire des difficultés du français moderne* (Duculot) recommends writing *chausse-trappe*.
** Meaning of course 'guardians', since for 'boats', the plural would be *des garde-pêche* (without an *s*).

THE SPELLING LESSON IN *LE BOURGEOIS GENTILHOMME*

If you read this original edition of *Le Bourgeois gentilhomme* carefully, you will be able to make out some of the characteristics of spelling in the seventeenth century: *foy, oüy, maistre, vray, r'aprochant*, etc.

52   LE BOURGEOIS
MONSIEUR JOURDAIN.
A, E, A, E Ma foy oüy. Ah que cela eſt beau !
MAISTRE DE PHILOSOPHIE.
Et la voix, I, en r'aprochant encore davantage
les machoires l'une de l'autre , & écartant les
deux coins de la bouche vers les oreilles, A, E, I.
MONSIEUR JOURDAIN.
A, E, I, I, I, I. Cela eſt vray. Vive la Science.
MAISTRE DE PHILOSOPHIE.
La voix, O, ſe forme en r'ouvrant les machoi-
res, & r'aprochant les levres par les deux coins,
le haut & le bas, O.
MONSIEUR JOURDAIN.
O, O. Il n'y a rien de plus juſte. A, E, I , O , I,
O. Cela eſt admirable ! I, O, I, O.
MAISTRE DE PHILOSOPHIE.
L'ouverture de la bouche fait juſtement com-
me un petit rond qui repreſente un O.
MONSIEUR JOURDAIN.
O, O , O. Vous avez raiſon , O. Ah la belle
choſe , que de ſçavoir quelque choſe !
MAISTRE DE PHILOSOPHIE.
La voix, V , ſe forme en r'aprochant les dents
ſans les joindre entierement, & allongeant les
deux levres en dehors , les aprochant auſſi l'u-
ne de l'autre ſans les joindre tout-à-fait, V.
MONSIEUR JOURDAIN.
V, V. Il n'y a rien de plus veritable, V.
MAISTRE DE PHILOSOPHIE.
Vos deux levres s'allongent comme ſi vous
faiſiez la mouë : D'où vient que ſi vous la vou-
lez faire à quelqu'un , & vous moquer de luy ,
vous ne ſçauriez luy dire que V.

The spelling lesson in *Le Bourgeois gentilhomme*. Facsimile of the original edition of Claude Barbin, 1673, plate of the Bibliothèque Nationale.

dictation of *cuisseaux* (de veau) and *cuissots* (de chevreuil), or again the *coquemars bosselés* and the *chlamydes défraîchies* served up to the sagacity of the candidates in the 1986 spelling championships.

NB Do I need to confess that in order to write this page I had to verify all of the words – from *chausse-trap(p)es* to *chlamyde* – in at least one (and sometimes two) dictionaries?

The fascination of spelling

In spite of its useless complications – and perhaps sometimes because of them – we can see the fascination with spelling of all French people today: the educated, those with little schooling, dialect speakers in search of an orthography for their language, those who love the French language, the representatives of the great cultural and political institutions. There is nothing rational in any of this, only an almost sentimental attachment, something like the feeling they have for the châteaux of the Loire, the Sainte-Chapelle or the Eiffel Tower. In these circumstances, one can begin to understand why it is that, in spite of the excellent reasons put forward by the reformers from the sixteenth century to our own day, no reform plan has ever really had any success other than the occasional simplification, which still allowed for the exceptions which, as we all know, prove the rule. Will the new supporters of gradual reform,[247] such as Nina Catach and her team, or of the complete elimination of spelling, such as Claire Blanche-Benveniste and André Chervel,[248] manage to convince those who write French every day that 'modern spelling conventions are not in the interests of the users'?[249]

André Martinet's experiment with *alfonic*

With *alfonic*[250] André Martinet was not proposing a spelling reform but a tool to make it easier to teach schoolchildren how to read and write French. By using the alfonic writing system, children could start from what they knew: their own pronunciation.

Working from the results of various phonological surveys which enabled him to establish the system of basic sounds common to most French usages, André Martinet developed a writing system which used only the characters available on the keyboard of French typewriters, thus making it possible to put off to a later stage the process of learning the difficult spelling system of French.

Diverging as little as possible from French habits, each French phoneme was assigned a letter of the alphabet, which might be modified by a diacritic (accent, diæresis, etc.). Thus, the diæresis added to the vowels *e, a, o* and *æ* provided a notation for the four nasal vowels: ë in *bain*, ä in *banc*, ö in

189

bon and œ̈ in *brun*; the circumflex provided a distinction between the closed vowel of *paume* (*pôm* in alfonic) and the open vowel of *pomme* (*pom* without an accent in alfonic); the grave accent distinguished between the final open vowel of *près* (*prè* in alfonic) and the final closed vowel of *pré* (*pre* with no accent in alfonic).

In this way, in alfonic each element of the phonological system had a corresponding written form:

Oral vowels			Nasal vowels		Consonants					
i	u	w			p	f	t	s	h	c
e	(œ̈)	ô	ë	(œ̈)	b	v	d	z	j	g
è	œ	o	ä	ö	m	n				g̈
	a	(â)								
									y	l r

It can be seen that *w* represents the vowel spelt by the sequence *ou* in the traditional spelling, whilst *h* represents the *ch* of normal spelling. The letters *c* and *g* always have the sounds that they normally have in words such as *cou* and *goût* (*cw* and *gw* in alfonic). Finally, *y* always represents the sound that is heard at the end of the word *abeille* (*abey* in alfonic), whilst the sound heard at the end of *montagne* is rendered by the sequence *ny* (*mötany* in alfonic), and the sound at the end of *camping* is represented by *g̈* (*cäpig̈* in alfonic).

Teachers under the supervision of Jeanne Martinet used this learning aid with children just beginning primary school (five years old) with results that were quite astonishing. The children very quickly learnt to write and to compose long stories in alfonic completely on their own. They developed a liking for the exercise, which also had the paradoxical effect of developing in them an intense curiosity for the oddities of spelling which turned into a kind of game rather than a source of inhibition.

THE MEANING OF WORDS

Analysing meaning

Unless you are talking nonsense – and even then – there is always meaning behind the words you utter, and meaning, like form, can be analysed. We have just seen that the form of words, whether written or phonic, can be decomposed into its constituent elements. Thus, the written form *botte* can be analysed into five letters and its phonic form into three phonemes /b ɔ t/. But how can we analyse the meaning of *botte*?

Dictionary definitions give descriptions rather than analyses: for example, for *botte* we find: 'leather or rubber footwear for covering the foot and leg and sometimes the thigh' (*Petit Robert*) or 'leather or rubber footwear extending beyond the foot to the knee' (*Petit Larousse*). Both of

SEVENTY-FIVE WORDS FOR SHOE

The wealth of French words for money is proverbial, but the same is true when it comes to footwear, as is shown by the following list, which is far from exhaustive.

après-ski	babouche	bain de mer	ballerine	basket
bateau	boot	bootee	botte	bottillon
bottine	botton	brodequin	camarguaise	Céline
Chanel	charentaise	Charles IX	chausson	chausson de lisière
chausson de pointe		chaussure	Church	clap-clap
Clarks	cothurne	creeper	croquenot	cuissarde
Derby	Doc Martens	écrase-merde	escafignon	escarpin
espadrille	galoche	gégène	godasse	godillot
grolle	Knep	Lamballe	méduse	mocassin
moon-boot	mule	mule du pape	Nike (roots)	nu-pieds
Oxford	pantoufle	pataugas	péniche	pigache
pompe	poulaine	rangers	ribouis	richelieu
sabot	Salomé	sandale	sandalette	santiag
savate	snow-boot	socque	sorlot	soulier
spartiate	tatane	tennis	tongue	trotteur
Weston				

these descriptions talk of leather and rubber, but those features are not inherent to the meaning of *botte*, since footwear can also be made of plastic or cloth. By contrast, the word *botte* cannot be applied to footwear which stops at the foot. Thus, the component of meaning 'rising above the foot' is specific to *botte* among all other types of footwear.

Seventy-five words for shoe

It is by comparing the various terms which express the concept of footwear in French that we can try to analyse the meaning of each one into its various components. A 1985 study[251] has shown that there are at least seventy-five different words to express this concept. (See the table above.)

We have seen that one essential feature of the meaning of *botte* is 'rising above the foot'. The *cuissarde* and the *bottine* are also types of *bottes*, but they each carry an additional component of meaning: 'rising to the thigh' in the case of *cuissarde* and 'stopping at the ankle' in the case of *bottine*. In none of these types of shoe does the material (leather, rubber, cloth) have a part to play in the choice of the word to use.

This is not the case with *galoche* or *sabot*, which can only be used for footwear with wooden soles, however, a recent innovation, *sabot de jardin*, means that the word *sabot* has lost the distinctive feature of meaning 'wooden-soled', since the new type of shoe is made of either rubber or plastic. Comparing *galoche* and *sabot* with *tennis* or *basket* brings out this component of meaning. The last two words refer to footwear with flexible soles and cloth uppers, and they differ from one another in that the *basket* comes up to the ankle while the *tennis* leaves the instep bare.

We could try to pursue the analysis and set up the 'system' of words designating footwear by grouping together in a table, as we did for the vowels and consonants, the lexical units which have at least one component of meaning in common with the rest of the system. We can easily see how *cuissarde*, *botte*, *bottine* and *boot* can be grouped together by their common component 'rising above the foot', just as *galoche* and *sabot* share the common feature 'having a wooden sole', and so on.

Unfortunately, we would have to leave out of the table many units which have no feature in common with the others apart from those which constitute the general notion of footwear: 'item of clothing worn on the foot and having a sole'. For example, the *santiag* groups together several components of meaning which are inseparable and form a whole: the feature 'rising above the foot' combines with 'made of leather' and 'with a pointed tip' and 'with a slanted heel'. This complex combination of meanings cannot be subdivided, since all of these features are necessary to define a *santiag*.

This characteristic of *santiag* (as also of *mule du pape*, *poulaine* and *espadrille*) is reminiscent of the phonemes /l/ and /r/ in French which share no pertinent feature with the other units of the phonological system. (See *r, l and ill are out on a limb*, p. 168.)

What makes the lexical system different from the phonological system is the fact that the links between lexical units – which are features of *meaning* rather than *articulation* – are far more numerous and therefore difficult to bring together into one table. Moreover, each component of meaning relates only to a small number of units (out of the many thousands in the language), whereas in phonology a small number of pertinent articulatory features applies to a large number of phonemes (which, in addition, are numbered in dozens rather than many thousands). If we did try to combine lexical units into a table, what would stand out most clearly would be the small number of common features and the large number of empty slots.

The meaning behind words

You will probably have noticed that, whereas a large part of the phonological system (what we have called the basic sounds of French) is shared and accepted with only a few exceptions by all speakers of French, there is far less agreement on the meaning of words.

Of the two dictionaries quoted above one says that the *botte* 'stops at the knee' (the *Petit Larousse*) while the other says that it may 'come up to the thigh' (the *Petit Robert*). In other words, the *Petit Robert* puts the *cuissarde* in the same group as *botte* while the *Petit Larousse* does not. Each dictionary gives the words a slightly different meaning. In the circumstances, you may begin to understand how a word may over time change meaning just as it changes form.

Forgotten meanings

If you look hard, you will find words which have remained virtually unchanged in meaning since the Latin.[252] That is the case with *barbe*, *bœuf*, *eau*, *fleur*, *fondre*, *mer*, *miel*, *nuire*, *rire*, *sain*, *saluer*, *sauver*, *tel*, *tonner*, *venin*, *vie*, *vieux*, *vouloir* and so on. But more often than not there are forgotten meanings lurking behind French words.

Who, other than experts in etymology, is aware of the presence of 'deux' in *diviser*, of 'trois' in *trancher*, of 'quatre' in *écarter*, *écarteler*, *équarrir*, *quartie*r, and *cahier*, of 'cinq' in *esquinter* or of 'dix' in *décimer*? (See the table on p. 194.)

Who thinks of 'vert' in *verger* (from the Latin VIRIDIARIUM)? Who recognises 'œuvrer', in other words 'travailler', in *jour ouvrable* (Latin OPERARE)?

Who can see 'eau' in *évier*? And who would suspect that *haschisch* is hiding an 'assassin'?

What's so special about 4, 22, 31 or 400?

Doing etymology means trying to find the history of words behind their present form and meaning. If you do not know that the public square in front of the Hôtel de Ville in Paris originally went all the way down to the banks of the Seine and that it was there on the water's edge (*grève*) that unemployed workers gathered to look for work, then you will not understand the link between the water's edge and the fact of not working in the expression *faire la grève*.

Why do we say *se mettre sur son trente et un* rather than *sur son vingt et un* or *son quarante et un*? Opinions differ on this, but the solution might be found in the deformation into *trente et un* of the word *trentain*, which used to refer to a high-quality material with a warp of thirty times a hundred threads. Putting on one's *trentain* must have been something people did only for the grand occasions, just as nowadays we put on our *trente et un*.

The expression *faire le diable à quatre* goes back to the fifteenth century. At that time stage plays showed not only saints but demons who indulged in devilry. There were 'little devilries' acted by two devils and 'large devilries' with four devils who created a tremendous noise to portray the torments of hell. When we use the expression *faire le diable à quatre*, we little suspect that we are talking about real devils.

The expression *faire les quatre cents coups* has existed only since the seventeenth century, more precisely since 1622, when Louis XIII ordered four hundred cannon shots to be fired to demonstrate his fighting power to

WHY *SOIXANTE-DIX*?

In Paris, and in France as a whole, *soixante-dix* and the rest of the series have supplanted the traditional forms *septante* and *nonante*, which are standard in Belgium and Switzerland, and *huitante* and *octante*, which are more rare in those countries.

To explain these innovations – *septante* was still common in Paris in the eighteenth century – André Martinet (in 'Soixante-dix and the others . . .', *Interlinguistica*: *Festschrift zum Geburtstag von Mario Wandruszka*, Tübingen, Niemeyer, 1971) recalls how these forms are learnt by children: not like ordinary words but by counting the units one by one. Children who know how to count (. . . *huit*, *neuf*, *dix*, *onze* . . .) may, when they get to *soixante-neuf*, be tempted to carry on with *soixante-dix* rather than *septante*. To begin with, their parents would have corrected them, but then the day came when neither children nor adults replaced *soixante-dix* by the correct form *septante*, and so *soixante-dix* became the accepted usage. French is not the only language to contain such aberrations. Danish has similar complications for numbers, starting with fifty which it expresses as 'two twenties plus half of the third twenty'.

We should also remember that there was a time when simple folk did their calculations by counting to twenty and then making a notch in a stick for twenty. (Compare the English *score* which means both 'twenty' and 'notch'.) They would then start again at *one* and count up to *two twenties* (two notches), and then again from *one* to *three twenties* (*trois vingts*), from *one* to *four twenties* (*quatre vingts*) . . . to *fifteen twenties* (*quinze vingts*), and so on, which explains the presence of the plural -*s* on *vingt*.

Beyond *soixante-dix-neuf* they landed on *soixante et vingt* which vied with the frequently used *quatre-vingts* to express the same number, and this finally won the day.

2, 3, 4 . . . 10, THINLY DISGUISED

Behind their modern form you can see more or less clearly:

2 in *diviser*
3 (Lat. TRES) in *trancher*
4 (Lat. QUATTUOR) *in équarrir*, *écarteler*
5 (Lat. QUINQUE) in *esquinter*
6 (Lat. SEXTA 'sixth' [hour]) in *sieste*
7 (Lat. SEPTEM) in *semaine*
8 (Lat. OCTO(BER) 'eighth' [Roman month]) in *octobre*
9 (Lat. NOVEM(BER) 'ninth' [Roman month]) in *novembre*
10 (Lat. DECEM) in *décimer*

---

the besieged people of Montauban. They weren't impressed. The expression has survived, although its military meaning has given way to another meaning which is just as rowdy.

The origin of the expression *vingt-deux!*, meaning 'watch out, here come the authorities', is much more incredible. It is said that the first typographers warned one another that the foreman (the 'chef d'atelier') was coming by using a coded signal that the latter could not understand. *Vingt-deux* means 'chef' because that word consists of a *c* (the third letter of the alphabet), an *h* (eighth letter), an *e* (fifth letter) and an *f* (sixth letter), and 3 + 8 + 5 + 6 = 22! *Se non è vero, è ben trovato!*

Words and the world

These few examples show us to what extent the signifying part of words and phrases is linked to the reality of the world, people, mentalities and history. If they are to try to analyse it, linguists must become historians, sociologists, psychologists and sometimes even detectives. Every word has its own history and goes immeasurably beyond language itself into the world around us.

Obviously, the hundreds of thousands of words in the French language cannot be presented even briefly in these few pages. I shall therefore follow the principle adopted throughout this book and look at just two series of words which, by their history have one point in common: the fact of having been a proper noun (surnames in the first case, geographical names in the second) before becoming a French noun, verb or adjective.

Eugène Poubelle, for example, was a *préfet* of the Seine, and it was he who, at the end of the nineteenth century, ordered Parisians to put their rubbish in containers which we now call *poubelles*. In the jargon of the grammarians, words such as *poubelle*, *lavallière*, *savarin* or *guillotine* are called *antonomasia*.

Among the examples taken from place-names we have the verb *limoger*, formed from Limoges, because a number of incompetent generals were sent to that town at the beginning of the First World War.[253]

Béchamel, Guillotin, Praslin and Co.

Let us take a look at words which come from the name of an historical person. First of all, we will find a large number of names of plants: *begonia*, *bougainvillée*, *camélia*, *dahlia*, *fuchsia*, *gardénia*, *hortensia* and *magnolia*, as well as *nicotine*, a substance extracted from tobacco or the 'herbe à Nicot'.

Another large group contains the units of measurement used in physics which have generally been derived from the names of scientists: *ampère*, *joule*, *newton*, *watt*, and so on.

Other words relate to:

– architecture: *mansarde, mausolée, vespasienne*;
– cookery: *béchamel, frangipane, parmentier, praline, sandwich, savarin*;
– technology: *bakélite, cardan, macadam, montgolfière, quinquet, rustine*;
– social life: *barème, belote, boycotter, gallup*;
– weaponry: *browning, chassepot, colt, lebel, guillotine*.

Other words, such as *guillemets, lapalissade*, etc., are difficult to classify.

I have gathered together for you in an 'imaginary cemetery' the names of people whose memory is preserved every day in the French language. 'Obituaries' are provided to explain how they got from the 'cemetery' to the dictionary. (See the table 'Obituaries' on pp. 197–9.)

Corbillard, mayonnaise, cravate and Co.

Words coming from the name of a place or a people have been put on maps. Because names of wines, alcoholic drinks and cheeses are so numerous in France and the Mediterranean basin, they have not been included in this list but have been given a map of their own.

You might like to see if you share the reputation the French are said to have of being duffers when it comes to geography. Read the words printed over their place of origin and try to guess the corresponding geographical name. It should be quite easy if you remember that changes may have to be made to allow for derivation, phonetic development or simply the distortions a word undergoes when it travels. (See maps pp. 200–3.)

Words from the four corners of the world

Not all the words that have made the transition from the atlas to the French language can be spotted at first glance. Whereas *apache* and *charleston* (North America), *indigo, madras* and *malabar* (India) and *bougie* (Algeria) are quite transparent, you have to begin thinking about the effects of derivation with *limousine* (from *Limousin*), *corbillard* (from *Corbeil*), *baïonnette* (from *Bayonne*) or *mousseline* (from *Mossoul*, the Iraqi town where the material was made).

You have to have some knowledge of the historical phonetics of French to recognise the word *beige* as the result of a development from *Bético*, a province of south-east Spain famous for its wool. We should add that the first meaning of *beige* was 'the colour of natural wool'. The same effort of transposition has to be made to understand that *pêche* (the fruit) comes from *persica* ('of Persia') or that *coing* comes from *Cydonea* (a town in Crete where this type of apple was grown).

Finally, *satin* and *kaolin* are French-style transpositions of the names of the Chinese towns *Zaitun* and *Kao-Ling*, just as *chicotin* is a modified form

'OBITUARIES'

The following 'obituaries' will remind those who might have forgotten why certain people bequeathed their name to the French language.

Al-Khowarizmi called Algorismi (780–850), Persian mathematician, inventor of algebra and introducer into Europe of 'Arabic' numerals and the decimal number system, known at the time as *algorithme*.

Ampère (André Marie) (1775–1836), French physicist, gave his name to the unit of electric current (*ampère*).

Baekeland (Leo Hendrick) (1863–1944), Belgian chemist who discovered *bakélite*.

Barrême (François) (1640–1703), French mathematician, author of 'Les comptes faits du grand commerce' from which was taken the word: *barème*.

Béchamel (Louis de) (1630–1703), financier and famous gourmet (sauce *béchamel*).

Bégon (Michel) (18th century), intendant of Saint-Domingue (*bégonia*).

Belot (F.) (20th century), devised the rules of a Dutch game: *belote*.

Bloomer (Amelia) (1818–94), made children's clothes fashionable (*bloomers*).

Bougainville (Louis Antoine, Count of) (1729–1811), French navigator, brought back from his voyages the *bougainvillées* or *bougainvilliers*.

Boycott (Charles) (1832–1897), Irish landowner placed in quarantine by his farmers, first example of a *boycott*.

Braille (Louis) (1809–1852), French teacher and organist, inventor of a system of writing for the blind: *braille*.

Browning (John) (1855–1926), American inventor of an automatic pistol (*browning*).

Calepino (Ambrogio) (1435–1511), Italian monk and lexicographer, author of a *Dictionnaire de la langue latine* (*calepin*, nowadays a notebook).

Camelli (18th century), Jesuit missionary who brought the *camellia* or *camélia* back from Asia.

Cardano (Girolamo) (1501–1576), Italian mathematician, inventor of a system of suspension (using a *cardan*) which made compasses insensitive to the movements of the ship.

Chassepot (Antoine Alphonse) (1833–1905), French gunsmith who developed the gun (*chassepot*) used during the war of 1870.

Colt (Samuel) (1814–1862), American inventor of a barrelled pistol, the *colt*.

Coulomb (Charles Augustin, de) (1736–1806), French physicist, gave his name to the unit of quantity of electricity: the *coulomb*.

Curie (Pierre and Marie) (1859–1906 and 1867–1934), French physicists, gave their name to the unit of radioactivity, the *curie*.

Dahl (18th century), Swedish botanist who introduced the *dahlia* from Mexico in 1789.

Faraday (Michael) (1791–1867), English physicist, gave his name to the unit of electrical capacity: the *farad*.

Frangipani (17th century), Italian marquis, inventor of the perfume used in cakes containing *frangipane*.

Fuchs (Leonhart) (1501–1566), Bavarian botanist to whom the French botanist Plumier dedicated the plant he called the *fuchsia*.

Gallup (George Horace) (1901–), American journalist and statistician, founder of an opinion poll institute, hence the name *gallup*.

Garden (Alexander) (18th century), Scottish botanist, gave his name to the *gardénia*.

Godillot (Alexis) (1816–1893), supplier in 1870 of military shoes called *godillots* (subsequently called *godasses*).

Guillemet or Guillaume, printer who suggested putting quotations between quotation marks or *guillemets*.

Guillotin (Joseph) (1738–1814), French doctor and politician, introduced the *guillotine* to cut short (*sic*) the suffering of those condemned to death.

Hertz (Heinrich) (1857–1894), German physicist (the *hertz* is the unit of frequency).

Hortense, wife of the famous clockmaker Lepaute (18th century) to whom the English botanist Commerson dedicated a variety of hydrangea, the *hortensia*.

Joule (James) (1818–1889), English physicist (the *joule* is the unit of energy).

La Palice (Jacques de Chabannes, seigneur de) (1470–1525), Marshal of France, subject of a song which ended with the line: 'A quarter of an hour before he died, he was still alive', the first *lapalissade*.

La Vallière (Louise Françoise) (1644–1710), mistress of Louis XIV, launched the fashion of cravats with a large knot, the *lavallières*.

Lebel (Nicolas) (1838–1891), French officer who helped to develop the gun (*lebel*) used in the Great War.

McAdam (John Loudon) (1756–1836), Scottish engineer, inventor of a system of road-surfacing known as *macadam*.

Magnol (Pierre) (1638–1715), French doctor and botanist whom Linnaeus honoured by giving his name to an American tree, the *magnolia*.

Mansart (François) (1598–1666), French architect who developed the roof known as the *mansarde*.

Massicot (Guillaume) (1797–1870), inventor of a machine for cutting paper (*massicot*).

Mausolus (377–353 BC), satrap of Caria (Asia Minor) whose magnificent tomb was one of the seven wonders of the world: the *Mausolée*.

Michelin (André) (1853–1931), French industrialist, creator of the first automated railway carriage mounted on tyres: the *micheline*.

Montgolfier (Joseph and Étienne) (1740–1810 and 1745–99), French industrialists, inventors of the first hot-air balloons: the *montgolfière*.

Morse (Samuel Finley) (1791–1872), American painter and physicist, inventor of the telegraph and the *morse* code.

Newton (Isaac) (1642–1727), English physicist (the *newton* is the unit of force).

Nicot (Jean) (1530–1600), French ambassador to Portugal, introduced into France the 'herbe à Nicot', in other words tobacco, from which *nicotine* is extracted.

Ohm (Georg Simon) (1789–1854), German physicist (the *ohm* is the unit of electrical resistance).

Parmentier (Antoine) (1737–1813), French agronomist, popularised the growth and consumption of potatoes by devising recipes for them (*parmentier*).

Pascal (Blaise) (1623–1662), French writer and scientist, gave his name to the unit of pressure, the *pascal* (and also, nowadays, to the 500 franc note).

Pasteur (Louis) (1822–1895), French chemist and biologist who specialised in the study of fermentation and *pasteurisation*.

Poubelle (Eugène René) (1831–1907), *préfet* of the Seine, he ordered Parisians to deposit their rubbish in containers: the *poubelles*.

Praslin (Gabriel de Choiseul, duc de Plessis-) (1805–1847), Marshal of France whose cook developed the recipe for *pralines*.

Pullman (George Mortimer) (1831–1897), American industrialist, developed the first railway sleeping cars known as *pullman*.

Quinquet (Antoine) (1745–1803), French pharmacist, perfected the oil lamp invented by Argand by adding a glass shade to it (the *quinquet*).

Raglan (Fitzroy James, Baron) (1788–1855), English general who made fashionable a kind of overcoat (the *raglan*) with the sleeve in one piece with the shoulder.

Rustin (20th century), French industrialist, inventor of a method for repairing inner tubes using *rustines*.

Sandwich (John Montagu, Earl of) (1718–1792), English admiral, a keen gambler, who had meat between two slices of bread (a *sandwich*) served at the gaming-table.

Savarin (Anthelme Brillat-) (1755–1826), French magistrate and gastronome, author of numerous cookery recipes, including one for the *savarin*.

Shrapnel (Henry) (1761–1842), English general and inventor of *shrapnel*, a shell filled with musketballs.

Silhouette (Étienne de) (1709–1767), general controller of finances, who was highly unpopular and caricatured in outline: the *silhouette*.

Vespasian (Titus Flavius) (9–79), Roman emperor who inaugurated the building of the first public urinals: the *vespasiennes*.

Volta (Alessandro, Count) (1745–1827), Italian physicist (the *volt* is the unit of electromotive force).

Watt (James) (1736–1819), Scottish engineer (the *watt* is the unit of power).

---

of *socotrin*, derived from *Socotra*, which is a small island in the south-east of the Red Sea where this variety of aloe used to come from.

Why *dinde* and *colchique*?

Reading these maps may leave you perplexed when you see, for example, that the word *dinde* (for *d'Inde*, compare *coq d'Inde* in Rabelais) is placed over . . . Mexico. And you might like to know why the word *colchique* 'poisonous plant' takes its name from *Colchis*, a former country to the south of the Caucasus famed more for its gold mines and the legend of the golden fleece.

As with antonomasia, each word has its own history. Here are a few indications that will provide some enlightenment on the origins of *dinde* and *colchique*.

Dinde is indeed an abbreviation of *coq d'Inde*, but the India in question

ESKIMOS

APACHES Charleston

Canaries

Sisal

Inde

Curaçao

Tolu

TUPINAMBAS

FRENCH WORDS AND GEOGRAPHICAL

Apaches :	*apache*	Charleston :	*charleston*
Cachemire :	*cachemire*	Curaçao :	*curaçao*
Calicut :	*calicot*	Eskimos :	*esquimaux*
Canaries :	*canari*	Gomen :	*goménol*
Chantoung :	*shantung*	Kao-Ling :	*kaolin*
	d'Inde :	*dinde*	

Mossoul
PERSE CACHEMIRE
CHANTOUNG
Zaitun
Kao-Ling
Moka
Madras
Socotra Calicut
MALABARS
Ternates
Gomen

OCATIONS (FAR-AWAY PLACES)

Madras :	*madras*		Sisal :	*sisal*
Malabar :	*malabar*		Socotra :	*chicotin*
Moka :	*moka*		Ternates :	*tarlatane*
Mossoul :	*mousseline*		Tolu :	*toluène*
Perse :	*pêche, persienne*		Zaitun :	*satin*
	Tupinambas :	*topinambours*		

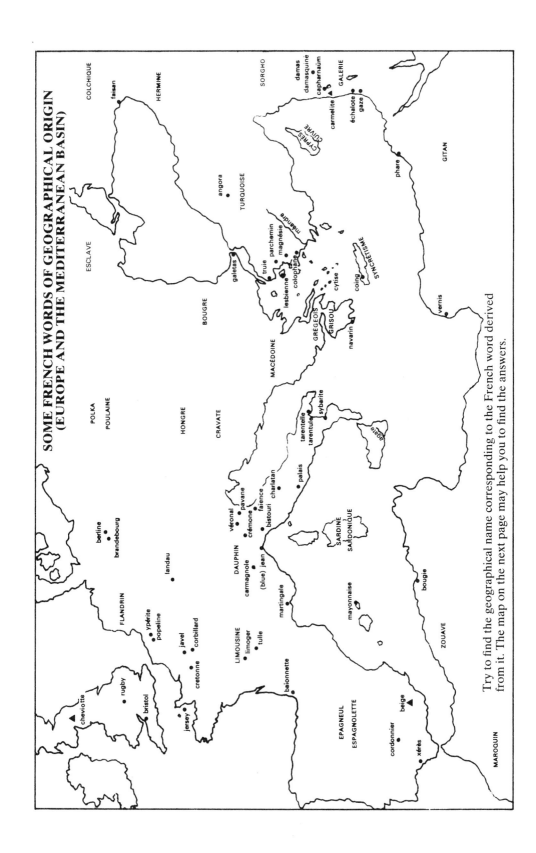

SOME FRENCH WORDS OF GEOGRAPHICAL ORIGIN
(EUROPE AND THE MEDITERRANEAN BASIN)

Try to find the geographical name corresponding to the French word derived from it. The map on the next page may help you to find the answers.

SOME GEOGRAPHICAL NAMES THAT HAVE ENTERED THE FRENCH LANGUAGE (EUROPE AND THE MEDITERRANEAN BASIN)

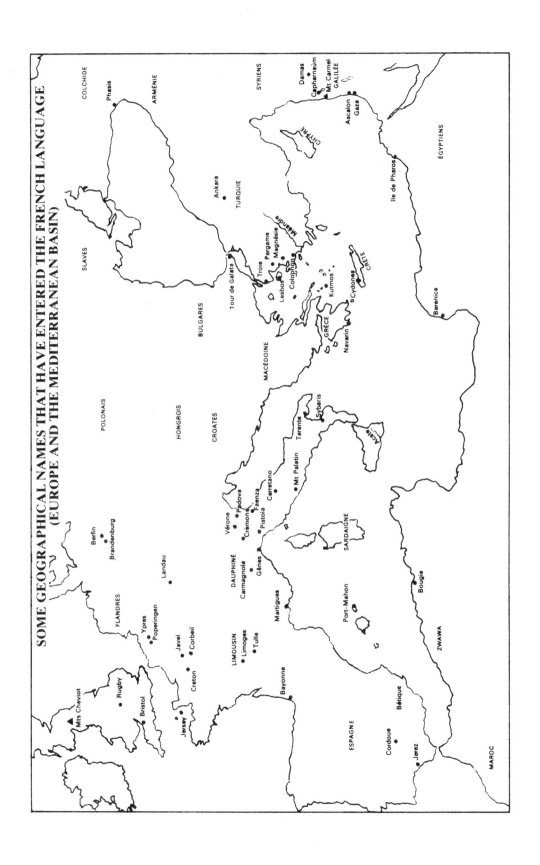

is not modern India but the West Indies which Christopher Columbus thought he had reached when he discovered America. The *coq d'Inde* is therefore the *dindon*, a species of bird discovered by the Spanish in Mexico. Originally, the diminutive *dindon* meant the young of the *dinde*, but in the seventeenth century a new diminutive was formed from *dindon*: *dindonneau*.

To understand why the name *colchique* was given to a poisonous plant, we have to call upon our knowledge of Greek mythology and Euripides' tragedy, *Medea*. It is because Medea came from Colchis and because she was a shameless poisoner that this poisonous plant was called *colchique*, so giving this far-away little region a small place in the vocabulary of French.[254]

Changing meanings

You can see that in the analysis of the meaning and evolution of a word, linguists must venture into a variety of areas, where they are less at ease and where they must call upon other disciplines: science and technology, literature, history, mythology, even politics and psychology. But when they try to understand how a word can change meaning, they are on their own ground.

The ancient art of rhetoric studied changes in meaning from the point of view of the art of writing. It classified with infinite subtlety a hundred figures of speech with the most impressive names,[255] the best known of which are repetition, apostrophe, litotes and irony, and the most scholarly of which are oxymoron and anacoluthon, not to mention synecdoche.

Do we need reminding that litotes consists of saying less to mean more (*Va, je ne te hais point*), that oxymoron is putting together two contradictory words (*cette obscure clarté*) and that anacoluthon is a breakdown in syntactical sequence (*Il dit, et déracine un chêne*)?

Since we are dealing not with the art of writing but with the structure and operation of language, we are only interested here in processes which may affect the meaning of words for the whole of the French community: for example, the passage of the meaning of *feuille* from the leaf of a tree to a leaf of paper, or of *orange* from the fruit to the colour, is a general phenomenon for all French speakers.

We can easily see how we get from one of these terms to the other: by comparison, by analogy, or by *metaphor*, in other words by using an image which is so obvious that it is accepted by everybody. Nobody thinks of the fruit now when we talk about an *orange* dress or *chestnut* hair. In going from the fruit to the colour we are making a *metonymy*, and we are guilty of a *catachresis* when we use an image which was originally based on a mistake but is no longer seen as such: a *wooden tile*, a *plastic glass*, or the phrase *saupoudrer de sucre* (because the correct meaning of *saupoudrer* is 'to sprinkle with salt').

It is usually through successive shifts in meaning, a succession of metaphors, that the meaning of a word evolves. Think, for example, of the development of the meaning of the word *bureau*: originally, *bureau* was a piece of *bure*, a kind of cloth placed on a piece of furniture. Through a succession of metaphors the same term came to mean the furniture itself (the part for the whole, which is a *synecdoche*), then the room in which the item of furniture stood, then the people who work together in the room (*tout le bureau s'est mis en grève*), and finally the abstract notion of an organisation (Le Bureau de l'Assemblée) or a service (Le Deuxième Bureau, the French Intelligence Service).

Whether they are called metaphor, metonymy, synecdoche or even catachresis is of no importance; what interests us is the fact that they are mechanisms for innovation which are an integral part of language. The synecdoches whereby we say *Corbeille* for the Stock Exchange, *petit écran* for television, or *salles obscures* for the cinema become a part of the language when everybody begins to use them.

Individual invention and the language of everybody

It is a characteristic of poets that they innovate, but their inventions usually remain specific to them and exceptional. They use the possibilities of the language in their own personal way and they produce art. In this way, they enrich literature and illustrate the language, but they do not really act on it. *Vêtue de probité et de lin blanc* or *ce toit tranquille où picoraient des focs* are phrases which belong to the realm of literature and art. They do not pass into the ordinary language. They are poetic creations which remain for the most part enshrined in the poem and do not leave it. But all it takes is for an image to be used by other writers or other speakers for it to take its place in everybody's language. Rabelais is said to have been the first to use the word *quintessence* with its new meaning of 'what is best in an idea or an object'. It should be remembered that since the fourteenth century it had been a term in alchemy designating a fifth essence, in other words a fifth element alongside air, water, earth and fire. But nowadays only the meaning initiated by Rabelais survives.

205

6

WHERE IS FRENCH GOING?
Present trends

DEVELOPMENTS IN VOCABULARY

New words

What changes most rapidly in a language is its vocabulary. All it takes is for some public figure to use a word that people had more or less forgotten, or to invent a new word – although that is far less usual since few people dare –, for everybody to feel the need to comment on it, and thereby increase the frequency with which it is used. Many French people will remember the words *volapük*, *chienlit* and *quarteron* made fashionable again by General de Gaulle, or the word *remue-méninges*, invented in 1965 by Louis Armand to replace *brain-storming*, which has virtually passed into everyday language. The mass of lexical units in use at any given time depends on the success of some of them and the balance which is set up between the known vocabulary and the vocabulary used by the community as a whole.

The inventory of words which are actually in use

It is extremely difficult to say how many words there are in a language unless we restrict ourselves to an inventory of the words used, for example, by one single author in just one of his works or in his entire output. The figures arrived at by that method are surprisingly low.

We know that for the spoken language a person needs only the 1,500 words or so of 'elementary French' or, at a more reasonable estimate, the 3,500 words of 'basic French'[256] to be able to hold an ordinary conversation. These estimates were obtained from studies carried out in the 1950s on oral texts spoken by people of all levels of education: the 300,000 words recorded consisted of only 8,000 different words, of which 2,700 appeared only once.

These figures are only slightly higher with a homogeneous, educated population. Twenty years ago an American professor of phonetics[257] recorded his conversations with fifty people from Paris (managers, professional people, academics), who gave him a total corpus of 68,000 words of which only 3,500 were different. And he found that for the entire twenty-four hours of recording with his fifty interlocutors, each of them had, in fact, used less than 2,000 different words in the course of a half-hour conversation.

Obviously, that does not mean that each individual knew only 2,000 words. There are the words we use and the words at our disposal, the words which do appear in speech and the words which might appear. There is a considerable disproportion between the two sets: 5,000 to 6,000 on the one hand and hundreds of thousands on the other. Between this minimum and maximum there is a whole world of possibilities for anybody wanting to write and speak French. And since, on the other hand, the vocabulary is enriched daily by new lexical units created by the needs of communication, it would be no exaggeration to say that the treasure trove of words we can call on is inexhaustible.

Indeed, the word *treasure* was used by the people who, in 1960, began the largest lexical trawl ever undertaken. The *Trésor de la langue française*, a historical lexicon of the French language of the nineteenth and twentieth centuries, the first volume of which appeared in 1971, is based on the analysis of ninety million examples taken from a thousand literary and technical texts of the last two centuries.

The general treasury of the French languages and dialects

Of the sixteen projected volumes, each 1,400 pages long, fourteen have now been published. As a continuation of this work, the documentation centre of the Institut National de la Langue Française in Nancy is overseeing a new programme, the *Trésor général des langues et parlers français*, which has already recorded on computer 260 million words gathered from 2,300 written texts: if we add the 175,000 different words taken from the literary works of the nineteenth and twentieth centuries to the 500,000 technical terms and then add to that the few hundred thousand neologisms recorded since 1960, we arrive at the truly staggering total of more than 1,200,000 different words.[258] To understand the meaning of these figures, which give one a slightly dizzy feeling, one must turn to the inventories themselves.

Two kinds of new word

Rather than drowning in this lexical immensity, let us try simply to see how the vocabulary renews itself nowadays, in what areas and by what means.[259]

Outside of the poets and writers, who have no complexes about creating neologisms but whose innovations tend to remain simply a mark of their personality, we see that the vocabulary is renewing itself in two directions:

207

on the one hand there are the technological innovations which produce new terms, and on the other there are the expressive needs of language users in their daily conversations. Neologisms of the first type are usually concerted, systematised and channelled; the second type are born in a more or less spontaneous, individualistic and disordered way, and their spread is governed by the whims of fashion or the needs of the moment.

As well as springing from a different motivation, these two types of lexical innovations make use of particular methods of formation.

Walkman or *baladeur*?

Generally speaking, modern technological terminology is often character-ised by borrowing purely and simply from English, the word being intro-duced along with the thing. This is the whole problem with words such as *tuner, walkman, compact-disc, video-clip*, etc., for which in 1983[260] the ministerial commissions on terminology proposed respectively *syntoniseur, baladeur, disque audionumérique* and *bande vidéo promotionnelle*.

Although *baladeur* had a short-lived success, the other terms have not been taken up by language users, who continue quite calmly to use the words *tuner, clips* (less often *video-clips*) and *disques compacts* (less often *compact-discs*). It should be noted that in the last case the loan word has been perfectly adapted to the standard type of word formation in French, with the noun preceding its determiner: *disque compact* as in *disque dur, route nationale* or *jambon fumé*.[260] What we are witnessing here is not a phenomenon of alienation but simply an effect of the law of least effort: since the replacements proposed by the commission were longer, more learned, and therefore more difficult to memorise, the loan word has been kept but modified and integrated into the more normal modes of word formation in French. It is especially in this technological area, where they serve a pressing need, that loan words are most frequently found.

Of fast food and franchising

Taking rational advantage of the possibilities of the French language, the scientists have also continued quite normally to forge new words using the prefixes and the suffixes they usually employ for French words (for example, *surgénérateur, radariste, microprocesseur, géostationnaire, anti-histaminique*, etc.).

As a result, we have in recent years witnessed the formation of many verbs ending in *-iser* such as *fidéliser, franchiser, gadgétiser, lyophiliser, médiatiser, publiciser*, and *transistoriser*, so increasing the frequency of use of this type of formation.

Many of these words have obviously been formed from English words. The word *gadget*, for example, has given rise to a whole series of derivatives in the purest French tradition: *gadgetière, gadgétisation, gadgétophile*, etc. On the other hand, as a kind of chauvinistic reaction to the *fast foods*, those American-style restaurants where you can get a quick meal at a reasonable price, there has been a veritable profusion of *briocheries*, *croissanteries* and *grilladeries*, neologisms based on French words.

The suffix *-erie* has thus taken on a new lease of life as a productive form: nowadays you can find *bagageries, jardineries, chausseries, sweateries* and *pulleries*, where you can buy sweaters, not to mention *dogueries*, which looks a bit like a joke, where you can buy everything for dogs.

Even in the realm of computers, where English normally dominates, the words *ordinateur* and *logiciel* have replaced the English words *computer* and *software* which were still frequently used in French ten years ago. The word *logiciel* itself has spawned a whole series of French formations on the same model: *didacticiel, ludiciel, progiciel*, etc. Similarly, *informatique* led to *bureautique, distributique, productique, promotique, télématique*, etc.

In this way the French language shows its capacity to adapt to the new needs of technology, using the resources it has within itself to provide the lexical units needed to name new concepts or new objects.

Among the lexical innovations of recent years let us also quote the term *zapping*, which originally meant 'to change channels' on the television when the commercials came on. The noun *zappeur* also exists and the verb *zapper* is conjugated in every tense. And the term has now widened its meaning to cover changing channels at any time. Surveys conducted among American and English colleagues show that these apparent Americanisms are a special kind of borrowing. Although 'to zap' already had the meaning to 'change TV channels' in English in the mid-eighties, most English and American people still knew it only with the meaning of 'kill, destroy'. What was therefore originally a restricted usage in English became common usage in French from the outset.

Professeure, professeuse, professoresse?

It was also the tendencies specific to French which the Commission de Terminologie[261] sought to use in its final report on the feminisation of job names, ordered by Yvette Roudy, the then Minister for Women's Rights, and presented in March 1986. This report, edited by Benoîte Groult, states that only fifteen out of 5,000 job names offered no immediately obvious feminine form.

Feminisation is obvious and simple for forms which are identical, the so-called epicene forms (un or une *architecte*, un *délégué*/une *déléguée*), as well as in those cases where the masculine ends in a consonant in the written form (*agent/agente, huissier/huissière, mécanicien/mécanicienne*).

209

The *-eur* suffix can be feminised as *-euse* (*monteur/monteuse*), and the *-teur* suffix as *-trice* (*dessinateur/dessinatrice*), with both solutions being possible in some cases (*enquêteuse, enquêtrice*). Some *-eur* nouns already exist in the feminine form (*danseur/danseuse, vendeur/vendeuse*), but *professeur, auteur* and *proviseur* are only used in the masculine. There are several possible solutions here: *professeure* (as in *prieure* or *meilleure*), *professeuse* (as in *danseuse* or *coiffeuse*), or maybe *professoresse* (as in *doctoresse* or *venderesse*) but this last suffix is scarcely productive nowadays.

It is clear, then, that the rejection of the feminine form is not related to some impossibility inherent in the language itself but to a resistance springing from prejudices very deeply rooted in the language users. In fact, the feminisation of forms is rejected, especially for the prestigious professions: *directeur, professeur, chirurgien, docteur* or *avocat*. People accept *repasseuse, bouchère* and even *greffière*, but they balk at the feminisation of *compositeur, ingénieur* and *metteur en scène*.

Women themselves bear some of the responsibility for this reticence: a recent survey showed that 80 per cent of women with a diploma in pharmacy preferred to be called *Madame le pharmacien* rather than *Madame la pharmacienne*. The terms *doctoresse, avocate* and *directrice* are also rejected.

If the French really do want to feminise job names, they will probably have to wait for a change in mentality like the one which has already taken place in Canada, where people are no longer upset by words like *professeure* and *auteure*.

The vocabulary of young people

Whereas word creations of the technical kind pay no attention to the French or foreign origin of the root term, following the rules of word formation which are standard in French, and producing word series which can be easily systematised, lexical creations of the expressive variety have different characteristics.

A new vocabulary originating among young people seems to have been making steady progress over the last few years among the population at large. The first to become aware of an increasing gap between the language of the younger and the older generations were the journalists: publications such as *20 ans*, *Lire*, *Le Nouvel Observateur*, *L'Express* and *Le Quotidien de Paris* have been offering lists of new words with comment and explanation since the beginning of the 1980s.

Assurer and *craindre*

From such publications the 'old folk' (meaning people over twenty-five or thirty) have learnt the meaning of certain words which they had often heard the younger generation using but which they had not understood till then. They were also surprised to discover the new meanings that young people were giving to old words such as *assurer, craindre, méchant* and *bonjour*. They learnt, for example, that although you could continue to *assurer* your car with an insurance company, you could also *assurer* full stop, something which has nothing whatsoever to do with insurance premiums.

In the language of the young, *assurer* is the opposite of *craindre*: speaking of somebody who is competent in a given area, the young say 'il/elle *assure*', but, more subtly – and more inexplicably – they will say that this person *craint* if he or she claims to be competent (claims to *assurer*) but is not really. In other words, if you want to *assurer* it is better to be *un bon*, otherwise you may *craindre*: in the world of young people it is far worse to *craindre* than not to *assurer* (are you still with me?).

Uncertainty among the parents

Nowadays, the use of *assurer* with this new meaning seems pretty well to have spread to the whole of the population and it has been adopted by the advertisers and the media, but *craindre* has not had the same success and is still restricted to the younger generation.

Older people are increasingly aware of the existence of these lexical neologisms. Modern authors frequently feel the need to add a glossary to books and articles about young people, thereby showing that they are dealing with a vocabulary which they understand but which is not familiar to them.

Christiane Collange's book *Moi, ta mère*, published in 1985, is a good example of the kind of attitude parents have towards these innovations. The book, which is about children who do not leave the parental home when they become adults, has an appendix listing some fifty words such as *assurer, buller, cool, dégager, être trop*, and so on. These words are also used in the body of the text, but they are always italicised to show that they are not the author's own words.

A breakdown in communication

The meaning given for *assurer* in Collange's book is 'faire de l'effet, se faire remarquer'. This is not quite the same as the meaning that I myself gave above and which appears in the lexis I compiled for *Les mouvements de mode expliqués aux parents* (1984).[262] This does not mean that one of us

211

has to be wrong. These differences merely illustrate one of the most remarkable features of the new vocabulary: its polysemy. Words have different meanings at the same time and some of these meanings may even be contradictory.[263]

Taken to extremes this polysemy could become dangerous for communication. We do not always know how to interpret *c'était trop* or *il est trop*, which means being impressed either favourably or unfavourably. With expressions such as *Passion!* or *Tu m'étonnes!* the situation is even more difficult for parents, who run the risk of making themselves look ridiculous to their children by taking them too literally. In fact, *Passion!* does not, as you might think, mean 'How interesting!', but is an ironical expression meaning the exact opposite. Similarly, *Tu m'étonnes* is roughly equivalent to an ironic 'Get away!' or 'Never!' in English. *Tu peux être plus flou*? means 'I don't understand a word you're saying, be more clear'. And if you do not know the rules of the game, you may run the risk of *se planter*!

The to-and-fro of lexical evolution

The history of the expression *Bonjour*, used in an advertising slogan on the dangers of alcohol, may serve to illustrate the uncertainties that arise in lexical evolution when an expression is interpreted differently by different users.

Originally, young people used this expression in a purely ironic way to mean 'au revoir, adieu' rather than 'bonjour': 'J'ai perdu mon portefeuille avec mon billet de train. Bonjour les vacances!'

After the much noticed advertisement on the dangers of alcohol, which uses the expression without irony in '. . . trois verres . . . bonjour les dégâts', every television viewer began to use the expression in all seriousness, and, in a boomerang effect, young people also now use the word without irony. It is not always young people who show the way.

Beware of negatives

There are many other words where it is best to be aware of deviations of meaning.

If somebody tells you you have a '*méchante veste*', take it as a compliment, and if you hear somebody say *ça va faire très mal*, expect a runaway success. If somebody says *un peu*, it means 'a lot', and if somebody says of a woman's son that when it comes to computers *c'est la bête*, she should be proud because it means he is a 'champion'. Could this be some kind of revolt against previous generations who were naïve enough to take words literally?

In the same vein, negative forms can be heard which do not mean exactly the opposite of the adjective which follows the negation: *pas évident* is not

212

the opposite of 'obvious' but of 'easy'; *pas aidé* is said of somebody who is slightly 'retarded' or 'not very beautiful'; *pas possible* describes something 'surprising' (which may be either good or bad). The expression *c'était pas triste* will be used to describe a lively and eventful meeting.

New meanings behind old forms

The processes for renewing meaning described above seem to be very common in the world of the young. This manner of speaking has the advantage (or the disadvantage, depending what side you are on) of functioning as a kind of secret language. I would even go so far as to call it doubly secret because it seems just like ordinary language. Thus, 'une fille *d'enfer*' has nothing infernal about her, but is simply very beautiful or highly intelligent; somebody described as *glauque* is 'weird and ambiguous', which is obviously a long way from the original meaning (which most people do not know) of *glauque*: 'greenish-blue'. These surreptitious innovations may go unnoticed for a long time by the uninitiated and create situations of confusion or conflict, so making dialogue between the generations even more difficult.

Changes of form

By contrast, neologisms based on a change of form are eye-catching and cause immediate reactions. One example is the word *galérer*, the meaning of which is not entirely clear but in which we can recognise the word *galère*, and that allows us to guess that it means something like 'to move about' or 'to work hard but get nowhere'. Likewise, the creation of the reflexive form *s'éclater* applied to people clearly excludes the meaning of 'to explode' or 'to shatter' but gives no clue to the fact that it means 'to enjoy thoroughly'. We must also now beware of the adjective *éclatant* which may have the meaning of 'giving enjoyment'.

As for abbreviations such as *accro*, *ado*, *appart*, *caric*, *cata*, *deb*, *doc*, *oc*, *p'tit dej*, *pro* or *pub*, they are harmless as long as they do not lead to ambiguity. But is that always the case? It may take a little while to realise that these are abbreviations for: *accroché*, *adolescent*, *appartement*, *caricature*, *catastrophe*, *débile*, *documentation*, *OK*, *petit déjeuner*, *professionnel*, and *publicité*.

A television crew shooting a documentary on microcomputers recently had a number of misunderstandings between *micro* (the new abbreviation for *micro-ordinateur*) and the old abbreviation *micro* (for *microphone*).

Back slang

We should also say a word or two about *verlan*, or back slang, which has recently been brought back into fashion by young people and which has left some traces in the everyday language thanks to a few hit songs such as *Laisse béton* and films such as *Les Ripoux*. Nowadays, this word-modifying process is less successful. It consists in inverting the syllables of a word (preferably one with fewer than three syllables), but the younger generation did not give their approval to just any innovation. Only those which had proved their effectiveness over a period of time were accepted. *Ripou* for 'pourri', *laisse béton* for 'laisse tomber', *zomblou* for 'blouson', *tromé* for 'métro', *meuf* for 'femme', and so on, have had their hour of glory.

Coded forms and standard language

Back slang is not a novelty. It is a well-known form of word travesty which, until quite recently, was restricted to the slang of certain professions: the *largonji* of the *loucherbems* (or *louchébems*), for example, was a code used by the butchers of La Villette to communicate with one another. The key to the code is simple and the process is effective since the uninitiated will not recognise the word *boucher* behind the word *loucherbem*: the initial consonant *b* is replaced by *l* and transferred to the end of the word, which takes on an extra syllable with a parasitic suffix to complicate matters a little.[264]

Similarly, the word *largonji* is a modified form of the word *jargon* in which the initial *j* is replaced by *l* and goes to the end of the word in its alphabetic form *-ji*. The process is hardly productive nowadays, but some forms have become established and passed into the standard language. Such is the case with *loufoque*, which is *largonji* for *fou* (*louf*) with the suffix *-oque* added to make it unrecognisable. The form was shortened to *louf* from which was subsequently derived *louftingue*. You can still hear the expressions *en loucedé* or *en loucedoque* for 'en douce'.[265]

The argots and argot[266]

The few examples of slang just given apply to a disguised lexis whose rules of formation could, in theory, be applied to all the words of the language. There are many other forms of slang with less systematic rules of formation and which are the secret language of a given body of people. The best known of these slangs is that of the criminal classes, which has left traces in the standard language: *abasourdir, amadouer, boniment, cambrioleur, drille, dupe, godiche, matois, polisson* and *trimer* are all originally slang words which have lost their secretive nature. A *cambrioleur* is a bedroom thief; a *camelot* is both a beggar and a travelling salesman; *amadouer* really means to rub with *amadon* (tinder), which is what the beggars in the Cour des Miracles put on their face to make themselves look ill; a *matois* is somebody facing the *mathe* or gallows; *trimer* comes from the vocabulary of mendicants and originally meant 'to walk'.[267]

Nowadays, there is a tendency to include in the term *argot* three very different types of vocabulary:

- the old *thieves' slang*, of which we have just given a few examples that have passed into ordinary usage;
- the various *modern slangs* which are ways of speaking specific to certain professions or groups of people (the slang of the *polytechniciens*, the *normaliens*, the prisons, etc.) and which are at the same time signals allowing the initiated to recognise one another;
- modern *unconventional* vocabulary which does not respect the traditional social conventions.

Unconventional vocabulary

Wishing to restrict themselves to a study of this last category, Jacques Cellard and Alain Rey preferred to avoid any ambiguity by calling their book the *Dictionnaire du français non conventionnel* (Paris, Hachette, 1980). The authors point in their foreword to the existence of a vocabulary which is indeed highly unconventional and publicly used by people who, for one reason or another, can be considered as authorised representatives of the French language: Professor Louis Leprince-Ringuet calling one of his works *Le Grand Merdier*; the president of the National Assembly exclaiming: *J'en ai marre de ce chahut*; the Prime Minister Raymond Barre declaring that he will *aller au charbon*; the academician Maurice Genevoix confessing: *Nous avons été baisés*, while his colleague Jean d'Ormesson says *l'assassin l'aura dans le cul*, both of them on television during the literary programme 'Apostrophes'. To these we can add, among others and more recently, the newspaper editor Serge July saying on TF1 on 13 May 1987 that Klaus Barbie *avait fait beaucoup de conneries*.

Into oblivion or into the dictionary?

It is too early to give an assessment of the neologisms quoted in this chapter. Some of them will suffer the fate of all fashions: they will become outmoded. Others which are today's exception will become tomorrow's norm. The history of languages has shown many examples of this.

The young have always had a slightly different way of speaking from that of older people, but as they grow older they begin to conform to the established usage. What is new nowadays is that the opposite is happening:

the older generation, with varying degrees of reluctance, are adopting some of the vocabulary of the young.

However, the uncertainties we have seen about the meaning of each word or phrase make this vocabulary fragile and vulnerable: a language containing words which mean two opposite things can function only if such words are the exception. In such cases, there will be a period of uncertainty, after which just one of the contradictory meanings will become accepted.

There is no shortage in the history of languages of cases where the meaning of a word developed into the opposite of what it meant to begin with: for example, *rien* comes from the Latin REM meaning 'something' and *école* comes from the Greek word SCHOLE which meant 'rest, leisure'.

SHIFTS IN GRAMMAR

The evolution of grammatical forms

We have just seen how easily the words in the vocabulary change form and meaning. Grammatical forms (articles, prepositions, conjunctions, etc.) develop much more slowly and the changes are not so readily spotted. The same is true of syntactic structures,[268] which allow us to take utterances made up of a *succession* of words in order to reconstitute the *global* meaning of the message.

Grammar does offer greater resistance to the pressures of society and fashion. There are far fewer grammatical units and they form a proper system, which means that modifying one element of the structure will sooner or later lead to a modification of neighbouring units. Changes in grammar, therefore, take place in a much more insidious manner than those in the lexis. It probably took generations, maybe even centuries, for French to develop adverbs ending in *-ment* from the Latin noun MENS 'mind, manner', or for a new future tense to appear. (See pp. 42–4.) Similarly, the double negative *ne . . . pas, ne . . . point* did not really become obligatory until the seventeenth century. (See p. 63.)

We therefore need to look at all the details of Modern French to locate the slightest indications which could prove, in a few years or a few generations, to be the precursory signs of more radical changes.[269]

A highly advanced development: the past historic

Television recently repeated a programme recorded in 1951 in which André Gide used the past historic to refer to the memory of a great pianist. Now the use of this tense in the spoken language was already rare more than thirty years ago. Nowadays it seems to be almost impossible to use it. Although we can still find modern uses of the tense in the written language, where it

216

remains the tense of narration, it is no longer heard in conversation. The French still write *il tomba à la renverse, ils vécurent très heureux, il vint me chercher* or *elle recousit son bouton*, but nobody would say such things in conversation: it would seem mannered and unnatural.

We can try to imagine how this development might have begun: faced with the variety of forms of the past historic, which are different for each type of verb, language users would probably have preferred to avoid the pitfalls of this difficult tense (je chant*ai*, je reç*us*, je *tins*, je cous*is*) and gradually replaced it with the more regular forms of the perfect tense (*j'ai chanté, j'ai reçu, j'ai tenu, j'ai cousu*),[270] given that this tense uses very common auxiliaries and a past participle learnt in early childhood. As a result, no difference is now made between a past which is over and done with (past historic) and a past with effects in the present time (perfect). *Ils mangèrent* and *ils ont mangé* have come to mean the same thing.

The process of eliminating the past historic from the spoken language is almost complete in all the regions of France, with the possible exception of those in which the local dialects collapsed by analogy the forms of the tense into just one. In the western Romance dialects, for example, the past historic has taken the same ending *-i* for most verbs (je *mangis*, je *tombis*, etc.). That is probably the reason why you can still occasionally hear the past historic in the French spoken in these regions.

In the written language, the past historic is still found in narrative, but rarely elsewhere. Linguists prefer to avoid it lest the use of these rare forms should distract the reader and turn their attention from the content to the form.

A television programme transmitted in early 1987 confirms this hypothesis: a writer on the programme used several past historics and imperfect subjunctives, all of them perfectly appropriate. The effect on the others taking part in the programme was such that an uproar ensued, clearly showing that their attention had been so focused on the manner of expression that they were unable for a few seconds to follow what he was saying.[271]

A little island of resistance: narrative

There are very few studies of the use of the tenses in spoken French, but you can always try a little experiment of your own: ask a few French people to tell you about a personal experience (such as a ceremony, an event, an accident, etc.) and then about a film or a novel. The chances are that the personal experience will be related in the perfect tense and the fictional story of the novel or film will be in the present.[272] If there are any past historics at all, they will be the exception. But it is far more likely that you will hear none at all.

217

Some not very relative pronouns

There is another section of grammar which deserves attention in modern spoken French: the relative pronouns are not what they used to be, or almost not, because their number is diminishing. Only the simple relatives *qui*, *que*, and *quoi* are still really frequent. The relative *dont* is becoming rare, and when it is used, – which is only by highly educated people – it is often used clumsily.[273] Out of a kind of hypercorrectness, people frequently come out with sentences such as *c'est de lui dont je te parle* or *c'est de l'âme dont il s'occupe*, without realising that *dont* already contains *de* ('de qui'). They could say more simply either *c'est lui dont je te parle* or *c'est de lui que je te parle*.

The long forms *lequel*, *auquel*, *duquel*, etc. are in no better state. The following sentences – produced by highly educated people because other people do not use these forms at all – were spoken by writers on the programme 'Apostrophes', and by academics, politicians or young intellectuals:

- *ils reçoivent* des *télégrammes de vingt mots dans* le*quel on leur dit* . . .
- une *légende révolutionnaire* au*quel je tiens* . . .
- *d'* une *carrière politique dans* le*quel on cherche à obtenir* . . .
- des *fictions sur* le*quel* . . .
- la *seule raison pour* les*quelles ils n'ont pas été* . . .
- *toutes* les *raisons pour* la*quelle* . . .

You will certainly have spotted the absence of agreement between the relative pronoun and its antecedent. That might seem to be no more than a slip of the tongue that can be easily corrected, but in fact it is remarkable that nobody usually notices, neither the speakers, who rarely correct themselves, nor the listeners, who do not point them out. I have myself asked friends who have just made this kind of mistake if they were aware of it. They always said no.

Grammatical 'novelties'

You should not be misled by the above remarks into thinking that grammatical development, however slowly it happens, always results in the elimination of something, the loss of a distinction. In reality, we have to accept that when a distinction is lost from the language, it is because it is no longer necessary for communication. In the sentence *des fictions sur lequel* . . ., nothing is lost by not having the relative pronoun *lequel* in the plural since the plural was already indicated by *des* (*fictions*). Its presence in the relative is a redundancy that can be done without. In this case, the agreement of the relative pronoun simply serves to remind us of information already supplied and its loss is no catastrophe.

By contrast, when the need arises to express a new concept or avoid an ambiguity, the language satisfies the need either by creating a new unit or by adding a new meaning to an existing one. When radio and television reporters speak *depuis* the Stock Exchange, *depuis* Canada or *depuis* a car,[274] they are right and 'correct usage' is wrong. Although it is true that in 'good French' the preposition *depuis* should be used only with adverbs of time and not place, expressions such as *parler de la Bourse, du Canada* or *d'une voiture* could be ambiguous and might encourage the interpretation of 'about' rather than 'from'. What some people call 'bad French' is, seen from this angle, an enrichment of the language because it allows for greater clarity of expression.

SHIFTS IN PRONUNCIATION

A humble feast of pasta in the living room

The four words *fête, humble, pâte* and *living* might serve as a mnemonic for the phonological shifts now taking place in French: the first three bear witness to the process of elimination of three vowels and the last one to the incorporation of a new consonant into the system (*living, parking, jogging, lifting*, etc.).

If we were to classify these phonological changes in chronological order, *fête* would head the list because it is the long vowel *ê* which will be the first to disappear given that fewer and fewer people now lengthen the vowel of *fête* to distinguish it from the vowel in *faite*.

Humble is also losing ground. The process of elimination is especially advanced in Paris, where the young and the not so young feel not the slightest bit of shame in pronouncing this vowel like the one in *simple* and see no incongruity in saying *l'ours brin* for 'l'ours brun'. It is true that there is little danger of misunderstanding in this context. In more perilous cases the adjective *marron* long ago took over from *brun*. This confusion of the vowels of *brin* and *brun*, which is widespread in the Paris region, has not yet reached the rest of the country (see the map of nasal vowels on p. 126) because the provinces are not so easily contaminated as that.

Pâte will probably be the last to go. The distinction between *pâte* and *patte* is disappearing more slowly than the other two, even though it is virtually unknown to young people in many regions.[275]

Paris is a town of provincials

The role played by Paris in the general development of French can be seen more clearly by trying to establish the points of departure of the shifts taking place in the common phonological system.

Since the twelfth century, when you had to be born in Paris to 'speak properly' (see p. 56), the capital has remained the model of 'good usage'. Nowadays, however, although we must still talk of the influence of Paris, it is with a slightly different meaning, because it is not always the tendencies specific to the traditional Parisian system which come to dominance. It is true that the distinctions *brin/brun* and *patte/pâte* are both in the process of disappearing, but the first distinction was a provincial one, while the distinction between the two *a* sounds was, on the contrary, deeply rooted in Parisian habits. Nowadays, in the cultural stew of Paris, the provincials are indeed tending to lose the vowel in *humble* which they used to have, but at the same time Parisians born and bred are letting themselves be contaminated by the provincials into retaining only the *a* of *patte* and no longer making a distinction with the *a* of *pâte*.

Generally speaking, the linguistic system will give at its weakest spot, with no regard to whether the feature being lost is traditionally Parisian or not.

The distribution of sounds in words

The already advanced elimination of three vowels, and the gradual introduction of a new consonant borrowed from English (the final consonant in *living*), affects the entire phonological system of French, in other words the inventory of phonic units available to users for pronouncing French words.

As well as the ongoing developments which are tending to modify the number of these units, we can also see changes in the pronunciation of certain words. Without reviewing all the words affected by this process, we can point out two great 'revivals':

- the 'revival' of certain consonants. Young people increasingly pronounce the *p* in *sculpter* or *dompter*. The word *cheptel* pronounced in the traditional way, in other words without the *p*, and the word *cric* pronounced without the final consonant would today pose problems of comprehension for most people under the age of sixty. Similarly, *baril* and *nombril* seem to have recovered their final consonant for most people;
- the 'revival' of a vowel that was until recently mute. This is the case with *e* in the first syllable of *belote*, *semelle* or *menu* which can be heard more and more frequently, especially among the younger generation, even when the preceding word ends with a vowel.

Stress and intonation

This regularised pronouncing of the so-called 'mute' *e* could be related to the increasingly widespread tendency to stress the first syllable of words.[276] This stress has been observed above all in people accustomed to speaking in public. Since they are the ones who are heard most frequently on the airwaves, they cannot fail to influence the rest of the population.

Furthermore, the characteristic of stressing all French words on the final syllable is no longer true today when, apart from the 'didactic' stress on the first syllable, only the last syllable of a breath group shows any prominence.

A few words should also be said about the types of intonation pattern which are frequently heard among young people. In particular, there is a rising modulation of the voice at the end of phrases or sentences which is especially perceptible in words ending in a consonant, words such as *grande* and *troupe* but also *but* and *bac*. Increasingly, you can hear a kind of vocalic echo which may be interpreted as a better way of making the final consonant audible. Since the phenomenon is general and affects both words ending in a consonant and words ending in *e*, it cannot be confused with the southern pronunciation of the 'mute' *e*.

The influence of writing

All of these observations lead us to a quite unexpected conclusion: in spite of the considerable disaffection of the young with anything that is written, – every parent has seen it and every teacher deplores it – these young people who are reading less and less have a pronunciation which is influenced more and more by writing, since they are pronouncing written letters that were once silent. This influence of spelling on pronunciation is not a new one,[277] but it was easier to understand at a time when reading did not have to compete with the audiovisual culture of the new media.

Could it be that the attraction of young people to computers, which rely on writing, is an opening through which the written language is in the process of regaining importance?

THE DYNAMICS OF CHANGE

Brakes and accelerators

Spoken for centuries by different people in the four corners of the world, the French language has demonstrated a real capacity to adapt to the new needs of communication. If today it displays both the discreet charm of its wrinkles and mobility of expression, and if it alternates between inertia and renewal, it is because of the duality pointed to in the preamble and which has been a constant theme of this book: on the one hand there are the schools, the institutions, the French Academy and the written language, which act as factors of stability, regularisation and unification; on the other hand there has developed a whole dynamic born of the changing needs of modern society and which, by contrast, makes French a language which

221

diversifies, renews itself and no longer hesitates to break the rules.

Of the different forces acting on the development of French, I have chosen to stress two extreme tendencies: tradition, symbolised by the French Academy, and change, which seems to find its most advanced expression in advertising.

The French Academy and its dictionary

The first volume of the ninth edition of the *Dictionnaire de l'Académie* finally saw the light of day in 1986, fifty-one years after publication of the eighth edition. This ninth edition, which, at the rate of one volume per year, should be completed around the year 2000, will contain 45,000 entries, some 10,000 more than the 1935 edition.

When you look at some of the new entries (*accordéoniste, acétone, activiste, actualiser, aérogare, aéroports*, etc.), you realise the full extent of the traditional delay with which words are accepted in dictionaries of good usage, which is defined in the preface as 'that which is accepted by the most enlightened people'.[278] But that is in the order of things and is no cause for surprise.

What is more unexpected is the discovery, as you leaf through the pages of this first volume, of entries like the following:

- *arsouille* n. Pop. Mauvais garçon aux mœurs crapuleuses;
- *badigoinces* n. f. pl. Argot. Lèvres, et par ext. bouche ou mâchoires;
- *baffe* n. f. Pop. Gifle;
- *bagnole* n. f. Pop. Voiture automobile;
- *balèze* adj. Argot. Costaud, d'une carrure impressionnante;
- *balle* n. f. (Toujours au pluriel.) Argot. Valeur d'un franc.

How are we to interpret the presence of such scarcely academic vocabulary, even with the indication *argot* or *populaire*, in this dictionary? Are we to understand that it has entered into usage – and good usage at that – sufficiently for it to be included? Might the Academy, as Maurice Druon says in the preface, really be 'more welcoming than is claimed'? But in that case what criteria did it use to make its selection? And can we really put on an equal footing a word like *balèze*, which really is known to everybody, and a word like *badigoinces*, which is at the very least used in much more restricted situations?

Novelties in spelling

As far as the written language is concerned, this first volume contains a few modifications to the spelling of certain words, and future candidates for the next spelling championships would do well to make themselves acquainted with the new degree of latitude now accepted by the Academy. People who have probably devoted a great deal of effort to memorising the incomprehensible use of an acute accent in *afféterie*, *allégement* and *allégrement* where the pronunciation called for a grave accent, will no doubt be relieved to learn that good usage now also accepts *affèterie*, *allègement* and *allègrement* with a grave accent. The verb *assener*, which previously had only one correct spelling with no accent on the first *e*, now has a second form: *asséner*, with an acute accent. But we will still have to wait several years before we have written confirmation of the fate which has been reserved for the acute accents in *crémerie* and *événement*.*

The true judges of usage

Or rather, to be more precise, nobody will wait for the Academy's pronouncements, since it long ago ceased to be the real standard setter. Who, other than historians of the language, consults the 1935 edition? And who can verify the meaning or even the existence of a word if all we have access to for the time being are the words contained in the first two volumes (from *a* to *chaînage*)?

All those who wish to know what the correct usage is have taken the habit of turning to other authorities. The Academy's dictionary was replaced a long time ago by standard dictionaries like the *Petit Robert* or the *Petit Larousse*, which are constantly updated, and by the many works[279] which list the difficulties of the French language. As for the French Academy, it remains a symbol and an abstraction.

The language and the state

There is one area which holds a large place in modern life: the area of scientific and technical terminology, where the concern is not with 'good usage' but with developing precise names for new concepts and new objects. The responsibility for this in France falls on the Commissariat Général de la Langue Française which, since 1984, has brought together various organisations concerned with terminology and which strives to coordinate the various existing term banks.[280]

Nowadays, people usually become acquainted with a new technology through the English word for it: among many others, terms such as *scanner* and *tuner* entered the language together with the inventions they designated. Faced with this persistent invasion of English words, which might give the impression that every scientific innovation is created by foreigners,

---

* We now have definitive (?) proof that *crémerie* and *événement* will keep their present spelling, since, at the time of first edition of this book going to press, the second volume of the *Dictionnaire de l'Académie française* appeared with the following note to the reader: 'The Academy, at its meetings of 12 and 19 March 1987, having noted that modifications in spelling that it agreed to in 1975 have not passed into general usage, has decided to reject them without exception.'

or that the French language is incapable of finding names for technological advances, the government decided to react, by assigning to various commissions for terminology the task of proposing French words to designate these new technologies.

As a result, problems of terminology are no longer purely linguistic matters and the French language becomes a political issue. The state also took protective measures by passing the Bas-Lauriol law of 31 December 1975[281] which requires the directions for use of any commercial product to be in French. This law concerned only the fraud detection squad. In 1985 the socialist government prepared an extension of the laws relating to language but did not in the event put forward any new legislation.[282]

It is true that public opinion is always hostile to measures of this kind which it sees as an infringement of individual liberty, even though the public itself is ready to alienate that same liberty both in its respect for a restrictive system of spelling and in its propensity for the unthinking adoption of the latest fashionable words.

Mass communication

If the French language today seems to be changing with increasing swiftness in spite of the checks placed on it by institutions, it is because other forces are acting in the opposite direction: the development of mass communications and the flourishing audiovisual technologies. Every message broadcast by radio or television is heard simultaneously by several thousand people who will naturally be tempted, in their turn, to use the word or phrase they have just heard. Through the mouths of politicians, journalists, entertainers and also through the commercials, new expressions are spread abroad, old ones are given a new lease of life, and lexical fashions rise and fall.

In a century in which the image is increasingly dominant, the spoken language nonetheless retains an important place in mass communication. There are, for example, the 'sound bites' thrown out by the politicians and repeated by the journalists because they give a focal point to their commentaries, and which find their way into every home. There are also the speech mannerisms of the radio and television presenters which are heard so frequently that they become contagious and spread out into the public at large.

It is also through the media that an abstract vocabulary with philosophico-psychoanalytical overtones contaminates the rest of the population: verbs like *interpeller*, *s'investir*, *assumer*, *privilégier*, *poser problème*, *sécuriser* and *responsabiliser* have seen their frequency of use inflated in recent years, and adjectives such as *fiable*, *gratifiant*, *mature*, *performant*, *obsolète* and *incontournable* punctuate the most familiar of

224

conversations. This vocabulary is no longer the sole reserve of the intellectuals, whose needlessly complicated phraseology has been derided by Claire Brétécher in her collected cartoon strips. It has spread from one journalist to the next, from magazine to magazine, and is now beginning to invade the modern novel. In 1987, it even became almost the most interesting character in a novel by Jean Dutourd, *Le Séminaire de Bordeaux*.

Innovation or barbarism?

It is easy to see how this vocabulary, which may be genuinely intellectual or no more than a sham, can get on people's nerves or make people laugh at its repetitive and pretentious nature, but from the point of view of the workings of the language it contains nothing to shock those who love French. Why not create the verb *privilégier* when the word *privilégié* has never caused a raised eyebrow? Why not create the word *fiable* from the verb *se fier* since there was no other adjective to fill the gap in French? Why not give new life to that old French word *obsolète*, even if it has come back via a detour through English? And finally, why not make full – and correct – use of the derivational resources of the language to form the words *incontournable* from *contourner*, *taciturnité* from *taciturne*, and *cohabitateur* from *cohabitation*?

The pessimists will say that these forms are barbarisms since they are not in the dictionary, but a more serene view would be to see them as signs of the good health of a language which has the capacity to renew itself by drawing on its own resources. When these new forms respond to a real need, they have every chance of becoming standard words that nobody will have difficulty remembering, because they conform completely to the rules of word formation in French. And ultimately nothing will prevent them from contributing to the enrichment of the lexical store of French vocabulary.

Advertising and language

We cannot leave the realm of linguistic creation without an analysis of the importance of advertising, since advertisements are a particular source of novelty in vocabulary and syntax nowadays. We could even go so far as to say that the poets – but how many people read poetry now? – and the ad men and women are the only ones who have no complexes about using the potentialities of French and who dare to innovate.

The public yields readily to the charms of the new words offered by adverts because they find these words amusing. Nonetheless, following the received wisdom that any word not in the dictionary is not French, they will begin by criticising the new word . . . only to adopt it after hearing it a few times.

225

What seems to be the striking element in an advert is precisely its linguistic formulation, since it sometimes happens that the advertising slogan is so successful that everybody remembers the words and forgets the name of the product.

It should be said in passing that in the space of a few decades, from the *réclame* to the *publicité* and now the *pub*, this new means of communication has developed an entire art of informing and convincing which brings together picture, sound and words. When the word used was *réclame*, it had its detractors who had nothing but scorn for it. Now, rebaptised *la pub*, it has its admirers, its enlightened fans, and even its fanatics.

The language of advertising: showing the way

In its desire to make the best possible use of all the potentialities of that instrument of communication which is language, the world of advertising really seems to have seized the initiative and dared to free the language from the straitjacket into which centuries of good usage had forced it.

One proof of this can be found in an article written by Etiemble almost thirty years ago called 'La Langue et la publicité'.[283] This text describes features which can be found in today's language but which at that time were specific to the language of advertising: as well as 'acronymania', which is less pervasive these days, we find abbreviations, unusual syntactic constructions and English loan words.

The acronyms quoted by Etiemble[284] in 1966, *BZF*, *TCF*, and *K2R* demonstrate that acronyms are often ephemeral, although *K2R* is still the name of a well-known stain-remover. Publicity nowadays no longer makes excessive use of acronyms, although French people do use the following, without always knowing what they stand for: *TUC*, *ZUP*, *RER* (since 1970), *PCV**, *CNCL*, and more recently *PAF*, not to mention some English acronyms which have become standard French words like *radar* and *laser*. (See table p. 227.)

Amongst the abbreviations quoted by Etiemble are *astap, OK d'ac* and *formid* which are nowadays totally unfashionable, not to say corny. The list of abbreviations used by French people nowadays is endless: trois heures du *mat*, le *petit dej*, l'*appart*, le *pro*, la *sécu*, etc. I have even recently heard *dem* for 'démission', *comm* for 'commission' and *provoc* for 'provocation'.

Amongst the unusual syntactic structures quoted by Etiemble were: *magasin pilote, initiative ORTF* and *tarif étudiant*. This process of formation by juxtaposition is so widespread nowadays that only the most finicky

* *PCV* is not really an acronym since the letters correspond to (taxe à) Per*Ce*Voir.

ACRONYMS AND THEIR MEANING

With EDF or SVP there is no difficulty in recovering *Electricité de France* and *S'il vous plaît* from the initials of the acronyms, but in other cases we understand the meaning of the acronym without knowing the words it is composed of.

The following list groups together some acronyms, such as *Cedex*, which are in everyday use but the composition of which is by no means obvious and sometimes even totally unknown.

Test your knowledge on the following:

ADN	AFNOR	ANPE	ASSEDIC	CAP	CEA
CEDEX	CEE	CERN	CES	CHU	CIA
CNCL	CNES	CNIT	CNPF	CNRS	CRS
ECU	FIAT	HLM	IBM	IFOP	INSEE
LASER	MIDEM	NASA	OPEP	OTAN	OVNI
PAF	QHS	RADAR	RER	SACEM	SIDA
SIMCA	SMIC	SOFRES	TUC	UHF	UHT
UNEDIC	UNESCO	UNICEF	URSSAF	VHF	ZUP

Acide désoxyribonucléique; Association française de normalisation; Agence nationale pour l'emploi; Association pour l'emploi dans l'industrie et le commerce; Certificat d'aptitude professionnelle; Commissariat à l'énergie atomique; Courrier d'entreprise à distribution exceptionnelle; Communauté économique européenne; Centre européen de recherches nucléaires; Collège d'enseignement secondaire; Centre hospitalier universitaire; Central Intelligence Agency; Commission nationale de la communication et des libertés; Centre national d'études spatiales; Centre national des industries et des techniques; Conseil national du patronat français; Centre national de la recherche scientifique; Compagnie républicaine de sécurité; European currency unit; Fabbrica italiana automobili Torino; Habitation à loyer modéré; International Business Machines Corporation; Institut francais d'opinion publique; Institut national de la statistique et des études économiques; Light amplification by stimulated emission of radiation; Marché international du disque et de l'édition musicale; National Aeronautics and Space Administration; Organisation des pays exportateurs de pétrole; Organisation du traité de l'Atlantique Nord; Objet volant non identifié; Paysage audiovisuel français; Quartier de haute sécurité; Radio detecting and ranging system; Réseau express régional; Société des auteurs, compositeurs et éditeurs de musique; Syndrome d'immunodéficience acquise; Société industrielle de mécanique et de carrosserie;

Salaire minimum interprofessionnel de croissance; Société française d'enquêtes par sondage; Travaux d'utilité communaux; Ultra high frequency; Ultra haute température; Union nationale pour l'emploi dans l'industrie et le commerce; United Nations Educational, Scientific and Cultural Organization; United Nations (International) Children's (Emergency) Fund; Union pour le recouvrement des cotisations de la Sécurité sociale et des Allocations familiales; Very high frequency; Zone à urbaniser en priorité.

---

of purists are shocked by expressions such as la *pause café*, le *problème vaisselle,* la *fiche cuisine* and le *match retour*. The following are a few more examples taken at random over one week from the advertisement pages of a number of magazines: *stratégie jeunesse, cuisson progrès, responsable formation, problème peau* and *directeur médias*.

In fact, this type of formation was not born yesterday: *hôtel-Dieu* goes back to the Middle Ages and *timbre-poste* to the nineteenth century. More recent formations such as *cousu main* and *assurance vieillesse* already have a classical air to them.

More daring formations

It is also in advertising copy that you will find most examples of syntactic formations – some will no doubt say deformations – borrowed from the usage of the younger generation. We have seen (p. 211) that young people use the verbs *assurer* and *craindre* intransitively, with no object. Nor do they hesitate to say that they are *branchés cinéma* or that somebody is *accro informatique* with no preposition. Thus, verbs which previously were purely transitive (you *insured* something or somebody) or intransitive (you thought *about* something or somebody) have lost their rigidity of use. Nowadays you are advised to *penser conserves*, you are invited to *voyager vacances*, somebody suggests that you *parler polaroïd*, that you *habiller confortable* and that you ought not to *bronzer idiot*. Some of the expressions still have the piquancy of novelty, but the young and the ad men have now enticed other people down the road to syntactic freedom. It is now quite common, for example, to hear *aimer* or *adorer* used with no reminder of the object: *(la mer), j'adore*!

Here again, the process is not in itself new. Even the most academic language contains verbs which at some point in their history acquired the capacity to be both transitive and intransitive:[285] *il réfléchit, il réfléchit la lumière, il réfléchit à son avenir*. It is only because the process is now being applied to such a large number of verbs at the same time that it becomes striking.

Advertising often becomes the vehicle for forms which begin by attracting attention because they are uncommon. As they are repeated and amplified by the posters, the press, radio and television, they become gradually familiar without the public realising it. If they correspond to a need, these innovations will then pass into the standard language with no difficulty.

Advertising plays with language

We have seen how readily the French language lends itself to puns, and the advertisers were quick to seize on that. Here are a few random examples of adverts which take advantage of the possibility: *une moquette qui a une réputation sans taches* (no circumflex and in the plural, of course), *nougâtez-vous* (where the circumflex is essential), *ceints et saufs* (which has to be read for the pun to be understood), *Synthol, protégez-nous* (where an antiseptic liquid is made to sound like a guardian angel), and *Mettez-vous Martell en tête* et *Hennessy soit-il* (where brand names for brandy are slipped into familiar expressions).

Allo tobus?

Several years ago, an entire publicity campaign was concentrated on puns. The Darty company wanted to publicise the setting up of twenty-seven after-sales service centres in the Paris region together with their telephone number. There is nothing more off-putting than a series of numbers, because the only thing a telephone number looks like is another telephone number. So on the sides and backs of Paris buses there appeared unexpected and attention-grabbing posters: *Allo bélisque? Non, ici l'un des 27 services après-vente Darty.* There were a variety of other slogans: *Allo tobus, Allo strogoth, Allo péra, Allo tarie, Allo rizon,* etc. People enjoyed the puns, looked more carefully at the ad, and found themselves racking their brains to find other puns.

The 'cultural' fall-out of advertising

Obviously the advertisers were not bent on reminding French people of every French word beginning with the phoneme /o/ or on educating the masses. Nonetheless, this advertising technique had the advantage of calling on the reader's intelligence, wit and, of course, knowledge of the language. That was also the case with the 1963 Perrier advert, which was a bit of a gamble because it was less immediately obvious: *Ferrier, c'est pou!* You had to realise it was a spoonerism in order to understand it.

A recent advert for Dim stockings also used a pun that took advantage of the present precarious situation of the two *a* sounds in French (see pp. 164, 219) when it launched the following slogan for men's underwear: *Dim: très mâle, très bien*!

Another campaign for Lee jeans can be thought of as typically French since it relies entirely on puns on the word *lit*: *On n'est bien que dans son Lee, Passons nos journées au fond d'un Lee, Mettons-nous au Lee,* and *Mon Lee est toujours bien fait.*

But there are still taboos

All these adverts which play on language can, to use an expression which is fashionable nowadays, offer a 'mieux-disant culturel' by evoking other words in the language while keeping the mind of the reader or listener alert.

However, other adverts have triggered reactions which led to them being

229

rejected. This happened with the poster campaign organised in 1985 by the Ministry of Transport around the following slogans: *On roule cool – On se calme , on se calme- On n'est pas aux pièces – Poussez pas, on n'est pas des bœufs.*

Judging, no doubt, that it was not desirable to give added vitality to expressions which it considered to be already too widespread, the French Academy went so far as to write to the President of the Republic to demand that the scandal cease forthwith. Of course the vocabulary existed, but it was not the job of a public organisation to help to spread it. And so the posters were withdrawn.

Still in 1985, the manager of a shop in Tours rejected a proposal from his advertising agency which he considered to be unseemly because it contained the word *con*. The ad was subsequently toned down to read: 'Ce serait *fou* d'attendre une année de plus.'

The young and the not so young

You will no doubt have recognised in the slogans chosen by the Ministry of Transport, *on roule cool* and *on se calme, on se calme*, expressions from the world of the young. And it is not by chance that young people love the adverts, which speak a language they understand because it is theirs. A few more random examples: '*Bonjour les dégâts!*', '*ça va fort*', '*elle assure* en Rodier', 'quatre nouveaux chocos pour *s'éclater* au goûter', 'L'Inde, *c'est géant!*', 'La 708 ça *fait très mal!*' All of these sentences are reminiscent of what was said earlier about the way of speaking of young people, which is beginning to work its way into other age groups.

The progression is a simple one to follow: originating among young people, these words and syntactic structures are repeated in advertisements and magazines, and on the airwaves, thus passing them on to older people. Initially, they shock the older generations, even though they have heard their children using them. But by dint of repetition they become familiar, and this process of conditioning leads adults to the point where they are ready to use them themselves.

And what now?

There are those who may be afraid that constant innovation and abbreviation will lead to a situation of mutual incomprehension. But in fact, when the danger of ambiguity becomes too great, the language reacts by eliminating one of the meanings: *deb* was the abbreviation for *débutante* in the 1960s, but now it is an abbreviation for *débile*, and the word *débutante* has reverted to its long form. It is too early to know if *micro* in the meaning of 'microcomputer' will supplant *micro* in the meaning of 'microphone' because the process is still under way.

The much older example of *radio*, which has remained the abbreviation for both *radiographie* and *radiophonie*, is ample demonstration that abbreviations are not always a danger to comprehension.

On the other hand, the spectre of *franglais* still terrifies the guardians of the purity of the language, who reject verbs such as *sponsoriser* or *nominer*. But the people who organise such things as boat races (and for whom the word *sponsoriser* does not have quite the same meaning as *commanditer*, *parrainer* or *patronner*), resist the suggestions made by the purists and continue, with a smidgin of guilt, to talk of *sponsors* rather than *parrains* because the *sponsor* always gives financial assistance whereas the *parrain* can be merely honorific.

Similarly, although they are asked to replace *nominer*, borrowed from English, by *nommer*, which is dyed-in-the-wool French, users baulk at using them as synonyms because they realise only too well that the two words do not mean the same thing. *Nominer* does indeed mean something different from *nommer* because the verb designates an earlier operation of selection, prior to the operation of choice which culminates in what the French call the *nomination*. To be more precise, we can say that the *nominés* are the selected competitors from whom the winner will be *nommé*. In spite of their desire to conform to good usage, the presenters and the commentators at the 1987 César awards found it difficult to avoid the word *nominer*, a better word than *nommer* because more restrictive, to designate the candidates who were in the first selection.

THE FRENCH LANGUAGE IN MOTION

At the end of this never-ending voyage around the French language, we rediscover the duality that we spoke of at the outset.

The French Academy, which is the guardian of the traditions, and advertising, which takes people out on to more adventurous terrain, are in fact no more than two extreme tendencies which should not be allowed to mask the other factors at work in the economy of the French language.

French speakers let themselves be more or less consciously caught up by the alternating fascination of these two opposed currents: *tradition*, which leads them to don with a shudder of delight the shackles of the rules and the prohibitions which impose 'good usage', and leads them also to enthuse over the spelling championships; and *modernity*, which impels them to break the rules and to set off down the forbidden pathways of innovation.

In a world where everything moves fast and where all languages are subject to the new conditions of mass communication, the French language, like all others, is launched upon a new age in its history: it will adapt or it will die.

The signs of movement that we can see passing through it are a discreet indication that it is already going in the right direction.

REFERENCES

1 Veikko Väänänen, *Introduction au latin vulgaire*, Paris, Klincksieck, 1963, pp. 4–6 and 57.
2 Nicole Gueunier, Emile Genouvrier and Abdelhamid Khomsi, *Les Français devant la norme*, Paris, Champion, 1978, pp. 167–73.
3 Ferdinand Brunot, *Histoire de la langue française*, Paris, Colin, 1966, vol. 1, p. 166.
4 André Martinet, *Des steppes aux océans. L'indo-européen et les 'Indo-Européens'*, Paris, Payot, 1986; and also Thomas V. Gamkrelidze and V.V. Ivanov, *Indoevropeiskii iazik i Indoevropeiskie'*, University of Tbilisi (USSR), 1986 (Eng. trans.: *Indo-European and the Indo-Europeans*, Berlin, Mouton, 1987).
5 Paul Viallaneix and Jean Ehrard (eds), *Nos ancêtres les Gaulois*, Actes du colloque international de Clermont-Ferrand, 1982, in particular the article by Christian Amalvi 'Vercingétorix dans l'enseignement primaire, 1830–1940', pp. 349–55.
6a Pierre Chaunu, *La France*, Paris, Robert Laffont, 1982, p. 65 *et seq.*;
6b Gabriel Camps, *La préhistoire*, Paris, Perrin, 1982, p. 342 *et seq.*;
6c Jean Guillaume, *La France d'avant la France*, Paris, Hachette, 1980.
7 André Martinet, 'Nos ancêtres les Gaulois', *Drailles* 5/6, Nîmes, 1986, p. 58.
8 Ferdinand Lot, *La Gaule*, Paris, Fayard, 1947, p. 77.
9 André Martinet, *Des steppes . . .* (Ref. 4), pp. 92–3.
10 François Falc'hun, *Perspectives nouvelles sur l'histoire de la langue bretonne*, Paris, PUF, 1963, p. 530.
11 René Goscinny and Albert Uderzo, *Astérix le Gaulois*, Paris, Dargaud, 1965.
12 Georges Dottin, *La langue gauloise, grammaire, textes et glossaire*, Geneva, Slatkine Reprints, 1980, p. 70.
13 J.J. Hatt, *Histoire de la Gaule romaine*, Paris, Payot, 1970, p. 191.
14 Oscar Bloch and Walther von Wartburg, *Dictionnaire étymologique de la langue française*, Paris, PUF, 1950.
15 Jacqueline Picoche, *Nouveau dictionnaire étymologique du français*, Paris, Hachette-Tchou, 1971, p. 416.
16 Emile Thévenot, *Les Gallo-Romains*, Paris, PUF, 'Que sais-je?', no. 314. l948, p. 51 and *Histoire des Gaulois*, Paris, PUF, 'Que sais-je?', no. 206, 1946, p. 86.
17 Alfred Fierro-Domenech, *Le pré carré*, Paris, Robert Laffont, 1986, p. 215.
18a Eric Vial, *Les noms de villes et de villages*, Paris, Belin, 1983, p. 76.
18b Francis Gourvil, *Langue et littérature bretonnes*, Paris. PUF, 'Que sais-je?',

no. 527, 1952, p. 13.

18c Fernand Braudel, *L'identité de la France – Les hommes et les choses*, Paris, Arthaud-Flammarion, 1986, p. 87.

19 Ferdinand Lot, *La Gaule* (Ref. 8), p. 37–61. Ernest Nègre, *Les noms de lieux en France*, Paris, Colin, 1963, pp. 49–50. Auguste Vincent, *Toponymie de la France*, Brionne, Montfort, 1984, pp. 108–13.

20 Père Gy, 'Histoire de la liturgie en Occident jusqu'au concile de Trente', in Martimort (ed.), *Principes de la liturgie*, Paris, ch. 3, p. 57.

21 M. Arondel *et al.*, *Rome et le Moyen Age jusqu'en 1328*, Paris, Bordas, 1966, p. 51.

22 Pierre Bec, *La langue occitane*, Paris, PUF, 'Que sais-je?', no. 1059, 1963, pp. 18–21.

23 M. Arondel *et al.*, *Rome* . . . (Ref. 21), p. 123.

24 Pierre Chaunu, *La France* (Ref. 6a), p. 91.

25 Alfred Fierro-Domenech, *Le pré carré* (Ref. 17), p. 34.

26 Walther von Wartburg, *La fragmentation linguistique de la Romania*, Paris, Klincksieck, 1967, pp. 81–96.

27 Pierre Chaunu, *La France* (Ref. 6a), p. 77.

28 Louis Guinet, *Les emprunts gallo-romans au germanique*, Paris, Klincksieck, 1982, p. 197.

29 André Martinet, 'Phonologies en contact dans le domaine du gallo-roman septentrional', *Festschrift für Johann Knobloch*, Innsbrucker Beiträge zur Kulturwissenschaft, Innsbruck, 1985, pp. 247–51.

30 Louis Guinet, *Les emprunts* (Ref. 28), pp. 203–5.

31 Louis Guinet, *Les emprunts* (Ref. 28), p. 26.

32 Jules Marouzeau, *La prononciation du latin*, Paris, Belles-Lettres, 1955, pp. 23–4.

33 Walther von Wartburg, *Évolution et structure de la langue française*, Berne, Francke, 1962 ed., p. 60.

34 Veikko Väänänen, *Introduction* . . . (Ref. 1), p. 57.

35 Compare for example André Martinet and Henriette Walter, *Dictionnaire de la prononciation française dans son usage réel*, Geneva, Droz, 1973, pp. 435–58.

36 Henriette Walter, *La dynamique des phonèmes dans le lexique français contemporain*, Geneva, Droz, 1976, pp. 450–1.

37 Charles Rostaing, *Les noms de lieux*, Paris, PUF, 'Que sais-je?', no. 176, 1969, pp. 71–2 and Nègre, *Les noms de lieux en France*, Paris, PUF, 1963, p. 102.

38 Camille Jullian, *Histoire de la Gaule*, Paris, Robert Laffont, 1971, p. 147 (abridged edition).

39 Henriette Walter, 'Toponymie, histoire et linguistique: l'invasion franque en Gaule', *Actes du XIIIe Colloque International de Linguistique Fonctionnelle* (Corfu, 1986), Paris, SILF, 1987.

40 J.J. Hatt, *Histoire* . . . (Ref. 13), p. 191.

41 Emile Thévenot, *Les Gallo-Romains* (Ref. 16), p. 94–5.

42 Emile Thévenot, *Les Gallo-Romains* (Ref. 16), p. 121.

43 M. Arondel *et al.*, *Rome* . . . (Ref. 21), p. 123.

44 Emile Thévenot, *Histoire* . . . (Ref. 16), p. 37.

45 Emile Thévenot, *Les Gallo-Romains* (Ref. 16), p. 119.

46 Charles Camproux, *Les langues romanes*, Paris, PUF, 'Que sais-je?', no. 1562, 1974, p. 64.

47 Pierre Miquel, *Histoire de la France*, Paris, Fayard, 1976, p. 51.

48   Pierre Miquel, *Histoire* . . . (Ref. 47), p. 53.
49   Ferdinand Brunot, *Histoire* . . . (Ref. 3), vol. 1, p. 142.
50   Ferdinand Brunot, *Histoire* . . . (Ref. 3), vol. 1, p. 136.
51   Pierre Miquel, *Histoire* . . . (Ref. 47), pp. 60 and 62.
52   Ferdinand Brunot, *Histoire* . . . (Ref. 3), vol. 1, pp. 139–41.
53   Frédéric Diez, *Anciens glossaires romans*, Paris, Klincksieck, 1876, p. 163.
54   Frédéric Diez, *Anciens glossaires* . . . (Ref. 53), pp. 64–117.
55   Oscar Bloch and Walther von Wartburg, *Dictionnaire* . . . (Ref. 14), p. 256.
56   Alphonse Juilland, *Dictionnaire inverse de la langue française*, London–The Hague–Paris, Mouton, 1965, pp. 16–37.
57   For example:
57a   Ferdinand Brunot, *Histoire de la langue française*, Paris, Armand Colin, new edition, 1966, 23 vols.
57b   Mildred K. Pope, *From Latin to Modern French*, Manchester, University Press, 1934 (new edition 1966).
57c   Marcel Cohen, *Histoire d'une langue: le français*, Paris. Éd. sociales, 1967.
57d   Walther von Wartburg, *Évolution* . . . (Ref. 33).
57e   Edouard and J. Bourciez, *Phonétique française*, Paris, Klincksieck, 1967.
58   For example:
58a   Jacques Chaurand, *Histoire de la langue française*, Paris, PUF, 'Que sais-je?', no. 167, 1969 (new edition 1977).
58b   Jacques Allières, *Formation de la langue française*, Paris, PUF, 'Que sais-je?', no. 1907, 1982.
59   Mildred K. Pope, *From Latin* . . . (Ref. 57b), § 383, p. 154.
60   Walther vonWartburg, *Évolution* . . . (Ref. 33), p. 73.
61   Eric Vial, *Les noms de villes* . . . (Ref. 18a), p. 213.
62   Paul Bacquet, *Etymologie anglaise*, Paris, PUF, 'Que sais-je?', no. 1652, 1976, p. 30.
63   Ferdinand Brunot, *Histoire* . . . (Ref. 3), vol. 1, p. 385, note 2.
64   Ferdinand Brunot, *Histoire* . . . (Ref. 3), vol. 1, p. 391.
65   Paul Bacquet, *Le vocabulaire anglais*, Paris, PUF, 'Que sais-je?', no. 1574, 1974, pp. 88, 101–12.
66   Ferdinand Brunot, *Histoire*. . . . (Ref. 3), vol. 1, pp. 286–87. Eric Vial, *Les noms de villes* . . . (Ref. 18a), pp. 215–19.
67   George D. Painter, *Marcel Proust*, Paris, Mercure de France, 1966, vol. 2, pp. 25 and 110.
68   Marcel Cohen, *Histoire* . . . (Ref. 57c), p. 85.
69   Ferdinand Brunot, *Histoire* . . . (Ref. 3), vol. 1, pp. 180–1, note 6.
70   Walther von Wartburg, *Évolution* . . . (Ref. 33), pp. 89–93.
71   Philippe Wolff, *Les origines linguistiques de l'Europe occidentale*, Paris Hachette, 1970, p. 154.
72   Jacques Monfrin, 'Les parlers en France', in Michel François (ed.) *La France et les français*, Paris, NRF, Encyclopédie de la Pléiade, p. 765.
73   Walther von Wartburg, *Évolution* . . . (Ref. 33), p. 121.
74   Ferdinand Brunot, *Histoire* . . . (Ref. 3), vol. 2, pp. 61, 42 and 58; Walther von Wartburg, *Évolution* . . ., (Ref. 33), p. 148.
75   Louis Meigret, *Le tretté de la grammere françoeze*, Paris, 1550, Geneva, Slatkine Reprints, 1970.
76   André Martinet and Henriette Walter, *Dictionnaire* . . . (Ref. 35), p. 430.
77   Charles Thurot, *De la prononciation française depuis le commencement du XVIᵉ siecle d'après les témoignages des grammairiens*, Paris, 1881–1883 and Geneva, Slatkine Reprints, 1966, vol. 2, pp. 11 and 12.

78   Marcel Cohen, *Histoire* . . . (Ref. 57c), p. 189.
79   Marcel Cohen, *Histoire* . . . (Ref. 57c), p. 225.
80   Albert Dauzat, *Phonétique et grammaire historiques de la langue française*, Paris, Larousse, 1950, pp. 73–5.
81   Charles Thurot, *De la prononciation* . . . (Ref. 77), vol. 1, pp. 162–74.
82   Albert Dauzat, *Le génie de la langue française*, Paris, Payot, 1947, pp. 21–2.
83   Charles Thurot, *De la prononciation* . . . (Ref. 77), vol. 2, pp. 271–3.
84   Guy Raynaud de Lage, *Manuel pratique d'ancien français*, Paris, Picard, 1970 edition, pp. 98 et 191; Albert Dauzat, *Phonétique et grammaire* . . . (Ref. 80), p. 228, note 2; Ferdinand Brunot, *Histoire* . . . (Ref. 3), vol. 2, pp. 379–80.
85   Ferdinand Brunot, *Histoire* . . . (Ref. 3), vol. 2, pp. 209–12 and 232–9; Pierre Guiraud, *Les Mots étrangers*, Paris, PUF, 1965, 'Que sais-je?', no. 1166, pp. 26, 31–3, 37 and 41 as well as pp. 9–20 for Arabic.
86   Claude Favre de Vaugelas, *Remarques sur la langue française utiles à ceux qui veulent bien parler et bien écrire*, Paris, 1647. New edition Paris, Champ Libre, 1981, pp. 10, 19 and 33.
87   Marcel Cohen, *Histoire* . . . (Ref. 57c), p. 195.
88   Ernest Bouvier, *Des perfectionnements que reçut la langue française au XVIIe siècle et des influences auxquelles il faut les attribuer*, Brussels, 1853; Geneva, Slatkine Reprints, 1970, p. 58.
89   Thomas Corneille, *Dictionnaire des Arts et des Sciences*, Paris, 1694.
90   Ferdinand Brunot, *Histoire* . . . (Ref. 3), vol. 4, p. 105.
91   Ferdinand Brunot, *Histoire* . . . (Ref. 3), vol. 4, ch. 7, pp. 119–26.
92   Ferdinand Brunot, *Histoire* . . . (Ref. 3), vol. 4, p. 107.
93   Marcel Cohen, *Histoire* . . . (Ref. 57c), p. 204.
94   Claude Favre de Vaugelas, *Remarques* . . . (Ref. 86), p. 170.
95   Ferdinand Brunot, *Histoire* . . . (Ref. 3), vol. 4, pp. 177–8.
96   Walther von Wartburg, *Évolution* . . . (Ref. 33), p. 187.
97   Walther von Wartburg, *Évolution* . . . (Ref. 33), p. 183.
98   Jean Duché, *Mémoires de Madame la langue française*, Paris, Olivier Orban, 1985, p. 107.
99   Jacques Chaurand, *Histoire* . . . (Ref. 58a), pp. 83–6.
100   Jean Orieux, *La Fontaine*, Paris, Flammarion, 1976, p. 243.
101   Augustin Gazier, *Lettres à Grégoire sur les patois de France, 1790–1794*, Paris, 1880, pp. 5–10 and 289–314.
102   Fernand Braudel, *L'identité* . . . (Ref. 18c), vol. 2, p. 161.
103   Marcel Cohen, *Histoire* . . . (Ref. 57c), p. 239.
104   Augustin Gazier, *Lettres* . . . (Ref. 101), p. 309.
105   André Martinet, *Économie des changements phonétiques*, Berne, Francke, 1955.
106   Gile Vaudelin, *Nouvelle manière d'écrire comme on parle en France*, Paris, 1713 and *Instructions crétiennes mises en ortografe naturelle pour faciliter au peuple la lecture de la Science du Salut*, Paris, 1715.
107   Giles Vaudelin, *Nouvelle* . . . (Ref. 106), p. 22.
108   Claude Favre de Vaugelas, *Remarques* . . . (Ref. 86), pp. 108–9.
109   N.N. Condeescu, *Traité d'histoire de la langue française*, Bucharest, 1975, pp. 334–5.
110   Albert Dauzat, *Phonétique* . . . (Ref. 80), p. 146, note 1, and Pierre Guiraud, *Le moyen français*, Paris, PUF, 'Que sais-je?', no. 1086, 1963, p. 111.
111   Jean Duché, *Mémoires* . . . (Ref. 98), p. 12.

112 Albert Dauzat, *Phonétique* . . . (Ref. 80), p. 146.
113 Jean-Pierre Seguin, *La langue française au XVIIIe siècle*, Paris, Bordas, 1972, pp. 186–214.
114 Eugène de Montbret, *Mélanges sur les langues, dialectes et patois*, Paris, 1831.
115 Jean Stefanini, *Un provincialiste marseillais, l'abbé Féraud (1725–1807)*, Aix-en-Provence, Ophrys, 1969, série 67, pp. 192–4.
116 Auguste Brun, *Recherches historiques sur l'introduction du français dans les provinces du Midi*, Paris, 1923, Geneva, Slatkine Reprints 1973.
117 Pierre Miquel, *Histoire* . . . (Ref. 47), p. 433.
118 André Chervel, *. . . et il fallut apprendre à écrire à tous les petits français*, Paris, Payot, 1977.
119 Ferdinand Brunot, *Histoire* . . . (Ref. 3), vol. 11, p. 565.
120 Ferdinand Brunot, *Histoire* . . . (Ref. 3), vol. 11, p. 537.
121 Ferdinand Brunot, *Histoire* . . . (Ref. 3), vol. 10, p. 723, note 1.
122 Henriette Walter, *Enquête phonologique et variétés régionales du français*, Paris, PUF, 1982.
123 Jean Egen, *Les tilleuls de Lautenbach*, Paris, Stock, 1979.
124 Albert Dauzat, *Dictionnaire étymologique*, Paris, Larousse, 1938. New edition 1946, p 775.
125 Dominique and Michel Frémy, *Quid*, Paris, Robert Laffont, 1988, p. 1508a.
126 Gérard Mermet, *Francoscopie*, Paris, Larousse, 1985, pp. 355, 356 and 363.
127 Georges Pastre, *Le français télé. . .visé*, Paris, Bellefond, 1986.
128 Anne Lefebvre, 'Les voyelles moyennes dans le français de la radio et de la télévision', *La linguistique* 24/1, Paris, PUF, 1988, and 'Le parler de la radio-télévision: comment sont perçues les voyelles moyennes', in Henriette Walter (ed.), *Diversité du français*, SILF, EPHE (4th section), Paris, Laboratoire de phonologie, 1982, pp. 13–14.
129 *Revue des patois gallo-romans*, vol. 5, suppl. 1893, p. 5.
130 Jacques Allières, *Manuel pratique de basque*, Paris, Picard, 1979, p. 105.
131 *Grand atlas de la France*, Paris. Selection from the *Reader's Digest*, 1969, p. 97.
132 Francis Gourvil, *Langue* . . . (Ref. 18b), pp. 106–7.
133 Yves Le Gallo, 'De Joseph Loth au GRELB', *La Bretagne linguistique. Trav. du groupe de rech. sur l'économie de la Bretagne*, Université de Bretagne occidentale, Brest, vol. 1, 1985, p. 12.
134 Jean Le Du, 'Pourquoi avons-nous créé le GRELB?' *La Bretagne linguistique* . . . (Ref. 133), vol. 1, 1985, p. 27.
135 Jean Markale, *Identité de la Bretagne*, Paris, Éd. Entente, 1985, p. 131.
136 Willem Pee, *Bulletin du comité flamand de France*, vol. 16, 1958, quoted in *Le guide de Flandre et Artois mystérieux*, Paris, Tchou, 1975, pp. 79–81.
137 Fernand Carton, 'Les parlers ruraux de la région Nord-Picardie: situation sociolinguistique', *International Journal of the Sociology of Language*, 29, New York, 1981, pp. 15–28.
138 Nicole Rousseau, *La situation linguistique à Hilbersheim (Moselle)*, Berne–Frankfurt–Las Vegas, Peter Lang, 1979, 130 pp. and especially ch. 4, pp. 37–53.
139 This same woman was an informant for French in Henriette Walter, *Enquête phonologique* . . . (Ref. 122), p. 114.
140 Nicole Rousseau, *La situation* . . . (Ref. 138), pp. 56–7.
141 Jules Ronjat lists nineteen. Quoted in Pierre Bec, *La langue occitane* (Ref. 22), pp. 24–33.

REFERENCES

142 Pierre Bec, *La langue occitane* (Ref. 22), p. 15.

143 Robert Lafont, *Clefs pour l'Occitanie*, Paris, Seghers, 1971, 1977 edition, p. 57.

144 For example, for Lozère and Haute-Loire:

144a France Lagueunière, 'La politique du bilinguisme en société rurale', *La Margeride: la montagne, les hommes*, Paris, Inst. nat. de la rech. agro., 1983, pp. 339–66;

144b *Pluralité des parlers de France, Ethnologie française*, vol. 3, 3–4, 1973, pp. 309–16. For Limousin: Henriette Walter, 'L'attachement au parler vernaculaire dans une commune limousine', *Communication au Colloque de la Sté d'Ethnologie française*, Nantes, June 1983.

145 For the west see Jean-Paul Chauveau, 'Mots dialectaux qualifiés de vrais mots . . .', *Les français régionaux* (Ref. 163), p. 109. For Beauce see Marie Rose Simoni, *Les français régionaux*, p. 73.

146 For the whole of this passage see Pierre Bec, *La langue occitane* (Ref. 22), pp. 100–19.

147 Walther von Wartburg, *La fragmentation . . .* (Ref. 26), p. 108.

148 Pierre Bec, *Manuel pratique de philologie romane*, Paris, Picard, 1971, vol. 2, p. 362.

149 Dany Hadjadj, *Parlers en contact aux confins de l'Auvergne et du Forez*, Université de Clermont-Ferrand, 1983, p. 152.

150 For Le Valais: Rose-Claire Schüle, 'Comment meurt un patois', *Actes du Colloque de Neuchâtel*, 1972, pp. l95–207 et 213–15; Maurice Casanova, 'Rapport', *Actes du Colloque de Neuchâtel*, 1972, pp. 207–13.

151 André Martinet, *La description phonologique avec application au parler franco-provençal d'Hauteville (Savoie)*, Paris–Geneva, Droz, l954, p. 58, 5–5.

152 For Saintonge see Henriette Walter, 'Patois ou français régional?', *Le Français Moderne*, 3/4, Oct. 1984, pp. 183–90.

153 For Haute-Bretagne see Jean-Paul Chauveau, 'Mots dialectaux . . .' (Ref. 145), p. 105.

154 For Picardy see Anne Lefebvre, 'Les langues du domaine d'oïl', in Geneviève Vermes (ed.) *Parler sa langue, 25 communautés linguistiques de France*, Paris, Magnart, 1988.

155 Patrice Brasseur, 'Le français dans les îles anglo-normandes', *Les français régionaux . . .* (Ref. 163), p. 100.

156 Pierre Bec, *Manuel pratique . . .* (Ref. 148), vol. 2, p. 25.

157 Jean-Paul Chauveau, *Le gallo: une présentation*, Faculté des Lettres de l'université de Brest, 1984, 2 vols, vol. 2, pp. 161–4.

158 Marguerite Gonon, 'État d'un parler franco-provençal dans un village forézien en 1974', *Pluralité . . .* (Ref. 144b), p. 283; Jean-Baptiste Martin, 'État actuel du bilinguisme à Yssingeaux (Haute-Loire)', *Pluralité . . .* (Ref. 144b), p. 309.

159 Patrice Brasseur, 'Le français dans les îles anglo-normandes'. *Les français régionaux . . .* (Ref. 163), p. 102.

160 Gérard Taverdet, 'Patois et français régional en Bourgogne', *Pluralité . . .* (Ref. 144b), pp. 320–2.

161 André Martinet and Henriette Walter, *Dictionnaire . . .* (Ref. 35).

162 For example:

162a *Pluralité . . .* (Ref. l44b).

162b Henriette Walter (ed.) *Phonologie des usages du français. Langue française*, no. 60, Paris, Larousse, 1983.

162c Henriette Walter, *Enquête phonologique . . .* (Ref. 122).

237

163 Gérard Taverdet and Georges Straka (eds), *Les français régionaux*, Paris, Klincksieck, 1977.

164 Gaston Tuaillon, *Les régionalismes du français parlé à Vourey, village dauphinois*, Paris, Klincksieck, 1983.

165 Claudette Germi and Vincent Lucci, *Mots de Gap, les régionalismes du français parlé dans le Gapençais*, Grenoble, Ellug, 1985.

166 Lucien Salmon, 'État du français d'origine dialectale en Lyonnais', *XVIIIe Congrès International de linguistique et philologie romanes*, Trèves (May 1986), Tübingen, Max Niemeyer, 1987. vol. 3.

167 See Gaston Tuaillon, *Les régionalismes* . . . (Ref. 164). p. 155; Claudette Germi and Vincent Lucci, *Mots de Gap* . . . (Ref. 165), p. 76; Lucien Salmon, *État du français* . . .', (Ref 166).

168 Gaston Tuaillon, 'Réflexions sur le français régional', *Les français régionaux* . . . (Ref 163), p. 23.

169 Quoted by Gaston Tuaillon, *Les régionalismes* . . . (Ref 164), p. 53.

170 Marcel Braunschvig, *Notre littérature étudiée dans les textes*, Paris, Armand Colin, 1921, pp. 516–17, note 2; André Lanly, 'Le français régional de Lorraine (romane)', *Pluralité* . . . (Ref, l44b), p. 305.

171 Pierre Guiraud, *Patois et dialectes français*, Paris, PUF, 'Que sais-je?', no. 1172, 1965, new ed. 1973, pp. 114–26.

172 Henriette Walter, 'Un sondage lexical en marge de l'enquête phonologique sur les français régionaux', *Actes du XVIIe congrès de linguistique et philologie romanes*, Université d'Aix-en-Provence, 1986, vol. 6, pp. 261–8.

173 Henriette Walter, 'Le surcomposé dans les usages actuels du français', *Actants, voix et aspects verbaux*, Université d'Angers, 1981, pp. 24–44.

174 René Jolivet, 'L'acceptabilité des formes verbales surcomposées', *Le français moderne*, 1984, no. 3/4, pp. 159–82.

175 Henriette Walter, 'Rien de ce qui est phonique n'est étranger à la phonologie', Vth International Phonology Meeting, *Wiener Linguistische Gazette, Discussion Papers*, University of Vienna (Austria), 1984, pp. 276–80.

176 Marc Blancpain, 'Géo-histoire du français', in Marc Blancpain and André Reboullet (eds) *Une langue: le français aujourd'hui dans le monde*, Paris, Hachette, 1976. p. 95.

177 *Qui-vive International*, magazine of the French language, Paris.

178 Gabriel de Broglie, *Le français, pour qu'il vive*, Paris, Gallimard, 1986.

179 Société Internationale de Linguistique Fonctionnelle (SILF), École Pratique des Hautes Études, 4th section, 45, rue des Écoles, 75005 Paris.

180 Marc Blancpain, 'Géo-histoire . . .' in *Une langue* . . . (Ref. 176), p. 94.

181 Albert Salon, 'Situation de la langue française par pays', in *Une langue* . . . (Ref. 176), p. 301.

182 David Hume, quoted by Pierre Burney, *Les langues internationales*, Paris, PUF, 'Que sais-je?', no. 968, 1962, p. 66.

183 Albert Salon, 'Situation de la langue francaise par pays', in *Une langue* . . . (Ref. 176), p. 302.

184 Thierry de Beaucé, interview with Denise Bombardier, *Le Point*, no. 762, 27 April 1987, pp. 158–66.

185 Gabriel de Broglie, *Le français* . . . (Ref. 178), pp. 29–32.

186a Marc Blancpain and André Reboullet (eds), *Une langue: le français aujourd'hui dans le monde*, Paris, Hachette, 1976.

186b Albert Valdman (ed.), *Le français hors de France*, Paris, Champion, 1979, 688 pp.

186c Auguste Viatte, *La francophonie*, Paris, Larousse, 1969.

186d *Le français en France et hors de France*, *Annales de la faculté des Lettres et des Sciences humaines de Nice*, no. 7, first quarter, 1969.

187 Jean-René Reimen, 'Esquisse d'une situation plurilingue, le Luxembourg', *La linguistique*, 1965/2, Paris, PUF, pp. 89–102.

188 Auguste Viatte, *La francophonie* (Ref. 186c), p. 40.

189 Jean-Pierre Martin, 'Le français parlé en vallée d'Aoste et sa situation linguistique par rapport à l'italien', *Le français hors de* . . . (Ref. 186b), pp. 271–84.

190 C. Thogmartin, 'Old Mines, Missouri et la survivance du français dans la haute vallée du Mississippi', *Le français hors de* . . . (Ref. 186b). pp. 111–18. Gérard- J. Brault, 'Le français en Nouvelle-Angleterre, *Le français hors de* . . . (Ref. 186b), pp. 75–91.

191 Pradel Pompilus, 'Le fait français en Haïti', (Ref. 186d), pp. 37–42 and 'La langue française en Haïti', *Le français hors de* . . . (Ref. 186b), pp. 119–43.

192 Abdallah Naaman, *Le français au Liban – Essai sociolinguistique*, Paris–Beirut, ed. Abdallah Naaman, 1979, p 64.

193 Sélim Abou, 'Le français au Liban et en Syrie', *Le français hors de* . . . (Ref. 186b), pp. 293–5.

194 R. Bemananjara, 'Situation de l'enseignement du français à Madagascar', *Le français hors de* . . . (Ref. 186b), pp. 528 et 532.

195 Flavien Ranaivo, 'La situation du français à Madagascar', *Le français hors de* . . . (Ref. 186b), pp. 513–16 and see also the recent article by Annette Tamuly, 'Le français à Madagascar, une seconde jeunesse', *Présence francophone*, 29, 1986, pp. 79–87.

196 Robert Chaudenson, 'Le français dans les îles de l'océan Indien (Mascareignes, Seychelles)', *Le français hors* . . . (Ref. l86b) pp. 567 et 575. Michel Carayol and Robert Chaudenson, 'Diglossie et continuum linguistique à la Réunion', *Les français devant la norme* (Ref. 2), p. 177.

197 Robert Chaudenson, 'Le français dans les îles . . .', *Le français hors de* . . . (Ref. 186b), pp. 567–70 (for Mauritius) and p. 595 (for the Seychelles).

198 Pierre Bandon, 'Situation du français dans les trois États d'Indochine', *Le français* . . . (Ref. 186b), pp. 664, 673 et 675.

199 Albert Salon, 'Situation de la langue . . .', *Une langue* . . . (Ref. 186a), p. 269.

200 Maurice Piron, 'Le français de Belgique', *Le français hors de* . . . (Ref. 186b), pp. 201–21.

201 Jacques Pohl, 'Quelques caractéristiques de la phonologie du français parlé en Belgique', *Phonologie* . . . (Ref. 162b), pp. 30–41.

202 Albert Doppagne, *Les régionalismes du français*, Paris-Gembloux, Duculot, 1978, pp. 50–68.

203 Pierre Knecht, 'Le français en Suisse romande: aspects linguistiques et sociolinguistiques', *Le français hors de* . . . (Ref. 186b), pp. 249–58; Ludmila Bovet, 'Le français en Suisse romande: caractéristiques et aperçu littéraire', *Présence francophone*, no. 29, Québec, Sherbrooke, 1986, pp. 7–26.

204 Gilles Gagné, 'Essai sur l'origine de la situation linguistique au Québec', *Le français hors de* . . . (Ref. 186b), pp. 33–59.

205 Jean-Claude Vernex, *Les Acadiens*, Paris, Entente, 1979, p. 59.

206 Jean-Claude Vernex, 'Espace et appartenance: l'exemple des Acadiens du Nouveau-Brunswick', in Dean R. Louder, Christian Morissonneau and Eric Waddell (eds), *Du continent perdu à l'archipel retrouvé*, Québec, Presses Université Laval, 1983, pp. 163–80.

207 Jean-William Lapierre and Muriel Roy, *Les Acadiens*, Paris, PUF, 'Que sais-

je?', no. 2078, 1983, pp. 9 and 32, and also Robert W. Ryan, *Une analyse phonologique d'un parler acadien de la Nouvelle-Écosse (Canada) (Région de la baie Ste-Marie)*, Centre international de recherches sur le bilinguisme, 1981, pp. 1–11.

208 Jean-Claude Vernex, *Les Acadiens* (Ref. 205), p. 64.

209 Gaston Dulong and Gaston Bergeron, *Le parler populaire du Québec et de ses régions voisines – Atlas linguistique de l'est du Canada*, Québec, La documentation québécoise, 1980, vol. 1, pp. 6–8.

210 Jean-Denis Gendron, *Tendances phonétiques du français parlé au Canada*, Paris, Klincksieck and Québec, Presses Université Laval, 1966, p. 120.

211 Alain Thomas, 'L'assibilation en franco-ontarien', *Information-Communication*, Lab. de phonét. expér. de l'univ. de Toronto, vol. 4, 1985, pp. 65–79.

212 Alexander Hull, 'Affinités entre les variétés de français', *Le français* (Ref. 186b), pp. 167–8.

213 Pierre R. Léon (ed.) *Recherches sur la structure phonique du français canadien*, Studia Phonetica no. 1, Montreal–Paris–Brussels, Didier, 1968, p. vi.

214a Hosea Phillips, 'Le français parlé de la Louisiane', *Le français hors de . . .* (Ref. 186b), pp. 93–110.

214b John Smith-Thibodeaux, *Les francophones de Louisiane*, Paris, Entente, 1977, pp. 48–51.

214c Patrick Griolet, *Cadjins et créoles de Louisiane*, Paris, Payot, 1986.

215 Eric Waddell, 'La Louisiane: un poste outre-frontière de l'Amérique française ou un autre pays et une autre culture', *Du continent . . .* (Ref. 206), pp. 196–211; Roland J.L. Breton and Dean R. Louder, 'La géographie linguistique de l'Acadiana, 1970', *Du continent . . .* (Ref. 206), pp. 214–34.

216 Gabriel Manessy, 'Le français en Afrique noire: faits et hypothèses', *Le français hors de . . .* (Ref. 186b), p. 334.

217 Jean-Pierre Caprile, 'Situation du français dans l'Empire centre-africain et au Tchad', *Le français hors de . . .* (Ref. 186b), pp. 496–7.

218 Jean-Pierre Makouta-Mboutou, *Le français en Afrique noire (Histoire et méthodes de l'enseignement en français en Afrique noire)*, Paris, Bordas, 1973, quoted in Gabriel Manessy, *Le français hors de . . .* (Ref. 186b), p. 343.

219 Jean-Pierre Caprile, 'Situation du français . . .', *Le français hors de . . .* (Ref. 186b), p. 501.

220 Sully Faïk, 'Le français au Zaïre', *Le français hors de . . .* (Ref. 186b), pp. 450–1.

221 Louis-Jean Calvet, *Les langues véhiculaires*, Paris, PUF, 'Que sais-je?', no. 1916, 1981.

222 Gabriel Manessy, 'Le français en Afrique noire . . .', *Le français hors de . . .* (Ref. 186b), p. 347.

223 Laurent Duponchel, 'Le français en Côte d'Ivoire, au Dahomey et au Togo', *Le français hors de . . .* (Ref. l86b), p. 413.

224 Jean-Pierre Caprile (Ref. 219), p. 493.

225 For Cameroon see Claude Hagège, 'A propos du français de l'Adamaoua', *La linguistique*, 1968/1, Paris, PUF, p. 125; Patrick Renaud, 'Le français au Cameroun', *Le français hors de . . .* (Ref. 186b), p. 429.

For the Ivory Coast see Gaston Canu, Laurent Duponchel and A. Lamy, *Langues négro-africaines et enseignement du français*, Abidjan, 1971, p. 60; Brigitte Tallon, 'Le francais de Moussa', in the review *Autrement*, no. 9, 1984.

For Mali see Jacques Blondé, 'La situation du français au Mali', *Le français hors de* . . . (Ref. 186b), p. 381.

For Niger see Equipe IFA, *Inventaires des particularités lexicales du fran-çais en Afrique noire*, Edicef AUPELF, Paris, 1992; Louis-Jean Calvet, 'Vocabulaire recueilli au cours d'une enquête en 1986', in 'Note sur l'argot et les formes populaires en français d'Afrique', *Documents du Centre d'Argoto-logie*, Université René Descartes, Paris, 1986, pp. 12–21.

For the Central African Republic see Luc Bouquiaux, 'La créolisation du français par le sango véhiculaire, phénomène réciproque', *Le français en France* . . . (Ref. l86d), p. 65.

For Rwanda and Burundi see Spiridion Shyirambere, 'Le français au Rwanda et au Burundi', *Le français hors de* . . . (Ref. 186b), pp. 485–6.

For Senegal see Pierre Dumont, 'La situation du français au Sénégal', *Le français hors de* . . . (Ref. l86b), pp. 368–9.

For Zaire see Sully Faïk, 'Le français au Zaïre', *Le français hors de* . . . (Ref. 186b), pp. 455–6; François Belorgey, 'Petit lexique kinois', in the review *Autrement*, special issue, no. 9, 1984.

A *Dictionnaire du français pour l'Afrique* is currently being prepared under the direction of Jacques David at the PEREF (Université Paris-La Sorbonne).

226 A. Lanly, *Le français d'Afrique du Nord. Étude linguistique*, Paris, PUF, l962, pp. 13–16.

227 Marcel Girard and Christian Morieux, 'La langue française en Algérie', *Le français hors de* . . . (Ref. 186b), p. 315.

228 Auguste Viatte, *La francophonie* (Ref. 186c), pp. 130–4.

229 Zohra Riahi, 'Emploi de l'arabe et du français par les élèves du secondaire', *Cahiers du CERES*, Tunis, Dec. 1970, pp. 99–165, and in particular pp. 107 and 133.

230 Zohra Riahi, 'Le français parlé par les cadres tunisiens', *Revue tunisienne des Sciences sociales*, Tunis, CERES, 1968, pp. 1–24.

231 For example, Discussion, in the *Revue tunisienne des Sciences sociales*, Tunis, CERES, 1968, pp. 19–24.

232 Dalila Morsly, 'Diversité phonologique du français parlé en Algérie: Réalisation de /r/', *Phonologie* . . . (Ref. l62b), pp. 65–72.

233 Quoted in A. Lanly, *Le français* . . . (Ref. 226), p. 38.

234 Henriette Walter, 'La nasale vélaire /ŋ/, un phonème du français?', *Phonologie* . . . (Ref. 162b), pp. 14–29.

235 Douglas C. Walker, 'On a Phonological Innovation in French', *Journal of the Phonetic Association*, 12/2, Dec. 1982, pp. 72–7. See also Nicol C. Spence, '*Faux amis* and *faux anglicismes*: problems of classification and definition', *Forum for Modern Language Studies*, vol. 23, no. 2, April 1987, pp. 169–83.

236 Henriette Walter, *La phonologie du français*, Paris, PUF, 1977, pp. 28–56.

237a André Martinet, *La prononciation du français contemporain. Témoignages recueillis en 1941 dans un camp d'officiers prisonniers*, Paris-Geneva, Droz, 1945 (new edition 1971).

237b Henriette Walter, *Enquête phonologique* . . . (Ref. 122). There are many other regional surveys, see Henriette and Gérard Walter, 'Orientation bib-liographique', *Phonologie* . . . (Ref. l62b), pp. 109–20.
For current trends see Henriette Walter. 'Les changements de prononciation en cours', Actes de la journée d'étude du GRELO, Université d'Orléans (June 1986) (distributed internally in the University).

238 André Martinet, *La prononciation* . . . (Ref. 237a), pp. 8–16.

239 Pierre Guiraud, *Les mots savants*, Paris. PUF, 'Que sais-je?', no. 1325. pp. 29–71.

240 Jacqueline Picoche, *Précis de lexicologie*, Paris, Nathan, 1977, p. 117–19.

241 Source: Audimat Plus, Sté Médiamétrie, 39, rue du Colisée, Paris.
242 Magazine *Lire*, 1985 championships, nos. 117, 118, 119, 120, 122. 1986 championships, nos. 126, 127, 128, 129, 136.
243a Nina Catach, *L'orthographe*, Paris, PUF, 'Que sais-je?', no. 685, 1978 (new edition 1982), pp. 72–95.
243b Hervé Bazin, *Plumons l'oiseau*, Paris, Grasset, 1966.
244 André Martinet, *Des steppes* . . . (Ref. 4), p. 65.
245 Charles Beaulieux, *Histoire de l'orthographe*, Paris, Champion, 1927 (new edition 1970), p. 149.
246a Nina Catach, 'Notions actuelles d'histoire de l'orthographe', *L'orthographe, Langue française*, no. 20, Dec. 1973, p. 3.
246b Nina Catach, *L'orthographe* (Ref. 243a), pp. 7–23.
246c Claire Blanche-Benveniste and André Chervel, *L'orthographe*, Paris, Maspero, 1969 (new edition 1978), pp. 45–112.
247 Compare Vincent Lucci and Yves Naze, *Enseigner ou supprimer l'orthographe*, Paris, CEDIC, 1979, p. 110–13 and Jacques Cellard, *Histoires de mots, II*, Paris, Éd. La Découverte-Le Monde, 1986, p. 125.
248 Claire Blanche-Benveniste and André Chervel, *L'orthographe* (Ref. 246c), pp. 207–23.
249 André Martinet, 'La réforme de l'orthographe française d'un point de vue fonctionnel', *Le français sans fard*, Paris, PUF, 1969, p. 62.
250 André and Jeanne Martinet, Jeanne Villard, with the collaboration of D. Boyer and A. and G. Dominici, *Vers l'écrit avec alfonic*, Paris, Hachette, 1983.
251 Henriette Walter, 'Sémantique et axiologie: une application pratique au lexique français', *La linguistique*, 21, 1985, pp. 275–95.
252 Arsène Darmesteter, *La vie des mots*, Paris, Delagrave, 1950, pp. 179–86 (a list of almost 300 words, some of which are disputable).
253 Jacqueline Picoche, *Nouveau dictionnaire* . . . (Ref. 15), pp. 716–39, and for algorithm see also Georges Ifrah, *Les chiffres ou l'histoire d'une invention*, Paris, Robert Laffont, 1985, p. 284.
254 The etymological dictionaries of Oscar Bloch and Walther von Wartburg (Ref. 14); Jacqueline Picoche (Ref. 15); Albert Dauzat (Ref. 124).
255 Henri Suhamy, *Les figures de style*, Paris, PUF, 'Que sais-je?', no. 1889, 1981.
256 Georges Gougenheim, *Dictionnaire fondamental*, Paris, Didier, 1958.
257 André Malécot, 'New Procedures for Descriptive Phonetics', *Papers in Linguistics and Phonetics to the Memory of Pierre Delattre*, The Hague–Paris, Mouton, 1972, pp. 1–11.
258 *TLF (Trésor de la Langue Française)*, review *Qui-vive International*, no. 5, Feb. 1987, pp. 88–9 and the brochure *L'Institut national de la langue française*, Feb. 1986, Nancy, CNRS, p. 1.
259 See for example, Georges Mounin, *Clés pour la langue française*, Paris, Seghers, 1975, pp. 81–93.
260 See 'Cent mots nouveaux de Fillioud, pour bien parler l'audiovisuel', in the newspaper *Libération*, Thursday 17 Feb. 1983; and Loïc Depecker and Alain Pagès, *Guide des mots nouveaux*, Commissariat Général de la Langue Française, Paris, Nathan, 1985.
261 See Benoîte Groult, 'La langue française au féminin', *Médias et langage*, nos 19–20, 1984, and Anne-Marie Houdebine, 'Le français au féminin', *La linguistique*, 23, 1987/1, pp. 13–34.
262 Hector Obalk, Alain Soral and Alexandre Pasche, *Les mouvements de mode expliqués aux parents*, Paris, Robert Laffont, 1984, with a lexis compiled by

Henriette Walter.

263   Henriette Walter, 'L'innovation lexicale chez les jeunes Parisiens', *La linguistique*, 20, 1984/2, p. 69–94.

264   Pierre Guiraud, *L'argot*, Paris, PUF, 'Que sais-je?', no. 700, 1958, pp. 66–9.

265   Pierre Perret, *Le petit Perret*, Paris, J.-C. Lattès, 1982, pp. 192–3; Géo Sandry and Marcel Carrère, *Dictionnaire de l'argot moderne*, Paris, Dauphin, 1984, p. 143.

266   Auguste le Breton, *Argotez, argotez, il en restera toujours quelque chose*, updated dictionary, Paris, Carrère, 1987, and Denise François, 'Les argots', in André Martinet (ed.), *Le langage*, Paris, NRF, La Pléiade, 1968, pp. 620–46.

267   Pierre Guiraud, *L'argot*, (Ref. 264), pp. 36–9.

268   André Martinet (ed.), *Grammaire fonctionnelle du français*, Paris, Crédif, Didier, 1979, in particular part 3, pp. 153–230.

269   An overview of work in progress can be found in Nicole Gueunier, 'La crise du français en France', in Jacques Maurais (ed.), *La crise des langues*, Québec, Conseil de la Langue Française, Paris, *Le Robert*, 1985, pp. 5–38. In addition, works intended for the general public often make pertinent comments on Modern French. For example: Robert Beauvais, *L'hexagonal tel qu'on le parle*, Paris, Hachette, 1970; Robert Beauvais, *Le français kiskose*, Paris, Fayard, 1975; Jean Thévenot, *La France, ton français fout le camp*, Gembloux, Duculot, 1976; Pierre Merle, *Dictionnaire du français branché*, Paris, Seuil, 1985; Pierre Daninos, *La France prise aux mots*, Paris, Calmann-Lévy, 1986; Orlando de Rudder, *Le français qui se cause*, Paris, Balland, 1986; Gilles Cahoreau and Christophe Tison, *La drogue expliquée aux parents*, Paris, Balland, 1987, with a glossary, pp. 263–78.

270   André Martinet, *Évolution des langues et reconstruction. Les changements linguistiques et les usagers*, Paris, PUF, 1975, ch. 2, pp. 11–23.

271   On the programme 'Apostrophes', Jan. 1987, with Yves Berger, Orlando de Rudder and Gabriel de Broglie.

272   André Martinet, see a corpus compiled in 1960 by Ivanka Cindric, quoted by André Martinet in *Évolution . . .* (Ref. 270), p. 18, and Søren Kolstrup, 'Les temps du passé du français oral. Le passé composé, l'imparfait et le présent historique dans les narrations', *Actes du VIIIe Congrès des Romanistes scandinaves*, Odense University Press, 1983, pp. 191–200. Another survey is being conducted by Christa Hombach in Rennes.

273   Marguerite Descamps, 'Synchronie dynamique et "pronoms relatifs" du français oral', *Actes* du 8e Colloque International de Linguistique Fonctionnelle (Toulouse, 6–11 July 1981), *Cahiers du Centre interdisciplinaire des sciences du langage*, no. 4, Université Toulouse-Le Mirail, 1982, pp. 126–8.

274   Examples quoted by Georges Pastre, *Le français télé . . . visé* (Ref. 127), p. 73, and André Goosse, *Façons de parler*, Gembloux, Duculot, 1971, pp. 101–3.

275   Among other work covering the country as a whole see Henriette Walter, *Enquête phonologique . . .* (Ref. 122) and Fernand Carton, Mario Rossi, Denis Autesserre and Pierre Léon, *Les accents des français*, Paris, Hachette, 1983.

276   Vincent Lucci, *Étude phonétique du français contemporain à travers la variation situationnelle*, Université de Grenoble, 1983, pp. 67–103.

277   Vladimir Buben, *Influence de l'orthographe sur la prononciation du français moderne*, Bratislava, 1935.

278 Maurice Druon, preface to vol. 1 of the *Dictionnaire de l'Académie française* (ninth edition), 1987, p. 1.
279 In particular:
279a Maurice Grevisse, *Le bon usage*, Paris-Gembloux, Duculot, 1980.
279b Joseph Hanse, *Nouveau dictionnaire des difficultés du français moderne*, Paris–Gembloux, Duculot, 1983.
279c Adolphe V. Thomas, *Dictionnaire des difficultés de la langue française*, Paris, Larousse, 1956.
280 Gabriel de Broglie, *Le français* . . . (Ref. 178), pp. 199–203.
281 Claude Hagège, *Le français et les siècles*, Paris, Odile Jacob, 1987, pp. 122–3, and Haut Comité de la Langue Française, *La loi relative à l'emploi de la langue française*, Paris, La documentation française, 1975.
282 Gabriel de Broglie, *Le français* . . . (Ref. 178), pp. 205–9.
283 Etiemble, 'La langue de la publicité', *Cahiers de la publicité*, Aug.–Sept. 1966, pp. 105–12.
284 Etiemble, *Le français dans la publicité*, 1966.
285 Maurice Grevisse, *Le bon usage* (Ref. 279a), no. 1348, p. 673.

INDEXES

INDEX OF PROPER NAMES

This index lists only those names which appear in the body of the text. It contains not only the names of real or mythical people but also the names of institutions, documents and branded products.

The names of authors of works corresponding to numbered references are to be found in the References (see pp. 232–44).

INDEX OF LANGUAGES, PEOPLES, PLACES

This index lists the names of languages, peoples and places referred to in the text. Words which have been looked at from the linguistic point of view are to be found in the Index of words (p. 255).

INDEX OF CONCEPTS

This index lists the linguistic concepts illustrated in the text. Consult the Index of words (p. 255) for terms which were the object of a specifically linguistic comment on their oral or written form or their meaning.

INDEX OF WORDS

This index contains all the words whose meaning or oral or written form are explained in the text. For that reason, it contains names of places and people which have been discussed from the linguistic point of view.

275